Cracking the AP® English Language and Composition Exam Premium

2020 Edition

The Staff of The Princeton Review

PrincetonReview.com

Penguin
Random
House

The Princeton Review
110 East 42nd St, 7th Floor
New York, NY 10017
Email: editorialsupport@review.com

Published in the United States by Penguin Random House LLC, New York, and in Canada by Random House of Canada, a division of Penguin Random House Ltd., Toronto.

ISBN: 978-0-525-56822-3
eBook ISBN: 978-0-525-56860-5
ISSN: 2641-3426

Printed in the United States of America.

10 9 8 7 6 5 4 3 2

2020 Edition

Editorial
Rob Franek, Editor-in-Chief
Deborah Weber, Director of Production
Gabriel Berlin, Production Design Manager
Selena Coppock, Managing Editor
Aaron Riccio, Senior Editor
Meave Shelton, Senior Editor
Chris Chimera, Editor
Eleanor Green, Editor
Orion McBean, Editor
Brian Saladino, Editor
Patricia Murphy, Editorial Assistant

Penguin Random House Publishing Team
Tom Russell, VP, Publisher
Alison Stoltzfus, Publishing Director
Amanda Yee, Associate Managing Editor
Ellen Reed, Production Manager
Suzanne Lee, Designer

Editor: Chris Chimera
Production Editors: Liz Dacey and Emily Epstein White
Production Artist: John Stecyk
Content Contributors: Corinne Dolci, Gina Donegan, Linda Kelley, Kevin Kelly, and Jason Morgan

Acknowledgments

The Princeton Review would like to thank Corinne Dolci, Gina Donegan, Linda Kelley, Kevin Kelly, and Jason Morgan for their thorough review of this title and useful updates to the 2020 edition. The editor of this edition would like to thank John Stecyk, Liz Dacey, and Emily Epstein White for their hard work on this edition, as well.

Contents

at PrincetonReview.com/prep

As easy as 1·2·3

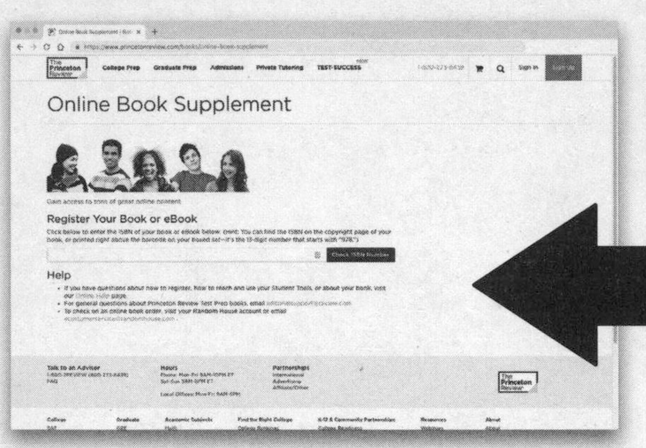

1 Go to PrincetonReview.com/prep and enter the following ISBN for your book:

9780525568223

2 Answer a few simple questions to set up an exclusive Princeton Review account. *(If you already have one, you can just log in.)*

3 Enjoy access to your **FREE** content!

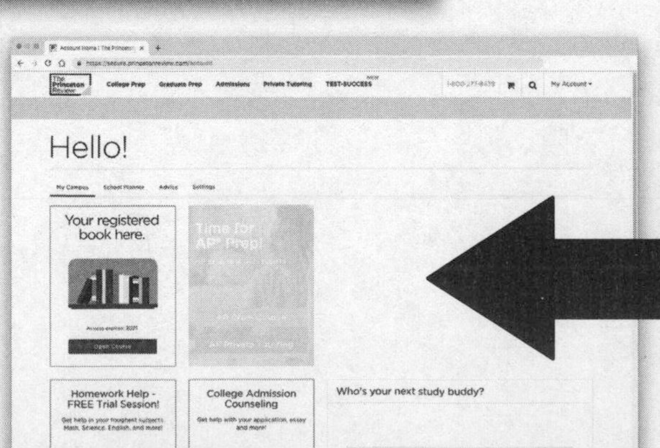

Once you've registered, you can...

- Get our take on any recent or pending updates to the Cracking the AP English Language and Composition Exam
- Take a full-length practice PSAT, SAT, and/or ACT
- Get valuable advice about the college application process, including tips for writing a great essay and where to apply for financial aid
- Use our searchable rankings of *The Best 385 Colleges* to find out more information about your dream school, if you're still choosing between colleges
- Access comprehensive study guides and a variety of printable resources, including: Online Articles, Applied Strategies, and Proven Techniques
- Check to see if there have been any corrections or updates to this edition

Need to report a potential **content** issue?

Contact **EditorialSupport@review.com** and include:

- full title of the book
- ISBN
- page number

Need to report a **technical** issue?

Contact **TPRStudentTech@review.com** and provide:

- your full name
- email address used to register the book
- full book title and ISBN
- Operating system (Mac/PC) and browser (Firefox, Safari, etc.)

Look For These Icons Throughout The Book

ONLINE ARTICLES

OTHER REFERENCES

APPLIED STRATEGIES

PROVEN TECHNIQUES

GOING DEEPER

CRITICAL CONNECTION

Part I
Using This Book to Improve Your AP Score

- Preview: Your Knowledge, Your Expectations
- Your Guide to Using This Book
- How to Begin

PREVIEW: YOUR KNOWLEDGE, YOUR EXPECTATIONS

Your route to a high score on the AP English Language and Composition Exam depends a lot on how you plan to use this book. Respond to the following questions.

1. Rate your level of confidence about your knowledge of the content tested by the AP English Language and Composition Exam.

    A. Very confident—I know it all
    B. I'm pretty confident, but there are topics for which I could use help
    C. Not confident—I need quite a bit of support
    D. I'm not sure

2. Circle your goal score for the AP English Language and Composition Exam.

    5 4 3 2 1 I'm not sure yet

3. What do you expect to learn from this book? Circle all that apply to you.

    A. A general overview of the test and what to expect
    B. Strategies for how to approach the test
    C. The content tested by this exam
    D. I'm not sure yet.

Not Sure Yet?
If you answered these three questions with "I'm not sure," you may need more time before you take the AP Exam. But don't be discouraged! Review the content chapters before you take the practice tests in this book and you'll see improvement in your confidence and even your test scores.

YOUR GUIDE TO USING THIS BOOK

This book is organized to provide as much—or as little—support as you need, so you can use this book in whatever way will be most helpful to improving your score on the AP English Language and Composition Exam.

- The remainder of **Part I** provides guidance on how to use this book and helps you determine your strengths and weaknesses.
- **Part II** contains Practice Test 1, its answers and explanations, and a scoring guide. (Bubble sheets can be found in the very back of the book for easy tear-out.) We strongly recommend that you take this test before going any further, in order to realistically determine:
    - your starting point right now
    - which question types you're ready for and which you might need to practice
    - which content topics you are familiar with and which you will want to carefully review

  Once you have nailed down your strengths and weaknesses with regard to this exam, you can focus your test preparation, build a study plan, and be efficient with your time.
- **Part III** of this book:
    - provides information about the structure, scoring, and content of the AP English Language and Composition Exam
    - will help you to make a study plan
    - points you toward additional resources

- **Part IV** explores various strategies, including:
  - how to attack multiple-choice questions
  - how to write effective essays
  - how to manage your time to maximize the number of points available to you
- **Part V** of this book is a review of the terms and rhetorical modes that will give you an edge on the AP English Language and Composition Exam.
- **Part VI and VII** contain Practice Tests 2 and 3, their answers and explanations, and a scoring guide. (Bubble sheets can be found in the very back of the book for easy tear-out.) If you skipped Practice Test 1, we recommend that you do all the tests (with at least a day or two between each of them) so that you can track your progress. Additionally, this will help to identify any external issues: if you get a certain type of question wrong each time, you probably need to review it. If you got it wrong only once, you may have run out of time or been distracted by something. In either case, this will allow you to focus on the factors that caused the discrepancy in scores and to be as prepared as possible on the day of the test.
- **Online Resources** contain two additional practice tests. Follow the study guide based on the amount of time you have to study for the 2019 exam. Use the key terms to improve your vocabulary by creating flashcards to help you learn words you might see on the test.

Once you register your book online, you can print the bubble sheets and scoring worksheets for your practice tests!

You may choose to use some parts of this book over others, or you may work through the entire book. Your approach will depend on your needs and how much time you have. Let's now look at how to make this determination.

HOW TO BEGIN

1. **Take a Test**
   Before you can decide how to use this book, you need to take a practice test. Doing so will give you insight into your strengths and weaknesses, and the test will also help you create an effective study plan. If you're feeling test-phobic, remind yourself that a practice test is a tool for diagnosing yourself—it's not how well you do that matters but how you use information gleaned from your performance to guide your preparation.

   So, before you read further, take Practice Test 1 starting at page 8 of this book. Be sure to do so in one sitting, following the instructions that appear before the test.

2. **Check Your Answers**
   Using the answer key on page 34, count the number of multiple-choice questions you answered correctly and how many you missed. Don't worry about the explanations for now, and don't worry about why you missed questions. We'll get to that soon.

Scoring Worksheets
We've included a scoring worksheet for the practice tests in this book at the end of each Answers and Explanations chapter. Remember that these worksheets are meant to serve as a rough guideline only. AP Exam scores are weighted according to a statistical process that varies slightly every year based on how students perform on the exam, but you can use the worksheets to approximate your score.

3. **Reflect on the Test**
After you take your first test, respond to the following questions:
    - How much time did you spend on the multiple-choice questions?
    - How much time did you spend on each essay?
    - How many multiple-choice questions did you miss?
    - Do you feel you had the knowledge to address the subject matter of the essays?
    - Do you feel you wrote well-organized, thoughtful essays?

4. **Read Part III and Complete the Self-Evaluation**
Part III provides information on how the test is structured and scored. As you read Part III, re-evaluate your answers to the questions above. At the end of Part III, you will revisit and refine the questions you answered above. You will then be able to make a study plan, based on your needs and time available, that will allow you to use this book most effectively.

5. **Engage with Parts IV and V as Needed**
Notice the word *engage*. You'll get more out of this book if you use it intentionally than if you read it passively, hoping for an improved score through osmosis.

    The Strategy chapters will help you think about your approach to the question types on this exam. Part IV opens with a reminder to think about how you approach questions now and then closes with a reflection section asking you to think about how or whether you will change your approach in the future.

    The Terms and Modes chapters in Part V are designed to provide a review of the terminology you are likely to encounter on the exam, and will help you to identify the rhetorical fallacies and modes used in both test passages and student essays. You will have the opportunity to assess your mastery of the content of each chapter through test-appropriate questions and a reflection section.

6. **Take More Practice Tests and Assess Your Performance**
Once you feel you have developed the strategies you need and gained the knowledge you lacked, you should take Practice Test 2, which starts at page 211. You should do so in one sitting, following the instructions at the beginning of the test.

    When you complete the test, check your answers to the multiple-choice sections against the answer key on page 237. If possible, find a teacher to read your essays and provide feedback.

    Once you have taken the test, reflect on what areas you still need to work on, and revisit the chapters in this book that address those deficiencies. Through this type of reflection and engagement, you will continue to improve. Then, take Practice Test 3 in this book and Practice Tests 4 and 5 online.

7. **Keep Working**
As we will discuss in Part III, there are other resources available to you, including a wealth of information on **AP Students:** apstudent.collegeboard.org/apcourse/ap-english-language-and-composition. You can continue to explore and engage in areas needing improvement right up to the day of the test.

Part II
Practice Test 1

- Practice Test 1
- Practice Test 1: Answers and Explanations

Practice Test 1

AP® English Language and Composition Exam

SECTION I: Multiple-Choice Questions

DO NOT OPEN THIS BOOKLET UNTIL YOU ARE TOLD TO DO SO.

At a Glance

Total Time
1 hour

Number of Questions
45

Percent of Total Grade
45%

Writing Instrument
Pencil required

Instructions

Section I of this examination contains 45 multiple-choice questions. Fill in only the ovals for numbers 1 through 45 on your answer sheet.

Indicate all of your answers to the multiple-choice questions on the answer sheet. No credit will be given for anything written in this exam booklet, but you may use the booklet for notes or scratch work. After you have decided which of the suggested answers is best, completely fill in the corresponding oval on the answer sheet. Give only one answer to each question. If you change an answer, be sure that the previous mark is erased completely. Here is a sample question and answer.

Sample Question	Sample Answer
Chicago is a (A) state (B) city (C) country (D) continent (E) village	Ⓐ ● Ⓒ Ⓓ Ⓔ

Use your time effectively, working as quickly as you can without losing accuracy. Do not spend too much time on any one question. Go on to other questions and come back to the ones you have not answered if you have time. It is not expected that everyone will know the answers to all the multiple-choice questions.

About Guessing

Many candidates wonder whether or not to guess the answers to questions about which they are not certain. Multiple-choice scores are based on the number of questions answered correctly. Points are not deducted for incorrect answers, and no points are awarded for unanswered questions. Because points are not deducted for incorrect answers, you are encouraged to answer all multiple-choice questions. On any questions you do not know the answer to, you should eliminate as many choices as you can, and then select the best answer among the remaining choices.

GO ON TO THE NEXT PAGE.

This page intentionally left blank.

ENGLISH LANGUAGE AND COMPOSITION
SECTION I
Time—1 hour

Directions: This part consists of selections from prose works and questions on their content, form, and style. After reading each passage, choose the best answer to each question and completely fill in the corresponding oval on the answer sheet.

Note: Pay particular attention to the requirement of questions that contain the words NOT, LEAST, or EXCEPT.

Questions 1–13. Read the following passage carefully before you choose your answers.

This passage is excerpted from a contemporary article in a scholarly journal.

The most obvious joke in the title of Swift's *Travels into Several Remote Nations of the World* is that what purports to be a chronicle of several excursions to remote nations turns out to be a satiric anatomy of specifically English attitudes and values. But there is a second joke. Many of the…supposedly unfamiliar and exotic sights Gulliver sees in his sixteen years and seven months of wandering in remote nations, and even the radically altered perspectives from which he sees them (as diminutive landscapes, giant people, intelligent animals, etc.), could have been seen or experienced in a few days by anyone at the tourists' sights, public entertainments, shows, spectacles, and exhibitions in the streets and at the fairs of London.

It is not surprising that *Gulliver's Travels* should be filled with the shows and diversions of London. All the Scriblerians were fascinated with popular entertainments; collectively and individually, they satirized them in many of their works. Swift shared this fascination with his fellow Scriblerians, and he transforms the sights and shows of London into an imaginative center of *Gulliver's Travels.*[1]

Gulliver himself senses that the wonders he sees in remote nations resemble popular entertainments back home in England when he notes that the capital city of Lilliput "looked like the painted Scene of a City in a Theatre."[1] And other popular entertainments would allow Londoners to see many of the same sights Gulliver saw in Lilliput. A Londoner could experience what a miniature city looked like to the giant Gulliver by going to see the papier-mâché and clay architectural and topographical models displayed at fairs and in inns, some of which were extraordinarily elaborate and detailed, such as the model of Amsterdam exhibited in 1710, which was twenty feet wide and twenty to thirty feet long, "with all the Churches, Chappels, Stadt house, Hospitals, noble Buildings, Streets, Trees, Walks, Avenues, with the Sea, Shipping, Sluices, Rivers, Canals &c., most exactly built to admiration."[2]

Miniature people, as well as miniature landscapes, could be seen in one of the most popular diversions in London, the peepshows, which were enclosed boxes containing scenes made out of painted board, paper flats, and glass panels and given the illusion of depth by mirrors and magnifying glasses. All of this was seen through a hole bored in one side. Among the most popular scenes were interiors, particularly palace interiors of European royalty, and so there is a direct analogy between peering in the hole of a peepshow and Gulliver's looking into the palace in Lilliput: "I applied my Face to the Windows of the middle Stories, and discovered the most splendid Apartments that can be imagined. There I saw the Empress, and the young Princes in their several Lodgings. Her Imperial Majesty was pleased to smile very graciously upon me, and gave me out the window her Hand to kiss." The queen's movements could have been seen in the peepshows, too, for clockwork animating the figures was introduced early in the century. And much the same illusion of a living, miniature world could be found in another popular diversion, the "moving picture," a device in which cutout figures were placed within a frame and activated by jacks and wheels. This curiosity fascinated contemporary Londoners: "The landscape looks as an ordinary picture till the clock-work behind the curtain be set at work, and then the ships move and sail distinctly upon the sea till out of sight; a coach comes out of town, the motion of the horses and wheels are very distinct, and a gentleman in the coach that salutes the company; a hunter also and his dogs keep their course till out of sight." Swift saw this same moving picture, or one very much like it, and was impressed.

1 *Gulliver's Travels*, in *The Prose Works of Jonathan Swift*, ed. Herbert Davis, 14 vols. (Oxford: B. Blackwell, 1939–68), XI:13

2 Quoted in John Ashton, *Social Life in the Reign of Queen Anne* (New York: Chatto and Windus, 1883), 219–20

GO ON TO THE NEXT PAGE.

1. The purpose of the passage is most likely to
   - (A) describe the cultural landscape in *Gulliver's Travels*
   - (B) draw a comparison between the fictional world Gulliver experienced and the similar imaginative elements of eighteenth-century London
   - (C) point out the superfluous nature of entertainment in Swift's London
   - (D) provide evidence that Swift's satire is derived from the natural curiosity of European royalty
   - (E) discredit the notion that *Gulliver's Travels* is a wholly original work

2. In the passage, the author's overall attitude toward *Gulliver's Travels* can best be described as
   - (A) cleverly subversive
   - (B) bitingly sarcastic
   - (C) generally appreciative
   - (D) halfheartedly engaged
   - (E) insistently dismissive

3. "Scriblerians" (line 16) refers to
   - (A) book craftsmen in London
   - (B) characters in Swift's novels
   - (C) English politicians and aristocrats
   - (D) historians of popular entertainment
   - (E) a London-based circle of English authors

4. It can be inferred from the second paragraph that Jonathan Swift was
   - (A) a citizen of London
   - (B) a producer of public entertainments
   - (C) a member of the Scriblerians
   - (D) a painter as well as an author
   - (E) a traveling salesman

5. The stylistic feature most evident in the first two paragraphs (lines 1–20) is the use of
   - (A) repeated syntactical patterns
   - (B) shifts in tense and person
   - (C) historical allusions
   - (D) a series of extended metaphors
   - (E) didactic analogies and asides

6. In describing miniature people and landscapes in the final paragraph, the author emphasizes their
   - (A) size
   - (B) obscurity
   - (C) magnificence
   - (D) commonness
   - (E) transience

7. In the fourth paragraph, the author includes long quotes primarily in order to
   - (A) refute the claims of his detractors that *Gulliver's Travels* was purely imaginative
   - (B) document the connection between *Gulliver's Travels* and popular entertainments
   - (C) challenge the prevailing scholarship on the miniature people and landscapes in *Gulliver's Travels*
   - (D) highlight the inconsistencies within *Gulliver's Travels* regarding miniature people and landscapes
   - (E) inform the reader of the sources for the study of miniature people and landscapes in *Gulliver's Travels*

8. Which of the following best describes the relationship between the first section (lines 1–20) and the second section (lines 21–66) of the passage?
   - (A) The second section answers the series of questions raised in the first section.
   - (B) The second section challenges the prevailing picture detailed in in the first section.
   - (C) The second section undermines the positions of scholars introduced in the first section.
   - (D) The second section expands on a technical definition introduced in the first section.
   - (E) The second section provides evidence for the claims introduced in the first section.

9. Footnote 1 in line 24 indicates that
   - (A) the article first appeared as an addendum to *Gulliver's Travels*
   - (B) *Gulliver's Travels* was first published in 1939
   - (C) the quotation "looked like the…Theater" was excerpted from *Gulliver's Travels*, part of a 14-volume set of Swift's works
   - (D) the quotation "looked like the…Theater" was originally written by Herbert Davis
   - (E) *Gulliver's Travels* was reprinted in its entirety in 1939, and credited to Herbert Davis instead of Swift

GO ON TO THE NEXT PAGE.

10. Footnote 2 in line 36 indicates

(A) the quotation was taken from a professional journal
(B) the quotation refers to a 1710 exhibit in Amsterdam
(C) the quotation originally appeared in *Gulliver's Travels* in 1883
(D) the quotation, describing a miniature exhibition of Amsterdam, first appeared in a book by John Ashton
(E) the quotation was originally published in a newspaper

11. The details in lines 46–52 suggest the scene is viewed by which of the following?

(A) An impartial anthropologist
(B) An intrigued visitor
(C) A critical literary scholar
(D) An argumentative architect
(E) A struggling writer

12. The speaker's tone might best be described as

(A) emphatic and insistent
(B) scholarly and enthusiastic
(C) dejected but hopeful
(D) erudite and cynical
(E) intransigent yet competent

13. In the final paragraph (lines 37–66), the writer mentions "peepshows" and "moving pictures" primarily to

(A) illustrate the fascination that Scriblerians had with popular curiosities of the era
(B) explain how Swift copied the literary styles and themes of his time
(C) emphasize the influence of popular entertainment on literature
(D) suggest that Gulliver's travels was purely allegorical in its significance
(E) highlight the obstacles Gulliver encountered in his voyages to Lilliput

GO ON TO THE NEXT PAGE.

Questions 14–25. Read the following passage carefully before you choose your answers.

This passage is from an eighteenth-century protofeminist work.

My own sex, I hope, will excuse me, if I treat them like rational creatures, instead of flattering their fascinating graces, and viewing them as if they were in a state of perpetual childhood, unable to stand alone. I earnestly wish to point out in what true dignity and human happiness consists—I wish to persuade women to endeavour to acquire strength, both of mind and body, and to convince them that the soft phrases, susceptibility of heart, delicacy of sentiment, and refinement of taste, are almost synonymous with epithets of weakness, and that those beings who are only the objects of pity and that kind of love, which has been termed its sister, will soon become objects of contempt.

Dismissing then those pretty feminine phrases, which the men condescendingly use to soften our slavish dependence, and despising that weak elegancy of mind, exquisite sensibility, and sweet docility of manners, supposed to be the sexual characteristics of the weaker vessel, I wish to show that elegance is inferior to virtue, that the first object of laudable ambition is to obtain a character as a human being, regardless of the distinction of sex; and that secondary views should be brought to this simple touchstone.

This is a rough sketch of my plan; and should I express my conviction with the energetic emotions that I feel whenever I think of the subject, the dictates of experience and reflection will be felt by some of my readers. Animated by this important object, I shall disdain to cull my phrases or polish my style;—I aim at being useful, and sincerity will render me unaffected; for, wishing rather to persuade by the force of my arguments, than dazzle by the elegance of my language, I shall not waste my time in rounding periods, nor in fabricating the turgid bombast of artificial feelings, which, coming from the head, never reach the heart—I shall be employed about things, not words!—and, anxious to render my sex more respectable to members of society, I shall try to avoid that flowery diction which has slided from essays into novels, and from novels into familiar letters and conversation.

These pretty nothings—these caricatures of the real beauty of sensibility, dropping glibly from the tongue, vitiate the taste, and create a kind of sickly delicacy that turns away from simple unadorned truth; and a deluge of false sentiments and overstretched feelings, stifling the natural emotions of the heart, render the domestic pleasures insipid, that ought to sweeten the exercise of those severe duties, which educate a rational and immortal being for a nobler field of action.

The education of women has, of late, been more attended to than formerly; yet they are still reckoned a frivolous sex, and ridiculed or pitied by the writers who endeavour by satire or instruction to improve them. It is acknowledged that they spend many of the first years of their lives in acquiring a smattering of accomplishments: meanwhile strength of body and mind are sacrificed to libertine notions of beauty, to the desire of establishing themselves—the only way women can rise in the world—by marriage. And this desire making mere animals of them, when they marry they act as such children may be expected to act—they dress; they paint, and nickname God's creatures—Surely these weak beings are only fit for a seraglio!—Can they govern a family, or take care of the poor babes whom they bring into the world?

14. In the initial paragraph, the author employs both
    - (A) apology and classification
    - (B) irony and exposition
    - (C) analogy and extended metaphor
    - (D) flattery and epithets
    - (E) induction and persuasion

15. In the initial paragraph, the author decries
    - (A) traditional feminine attributes
    - (B) traditional male attributes
    - (C) modern sexuality
    - (D) the importance of love
    - (E) the importance of sentiments

16. In the initial paragraph, the author suggests that
    - (A) men prefer strong women
    - (B) a man will never truly love a strong woman
    - (C) men never respect strong women
    - (D) women need emotional and physical strength
    - (E) women need intellectual and physical strength

17. The author ties the second paragraph to the first by using the words
    - (A) "vessel" and "touchstone"
    - (B) "soften" and "inferior"
    - (C) "laudable" and "sex"
    - (D) "slavish" and "virtue"
    - (E) "soften" and "weak"

GO ON TO THE NEXT PAGE.

18. The word "vessel" (line 17) is a metaphor for

(A) sex
(B) woman
(C) man
(D) phrase
(E) character

19. The author suggests that a woman's worth may be best judged by

(A) comparing her with a praiseworthy man
(B) examining the elegance of her writing
(C) evaluating the strength of her character
(D) evaluating her physical beauty
(E) examining her manners

20. The author proposes to write in a manner that is both

(A) cogent and emotional
(B) polished and intellectual
(C) ornate and rhetorical
(D) elegant and cerebral
(E) convincing and flowery

21. The words "pretty nothings" (line 38) are a reprise of

(A) "letters and conversation" (lines 36–37)
(B) "essays" and "novels" (line 36)
(C) "flowery diction" (line 35)
(D) "rounding periods" (line 30)
(E) "members of society" (line 34)

22. With the phrase "dropping glibly from the tongue" (line 39) the author begins

(A) a caricature of women
(B) a critique of turgid bombast
(C) a panegyric of sugary writing
(D) an analysis of sentimental writing
(E) an extended metaphor

23. One can infer from the passage that to become strong human beings, rather than mere children, young women need

(A) an education different from that of young men
(B) more understanding husbands
(C) obliging husbands
(D) a good marriage
(E) the same education as that of young men

24. The tone of the final paragraph is

(A) sardonic
(B) lyrical
(C) condescending
(D) frivolous
(E) reserved

25. Which of the following best describes the writer's exigence in the passage?

(A) A low turnout rate among eligible voters in recent national elections
(B) The trend toward violence in feminist political movements
(C) Social inequality among men and women
(D) Widening disparities in the socioeconomic circumstances of wealthy and poor women
(E) Public resentment of increasing political power granted to women

GO ON TO THE NEXT PAGE.

Questions 26–33. are based on the following passage.

The passage below is a draft.

Throughout her life, "Dolly" chose to speak in her native Cornish, a language that dates back to at least the early Roman occupation of Great Britain. (2) When Dolly died in 1777, she gained fame as the last fluent, native speaker of the Cornish language, which would then remain extinct for over one hundred years.

(3) Born in 1692, Dolly was one of six children born to a poor fisherman and his wife in the charmingly-named village of Mousehole in Penzance. (4) Dolly never married and lived in a shabby hut in a drab corner of Mousehole, making her living as a travelling fishwife and sometime fortune-teller. (5) By the 1760s, when the Cornish people around her had largely traded their native language for English, Dolly became known for gabbing in Cornish with whomever she could find. (6) She was especially known for singing in her language of choice.

(7) There is some controversy as to whether Dolly was, in fact, the last native speaker of Cornish. (8) Modern historians now believe that there may have been half a dozen people in the vicinity of Mousehole, all of whom died before 1800, who continued to speak Cornish after Dolly's death.

(9) What we know for sure is that Dolly Pentreath was *not* the last speaker of the Cornish language. (10) In 1904, Celtic linguist Henry Jenner published *A Handbook of the Cornish Language*.

(11) This sparked a massive revival in interest in the ancient language throughout the 20th Century. (12) Devotees taught classes, published educational materials, and coined new words. (13) It is estimated that around 600 people in Cornwall speak their ancestral tongue.

26. Which of the following sentences, if placed before sentence 1, would provide the most effective introduction to the topic of the paragraph and the passage as a whole?

(A) The eccentric Dolly Pentreath was born in 1692 in a small fishing village in Cornwall, England.
(B) According to legend, the dying words of Cornwall native Dorothy Pentreath were "*My ny vynnav kewsel Sowsnek!*" ("I don't want to speak English!").
(C) To their surprise, as part of a 1994 research project, graduate students at the University of Exeter discovered the last known speaker of the Cornish language, Dolly Pentreath.
(D) Ironically, when Dorothy Pentreath suffered brain injuries after a mining accident, she immediately started speaking English again.
(E) There are three languages which are nearly extinct in modern Britain: Breton, Manx, and Cornish.

27. The writer wants to add the following sentence to the second paragraph (sentences 3–6) to provide additional explanation.

She was not taught any English, since Cornish was the language of coastal Cornwall fish-traders in the 1690s.

Where would the sentence best be placed?

(A) Before sentence 3
(B) After sentence 3
(C) After sentence 4
(D) After sentence 5
(E) After sentence 6

28. In the third paragraph (sentences 7–8), the writer wants to expand on the controversy surrounding Dolly Pentreath. Which of the following claims would best achieve this purpose?

(A) Dolly Pentreath is not, in fact, the last speaker of Cornish, but rather its last fluent native speaker.
(B) In 1775, a fisherman in Mousehole named William Bodinar stated that he knew of five people who could speak Cornish.
(C) Dolly Pentreath was often known for cursing at people in Cornish whenever she became angry.
(D) Some people in Great Britain wish to revive rare languages such as Manx and Cornish.
(E) In 1768, researcher Daines Barrington wrote of a man from Marazion named John Nancarrow who was a native speaker and survived into the 1790s.

GO ON TO THE NEXT PAGE.

29. In the third paragraph (sentences 7–8), the writer wants to provide further evidence to rebut the claim made by modern historians. Which of the following pieces of evidence would best achieve this purpose?

(A) A 2012 petition, signed by over 25,000 Cornish people, urging Parliament to adopt Cornish as the second official language of the United Kingdom
(B) An interview of a modern Cornish speaker who claims Dolly Pentreath as his ancestor
(C) A personal anecdote about the author's travels around Cornwall in the 20th century
(D) A quote from an inscription on Dolly Pentreath's gravestone declaring her to be the last speaker of ancient Cornish
(E) An exposé of incompetence among certain modern scholars of British languages

30. The writer wants to add more information to the fourth paragraph (sentences 9–10) to support the main argument of the paragraph. All of the following pieces of evidence help achieve this purpose EXCEPT which one?

(A) The name of a 19th century book written in Cornish
(B) Census records indicating how many Cornish speakers there were in Penzance in 1850
(C) A quote from Dolly Pentreath's 18th century diary written in Cornish
(D) A Cornish dictionary published in 1920
(E) Evidence suggesting a revival of interest in Cornish in Victorian England

31. Which one of the following true statements, if inserted after sentence 13, would provide the best evidence for the idea that the revival of Cornish was successful?

(A) By 2010, UNESCO had removed Cornish from its list of "extinct" languages.
(B) Many people in 1904 believed that the Cornish language was an important part of Cornish culture and heritage.
(C) Along with Welsh and Breton, Cornish originally derived from the Brittonic language.
(D) Most modern residents of Cornwall continue to consider English their primary language.
(E) In 1929, Robert Morton Nance published his Unified Cornish system, based on available Middle Cornish sources.

32. The working title of this passage is "Dolly Pentreath: The Last Speaker of Cornish?". The fourth and fifth paragraph (sentences 9–13) answer the question posed in the title of the passage in which of the following ways?

(A) It provides evidence that Dolly Pentreath was not historically considered the last native speaker of Cornish.
(B) It shows that, despite Dolly Pentreath's legendary status in Cornwall, the Cornish language continues to be spoken today.
(C) It reaffirms the role that Cornish linguists and historians have played in perpetuating the Dolly Pentreath myth.
(D) It provides evidence to finally settle the question of whether Dolly Pentreath was a real historical figure.
(E) It does not answer the question posed in the title.

33. The writer wants to add a phrase at the beginning of sentence 13 (reproduced below), adjusting the capitalization as needed, to set up a continuation of the idea discussed earlier in the paragraph.

It is estimated that around 600 people in Cornwall speak their ancestral tongue.

Which of the following choices best accomplishes this goal?

(A) Furthermore,
(B) For example,
(C) Similarly,
(D) By contrast,
(E) Today,

GO ON TO THE NEXT PAGE.

Questions 34–41 are based on the following passage.

The passage below is a draft.

(1) Sherwood Anderson saw his first novel, *Windy McPherson's Son*, published in 1916, but it was not until 1919 with the publication of his masterpiece *Winesburg, Ohio* that Anderson was pushed to the forefront of a new movement in American literature. (2) The latter book, something between a short-story collection and a novel, helped to inaugurate an age of a truly homespun American Modernism.

(3) As other writers began to supplant him in the popular imagination, Anderson continued his tireless literary experimentation until his death in 1941. (4) It takes only a few pages of *Winesburg, Ohio*, however, or many of his other short stories, articles, and novels to see that Anderson is still very much with us today and that much of what we understand about ourselves as Americans was made clear to us only by the pen of the advertising man from Ohio.

(5) Sherwood Anderson would be seen by a new generation of American writers as the first author to take a real step toward creating a type of literature that was in tune with something previously only associated with Europe. (6) Anderson was able to fuse his sense of the passing of the Industrial Age in America with a type of uniquely American expression that sought to replace previous literary conventions with more local expressions of fragmentation and alienation.

(7) With *Winesburg, Ohio*, Anderson inspired a younger group of writers, among whose ranks were Ernest Hemingway and William Faulkner, to embrace their American experiences and to express them in ways separate from those being expressed by European writers or American expatriates, as American writers living abroad were known. (8) When *Winesburg, Ohio* finally appeared in 1919, its general reception was positive, but limited to those who were able to find copies of the book.

(9) In the 1920s, Anderson wrote some direct responses to the more explicit examples of literary Modernism in Europe. (10) In the 1930s, Anderson wrote *Beyond Desire*. (11) But Anderson's most important contributions in the 1920s and 1930s are best felt indirectly through the works of the various writers he inspired. (12) Anderson was among the first to explore the troubled relationship between the city and the rural town, the direct style to which we so often apply the name, "American," and the idea that deeply intellectual concerns can be relevant to everyday people as much as they can to academics. (13) Even today, Anderson's initial treatment of these themes remains an important starting point for anyone interested in American culture.

34. The writer wants to add a sentence to create an effective transition from sentence 3 to sentence 4. Which of the following sentences, if added between sentences 3 and 4, would best achieve this purpose?

(A) In the contemporary popular imagination, Anderson's influence often appears to be diminishing.
(B) In 1912, Anderson had had a nervous breakdown that led him to abandon his business and family and to become a writer.
(C) Before he died, though, he had moved to Chicago and was eventually married four times.
(D) Even Anderson scholars often overlook the fact that *Dark Laughter*, a novel inspired by Anderson's time in New Orleans, was his only bestseller.
(E) He died at the age of 64 during a cruise to South America.

35. After sentence 8, the writer wants to add a sentence to provide support for the main claim made in sentence 8. Which of the following sentences best accomplishes this goal?

(A) Anderson's later books, such as *Dark Laughter*, would go on to sell many more copies.
(B) Despite the success of *Winesburg, Ohio* many critics still preferred the older European models of writing.
(C) *Winesburg, Ohio* remains one of Anderson's best-loved books.
(D) Those who did secure a copy of *Winesburg, Ohio* felt that it inaugurated a new age in American literature.
(E) *Winesburg, Ohio*, which launched Anderson's career, has been lauded as a masterwork of American literature.

36. For the sake of the logic and coherence of this essay, the second paragraph (sentences 3–4) should be placed:

(A) (where it is now)
(B) Before the first paragraph (sentences 1–2)
(C) After the third paragraph (sentences 5–6)
(D) After the fourth paragraph (sentences 7–8)
(E) After the fifth paragraph (sentences 9–13)

GO ON TO THE NEXT PAGE.

37. At the end of sentence 10 (reproduced below), the writer wants to provide clear and effective support for the claim made in Sentence 4, adjusting punctuation as needed.

In the 1930s, Anderson wrote Beyond Desire.

Which of the following additions to the end of the sentence 10 best achieves this purpose?

(A) which addressed social questions that only social scientists and propagandists dared touch.
(B) which was heavily influenced by the literature of the Southern Populist movement.
(C) which has been named by many literary critics as a highlight from Anderson's later work.
(D) which was not as highly revered as *Winesburg, Ohio*.
(E) which is now considered to have been highly influential on later writers of the 20th century.

38. The writer wants to provide additional detail to clarify information that is crucial to the overall topic but may be unfamiliar to the average reader. Which of the following additions would best be most effective?

(A) A definition of literary Modernism in the first paragraph (sentences 1–2)
(B) More detail about Anderson's advertising career in second paragraph (sentences 3–4)
(C) An expanded discussion of the Industrial Age in third paragraph (sentences 5–6)
(D) A list of the major works of Hemingway and Faulkner in the fourth paragraph (sentences 7–8)
(E) A detailed plot description of *Beyond Desire* in the fifth paragraph (sentences 9–13)

39. How does the writer's purpose in the first paragraph (sentences 1–2) compare to the writer's purpose in the fifth paragraph (sentences 9–13)?

(A) The first paragraph is expository, while the fifth paragraph is analytical.
(B) The first paragraph provides evidence for the conclusion drawn in the fifth paragraph.
(C) The fifth paragraph provides additional detail about a general claim made in the first paragraph.
(D) The first paragraph provides objective analysis, while the fifth paragraph provides subjective advice.
(E) The first paragraph raises questions, while the fifth paragraph makes assertions.

40. The writer is considering adding the following quote from literature scholar Daniel Mark Fogel:

"Instead of emphasizing plot and action, Anderson used a simple, precise, unsentimental style to reveal the frustration, loneliness, and longing in the lives of his characters. These characters are stunted by the narrowness of Midwestern small-town life and by their own limitations."

Where would be the most effective place to add this quote?

(A) After sentence 2
(B) After sentence 4
(C) After sentence 6
(D) After sentence 8
(E) After sentence 9

41. All of the following sentences help to establish the writer's main argument EXCEPT

(A) sentence 1
(B) sentence 2
(C) sentence 7
(D) sentence 10
(E) sentence 11

Questions 42–45 are based on the following passage.

The passage below is a draft.

Siena is an old, picturesque city located in the hills of Tuscany. (2) Many historical markers from as far back as medieval Italy still remain throughout the city. (3) Another remnant from Siena's rich history that still plays a very prominent role today is the tradition of *Il Palio*.

(4) *Il Palio di Siena* is held twice a year: once in July and once in August. (5) A field of ten bareback horses races three laps, each with two dreaded right-angle turns, around a dangerously steep track circling the city's central plaza, the *Piazza del Campo*. (6) Even though *Il Palio* lasts only about 90 seconds, its importance in Siena goes far beyond the race itself.

(7) Members are fiercely committed emotionally, socially, and financially to their own *contrada*. (8) They voluntarily tax themselves to support their own *contrada* and to invest in a good horse and jockey for the biannual race. (9) Jockey salaries for a single race often exceed 250,000 euros! (10) This is, however, a small price to pay to achieve victory at *Il Palio*. (11) Seeing the colors and arms of their *contrada* in the winner's circle is the most glorious event—even more so than getting married—for many Sienese citizens. (12) Old men weep openly out of sheer joy, and elated adults and children parade throughout the city with their newly won silk banner, also called the *palio*.

(13) The brief race is a spectacular culmination of an entire way of life in Siena. (14) Every citizen belongs to one of seventeen city districts, collectively known as the *Contrade*. (15) *Contrada* is the term for a single district that has its own color and arms, such as the *Aquila* (the eagle) or *Bruco* (the caterpillar). (16) A contrada is the source of so much local patriotism that every important event, from baptisms to food festivals, is celebrated only within one's own contrada and fellow members, who become more like family.

(17) After the actual race day, the *Palio* festivities continue for a minimum of two weeks. (18) Thousands of visitors from around the world travel to Siena during the summer, not only to witness the exciting race but also to attend the after-parties thrown by the locals. (19) While the Palio is not important to outsiders who do not live in Siena, the race and the festivities that follow are a spectacular experience.

42. The writer wants to add a phrase at the beginning of sentence 2 (reproduced below), adjusting the capitalization as needed, to set up a contrast within the paragraph.

    Many historical markers from as far back as medieval Italy still remain throughout the city.

    Which of the following choices best accomplishes this goal?

    (A) In contrast to cities in nearby Greece,
    (B) As examples of modernity,
    (C) As with many European cities,
    (D) Even though its inhabitants live modern lives,
    (E) Despite what many may assume,

43. Which of the following true statements, if inserted after sentence 2, would best connect the first part of the first paragraph with the last part while illustrating the main idea of this paragraph?

    (A) Like most Italian cities, Siena is very serious about soccer, a modern sport codified in England in the 1800s.
    (B) Cobblestone streets and Gothic architecture are blended with modern sidewalk cafes and trendy designer stores.
    (C) The city of Siena is certainly a mixture of ancient and contemporary practices.
    (D) Siena is a major cultural center that offers numerous examples of art and architecture by Renaissance masters.
    (E) UNESCO has declared the historic centre of Siena a World Heritage Site.

44. For the sake of the logic and coherence of this essay, what would be the best placement for the third paragraph (sentence 7–12)?

    (A) (where it is now)
    (B) before the first paragraph (sentence 1–3)
    (C) before the second paragraph (sentence 4–6)
    (D) before the fifth paragraph (sentence 17–19)
    (E) delete the third paragraph

GO ON TO THE NEXT PAGE.

45. In sentence 19 (reproduced below), which of the following versions of the underlined text best establishes the writer's position on the main argument of the passage?

While the Palio is not important to outsiders who do not live in Siena, the race and the festivities that follow are a spectacular experience.

(A) (as it is now)
(B) It is no wonder:
(C) Although the Sienese have often been suspicious of outsiders,
(D) Despite outside efforts to stop the *Il Palio*,
(E) As I have witnessed myself on numerous occasions,

END OF SECTION I

AP® English Language and Composition Exam

SECTION II: Free Response Questions

DO NOT OPEN THIS BOOKLET UNTIL YOU ARE TOLD TO DO SO.

At a Glance

Total Time
2 hours, plus a 15-minute reading period

Number of Questions
3

Percent of Total Grade
55%

Writing Instrument
Pen required

Instructions

Section II of this examination requires answers in essay form. To help you use your time well, the coordinator will announce the time at which each question should be completed. If you finish any question before time is announced, you may go on to the following question. If you finish the examination in less than the time allotted, you may go back and work on any essay question you want.

Each essay will be judged on its clarity and effectiveness in dealing with the requirements of the topic assigned and on the quality of the writing. After completing each question, you should check your essay for accuracy of punctuation, spelling, and diction; you are advised, however, not to attempt many longer corrections. Remember that quality is far more important than quantity.

Write your essays with a pen, preferably in black or dark blue ink. Be sure to write CLEARLY and LEGIBLY. Cross out any errors you make.

The questions for Section II are printed in the green insert. You are encouraged to use the green insert to make notes and to plan your essays, but be sure to write your answers in the pink booklet. Number each answer as the question is numbered in the examination. Do not skip lines. Begin each answer on a new page in the pink booklet.

GO ON TO THE NEXT PAGE.

ENGLISH LANGUAGE AND COMPOSITION
SECTION II
Total Time—2 hours, 15 minutes

Question 1

Suggested reading and writing time—55 minutes.
It is suggested that you spend 15 minutes reading the question, analyzing and evaluating the sources, and 40 minutes writing your response.
Note: You may begin writing your response before the reading period is over.

(This question counts for one-third of the total essay section score.)

Throughout much of history, humans have defined themselves as members of their tribe. With the growth of civilization in the Neolithic period, humans began to define themselves by their village or state. By the nineteenth century, humans were defining themselves by their nation. Today, in the twenty-first century, humans are being asked to define themselves as citizens of the world.

Carefully read the following seven sources, including the introductory information for each source. Then synthesize the information from at least three of the sources and incorporate it into a coherent, well-developed essay that argues a clear position on the extent to which people are able to define themselves as global citizens.

Your argument should be the focus of your essay. Use the sources to develop your argument and explain the reasoning for it. Avoid merely summarizing the sources. Indicate clearly which sources you are drawing from, whether through direct quotation, paraphrase, or summary. You may cite the sources as Source A, Source B, and so forth, or by using the descriptions in parentheses.

Source A (Hassanpour)
Source B (graph)
Source C (Symons)
Source D (Kennedy)
Source E (Pirie)
Source F (Yeo)
Source G (map)

GO ON TO THE NEXT PAGE.

Source A

Hassanpour, Amir. "The Kurdish Experience." *MERIP* 189. Middle East Research and Information Project. July 1994. Web. 31 Jan. 2017.

The following is excerpted from an article on a website that provides analysis and information on the Middle East.

Numbering over 22 million, the Kurds are one of the largest non-state nations in the world. Their homeland, Kurdistan, has been forcibly divided and lies mostly within the present-day borders of Turkey, Iraq and Iran, with smaller parts in Syria, Armenia and Azerbaijan. The greatest number of Kurds today still live in Kurdistan, though a large Kurdish diaspora has developed in this century, especially in the main cities of Turkey and Iran and more recently in Europe as well. Between 10 and 12 million Kurds live in Turkey, where they comprise about 20 percent of the population. Between 5 and 6 million live in Iran, accounting for close to 10 percent of the population. Kurds in Iraq number more than 4 million, and comprise about 23 percent of the population.

In the modern era, the Kurdish nation, with its distinctive society and culture, has had to confront in all of the "host" states centralizing, ethnically-based nationalist regimes—Turkish, Arab and Persian—with little or no tolerance for expressions of national autonomy within their borders. While the modes and scale of oppression have varied in time and by place, the conditions of Kurds share some important features. First, the Kurdish areas overlap nation-state borders: They thus acquire significance for "national security" and are vulnerable to interference and manipulation by regional and international powers. Second, the Kurdish regions of these countries are usually the poorest, least developed areas, systematically marginalized by the centers of economic power. Third, the dynamics of assimilation, repression and Kurdish resistance in each country have affected the direction and outcome of the Kurdish struggles in the neighboring countries. A fourth shared feature is that these Kurdish societies are themselves internally complex, and fraught with differences of politics and ideology, social class, dialect and, still in a few places, clan.

In spite of a long history of struggle, Kurdish nationalism has not succeeded in achieving its goal of independence or even enduring autonomy. Do recent events require us to change this assessment? In 1992, a Regional Government of Iraqi Kurdistan was established, but it is economically besieged and functions very much at the sufferance of a Western military umbrella. In Turkey, a ten-year-old armed struggle has effectively defied the unrestrained efforts of the Turkish state to impose a military solution, but a political solution acceptable to the Kurds does not appear imminent. The Kurdish movement, in contrast to many other national liberation movements, has experienced a persistent contradiction between its traditional leadership and the relatively developed society it seeks to liberate. Only to the extent that this may be changing does the future hold some promise for Kurdish aspirations. Today, about half the population lives in urban centers, and feudal relations of production in rural areas have almost disappeared. Yet the politics and ideology of much of the leadership can hardly be distinguished from the worldview of landed notables of the past.

GO ON TO THE NEXT PAGE.

Source B

Investing.com. Untitled graph. June 2016. Web. 31 Jan. 2017.

The following is a graphic depicting the value of the British pound sterling on June 24, 2016, the day that England voted to leave the European Union.

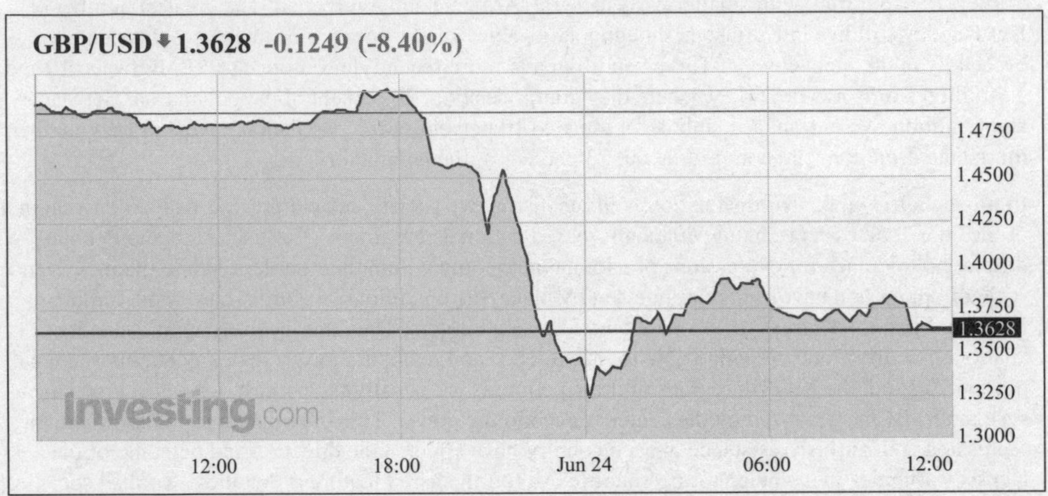

GO ON TO THE NEXT PAGE.

Source C

Symons, Emma-Kate. "Marine Le Pen's New York Times op-ed is a knife in the back for France." *Qz.com.* 19 Jan. 2015. Web. 31 Jan. 2017.

The following is excerpted from an article taking exception with The New York Times' *publication of an op-ed by Marine Le Pen, the leader of the French far-right political party Front National.*

Since 17 people were murdered in the Paris terror attacks that started with a massacre of cartoonists, staff, and police at Charlie Hebdo magazine, The New York Times has not deemed fit to print even one caricature by the French satirical weekly, citing Muslim sensitivities.

But today the Times opened up her august op-ed pages to France's extreme right Front National (FN) party president, Marine Le Pen, the chief Gallic spokesperson for Islamophobia and racism.

We must explain who Le Pen is here because the Times did not include even a phrase qualifying its op-ed contributor as a far right party boss, nor explaining her movement's long history of Muslim-baiting, incitement to racial hatred, Holocaust denial, and generalized anti-foreigner bile stretching back to the grimmest days of World War II collaborationist Vichy France.

The deliberately divisive FN leader is less Pat Buchanan, the renegade Republican, as she is white supremacist David Duke, and it is highly doubtful the Times would give an op-ed to either, especially on the Martin Luther King Jr. holiday weekend.

The daughter of party founder Jean-Marie Le Pen, an avowed Algerian war-torturer, she appropriated the legacy of Albert Camus and Georges Clemenceau, then purported to speak for "The French people," "French values," and the national value of "laicité," secularism built upon the strict separation of church and state.

In 2010, to cite one notorious example among many, Le Pen compared Muslims praying in French streets (for lack of mosques) to an "occupying force" akin to the Nazis, though such outrages were airbrushed from her carefully-worded Times screed.

Her op-ed, littered with half-truths and lies, distorts the position of the French government, which strongly condemned the Charlie Hebdo attacks, the murder of police, and the attack on a Kosher market as terrorism, driven by Islamism, and as fundamentally anti-Semitic.

Of course Le Pen did not dare mention anti-Semitism, and she conveniently neglected to detail that her party promises to end all immigration, send migrants "home," strip non-white French people arbitrarily of citizenship, close mosques and prayer halls, deport Roma peoples, close France's borders and Europe's free movement of peoples, leave the euro zone, and install the "national preference" for only "real" French i.e., white, nationals, thus forcing out millions of French people with dual nationality.

Le Pen is hoping to having a real shot at the French presidency in the 2017 elections, and her popularity is soaring, with more than one third of French agreeing with her views. Her success would mean a hijacking of French democracy as we know it.

The FN's DNA is firmly fascist and Le Pen has never renounced the core of her father's ideology; she has just presented a more acceptable face, refocused the hatred on Muslims, and calibrated her incoherent economic "platform" to sound like far-left anti-globalization populism.

But the leopard has not changed its spots. The FN remains what it always has been. It is a fascist-derived front party that capitalizes on hatred of the other, chiefly immigrants, and today, especially Muslims. Its platform espouses a monocultural white France, and its supporters are among France's most virulently anti-Semitic voters.

Le Pen's values are an insult to French values—the Front National abhors the legacy of the French revolution, and the universalist notion of French citizenship, as something that is not tied to race, but tied to republican French values of liberty, equality and fraternity.

GO ON TO THE NEXT PAGE.

Source D

Kennedy, Patrick F. Statement on Sri Lanka Day. 4 Feb. 2016.

The following are remarks given on Sri Lanka Day in 2016 from the Under Secretary of Management, Organization of American States, U.S. Department of State.

Thank you, Ambassador Kariyawasam, for that kind introduction, and the honor of your invitation. And I must say that I'm incredibly excited to visit your beautiful country later this month and see the progress already made on our new embassy complex.

68 years ago today, Sri Lanka found itself in good company when it joined the rather exclusive club of great nations that chose the fourth day of the month to declare independence from the United Kingdom.

Like Sri Lankans are doing today, in a few months Americans will mark our anniversary of independence, when we will also remember the heroes and patriots of years past, and reflect on how far we've come in our long quest for a more perfect union.

And like Sri Lankans of today, Americans are still striving to address some of the very challenging problems that have long bedeviled us. Problems like poverty, discrimination, and injustice.

But Sri Lankans and Americans both understand that these problems can only be solved through the use of the ballot box, the voice of a free press, the strength of a healthy civil society, and the actions of an empowered citizenry that is committed to democracy, human rights, and progress for all.

Yes, our nations share many interests in global affairs, and that makes us strong partners. We also have many of the same core values, and face many of the same hard problems. And that, I believe, makes us strong friends. For, in the words of the Roman poet Sallust, "to like and dislike the same things, that is indeed true friendship."

We love to see our friends succeed, and the accomplishments of the Sri Lankan people and their government over the past year have made all of us rightly proud.

GO ON TO THE NEXT PAGE.

Source E

Pirie, Dr. Madsen. "Ten Very Good Things: 9. Globalization." *AdamSmith.org*. 12 Oct. 2012. Web. 31 Jan. 2017.

The following is excerpted from a blog of a nonprofit organization dedicated to economic policy.

Over the course of decades globalization is turning the world into an integrated economy instead of what it has been for most of its history, a series of relatively isolated economies. The more trading that takes place, the more wealth is created, and global trade across international frontiers has created more wealth than ever before in human history, and has helped lift more people out of mere subsistence than ever before.

To poorer countries, globalization brings the chance to sell their relatively low cost labour onto world markets. It brings the investment that creates jobs, and although those jobs pay less than their counterparts in rich economies, they represent a step up for people in recipient countries because they usually pay more than do the more traditional jobs available there.

To people in richer countries, globalization brings lower cost goods from abroad, which leaves them with spending power to spare and a higher standard of living. It also brings opportunities for productive investment in high growth industries in developing countries.

Those adversely affected by the global exchanges are the people in rich countries whose output is now undercut by the cheaper alternatives from abroad. They often need to find new jobs or to be retrained to do work that adds higher value. The extra wealth generated by globalization has brought an increase in service sector employment, which provides many of the new jobs needed.

Competition from abroad forces firms to become more efficient and to use resources more efficiently. Often they choose to go upmarket, seeking higher added value products that face less competition from relatively unskilled labour. Thus firms which once sold cheap textiles move into fashion and design, and find customers among the rising middle classes in developing countries.

The integration of the world economy has brought with it an interdependence. As countries co-operate in trade with each other, they get to know each other and grow into the habit of resolving disputes by negotiation and agreement instead of by armed conflict. The 19th century French economist Frederic Bastiat expressed this pithily: "Where goods do not cross frontiers, armies will."

GO ON TO THE NEXT PAGE.

Source F

Yeo, Sophie. "China Air Pollution Blankets U.S. West Coast." *ClimateChangeNews.com.* 21 Jan. 2014. Web. 31 Jan. 2017.

The following is excerpted from an article on a website devoted to matters of climate change.

Air pollution in China is blowing over the Pacific Ocean and settling on the west coast of America, causing at least one extra day of dangerous smog in Los Angeles every year.

This is a case of getting what you pay for, according to a new study led by researchers from Peking University in Beijing.

They have calculated that approximately one quarter of the sulphate pollutants that cross into the US are tied to products created within China but destined for American consumers.

"We've outsourced our manufacturing and much of our pollution, but some of it is blowing back across the Pacific to haunt us," said co-author Steve Davis from the University of California Irvine.

"Given the complaints about how Chinese pollution is corrupting other countries' air, this paper shows that there may be plenty of blame to go around."

One of the drivers of the economic boom in China over the past ten years has been the demand for its exports. Between 2000 and 2007, the volume of Chinese exports grew by 390%.

At the same time, discontent over hazardous levels of air pollution in cities such as Beijing has been growing. Today, the governor of Hebei, the province surrounding Beijing, threatened to fire any officials who add new steel capacity, and thus increase the amount of coal being burnt.

GO ON TO THE NEXT PAGE.

Source G

"International Space Station Operation and Management." *NASA.gov*. Web. 31 Jan. 2017.

The following map shows the various international facilities that support the operation and management of the International Space Station, launched in 1998.

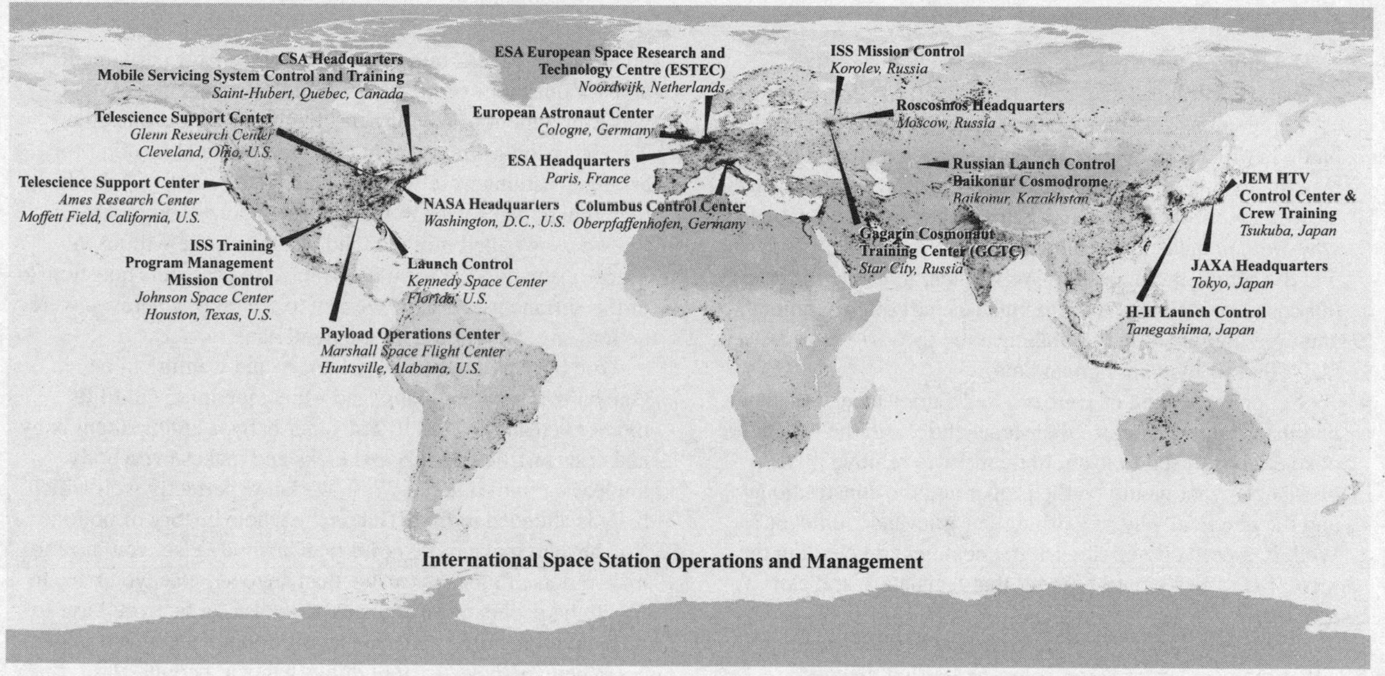

International Space Station Operations and Management

GO ON TO THE NEXT PAGE.

Question 2

Suggested time—40 minutes.

(This question counts for one-third of the total essay section score.)

The passage that follows is an excerpt from Emmeline Pankhurst's "Freedom or Death" speech, delivered in Hartford, Connecticut, on November 13, 1913. Pankhurst was a British political activist and leader of the women's suffrage movement in Britain who was widely criticized for her militancy. The following speech addresses her critics and defends the tactics of the suffragettes. Read the passage carefully. Then, in a well-developed essay, analyze the rhetorical strategies Pankhurst uses to convey her message.

Tonight I am not here to advocate woman suffrage. American suffragists can do that very well for themselves.

I am here as a soldier who has temporarily left the field of battle in order to explain—it seems strange it should have to be explained—what civil war is like when civil war is waged by women….Since I am a woman it is necessary to explain why women have adopted revolutionary methods in order to win the rights of citizenship. We women, in trying to make our case clear, always have to make as part of our argument, and urge upon men in our audience the fact—a very simple fact—that women are human beings.

Suppose the men of Hartford had a grievance, and they laid that grievance before their legislature, and the legislature obstinately refused to listen to them, or to remove their grievance, what would be the proper and the constitutional and the practical way of getting their grievance removed? Well, it is perfectly obvious at the next general election the men of Hartford would turn out that legislature and elect a new one.

But let the men of Hartford imagine that they were not in the position of being voters at all, that they were governed without their consent being obtained, that the legislature turned an absolutely deaf ear to their demands, what would the men of Hartford do then? They couldn't vote the legislature out. They would have to choose; they would have to make a choice of two evils: they would either have to submit indefinitely to an unjust state of affairs, or they would have to rise up and adopt some of the antiquated means by which men in the past got their grievances remedied.

Your forefathers decided that they must have representation for taxation, many, many years ago. When they felt they couldn't wait any longer, when they laid all the arguments before an obstinate British government that they could think of, and when their arguments were absolutely disregarded, when every other means had failed, they began by the tea party at Boston, and they went on until they had won the independence of the United States of America.

It is about eight years since the word *militant* was first used to describe what we were doing. It was not militant at all, except that it provoked militancy on the part of those who were opposed to it. When women asked questions in political meetings and failed to get answers, they were not doing anything militant. In Great Britain it is a custom, a time-honored one, to ask questions of candidates for parliament and ask questions of members of the government. No man was ever put out of a public meeting for asking a question. The first people who were put out of a political meeting for asking questions were women; they were brutally ill-used; they found themselves in jail before 24 hours had expired.

We were called militant, and we were quite willing to accept the name. We were determined to press this question of the enfranchisement of women to the point where we were no longer to be ignored by the politicians.

You have two babies very hungry and wanting to be fed. One baby is a patient baby, and waits indefinitely until its mother is ready to feed it. The other baby is an impatient baby and cries lustily, screams and kicks and makes everybody unpleasant until it is fed. Well, we know perfectly well which baby is attended to first. That is the whole history of politics. You have to make more noise than anybody else, you have to make yourself more obtrusive than anybody else, you have to fill all the papers more than anybody else, in fact you have to be there all the time and see that they do not snow you under.

When you have warfare things happen; people suffer; the noncombatants suffer as well as the combatants. And so it happens in civil war. When your forefathers threw the tea into Boston Harbor, a good many women had to go without their tea. It has always seemed to me an extraordinary thing that you did not follow it up by throwing the whiskey overboard; you sacrificed the women; and there is a good deal of warfare for which men take a great deal of glorification which has involved more practical sacrifice on women than it has on any man. It always has been so. The grievances of those who have got power, the influence of those who have got power commands a great deal of attention; but the wrongs and the grievances of those people who have no power at all are apt to be absolutely ignored. That is the history of humanity right from the beginning.

Well, in our civil war people have suffered, but you cannot make omelettes without breaking eggs; you cannot have civil war without damage to something. The great thing is to see that no more damage is done than is absolutely necessary, that you do just as much as will arouse enough feeling to bring about peace, to bring about an honorable peace for the combatants; and that is what we have been doing.

GO ON TO THE NEXT PAGE.

We entirely prevented stockbrokers in London from telegraphing to stockbrokers in Glasgow and vice versa: for one whole day telegraphic communication was entirely stopped. I am not going to tell you how it was done. I am not going to tell you how the women got to the mains and cut the wires; but it was done. It was done, and it was proved to the authorities that weak women, suffrage women, as we are supposed to be, had enough ingenuity to create a situation of that kind. Now, I ask you, if women can do that, is there any limit to what we can do except the limit we put upon ourselves?

GO ON TO THE NEXT PAGE.

Question 3

Suggested time—40 minutes.

(This question counts for one-third of the total essay section score.)

In response to the issue of racial imbalance, a sociologist argued, "Neutrality in our society is supposed to be the great equalizer because we believe that, if we don't favor any one group, things will work themselves out and become more equal. But the thing is this: neutrality has this effect only if there is no previous social or historical context. But that's not how the real world is. There is, in fact, a social and historical context for every situation. So if I were being "neutral" and viewing everyone as being the same, ignoring personal contexts, I wouldn't be promoting equality because I would be ignoring the differences that exist and allowing the inequalities to continue to exist, given that I wouldn't do anything to help change them. Identifying problems and actively promoting solutions are necessary to effect useful change; being neutral is consenting to the status quo."

In a well-written essay, develop your position on whether a "neutral" stand on race perpetuates racial imbalance today. Use appropriate evidence from your reading, experience, or observations to support your argument.

STOP

END OF EXAM

Practice Test 1: Answers and Explanations

PRACTICE TEST 1 ANSWER KEY

1. B
2. C
3. E
4. C
5. A
6. D
7. B
8. E
9. C
10. D
11. B
12. B
13. A
14. B
15. A
16. E
17. E
18. A
19. C
20. A
21. C
22. E
23. E
24. A
25. C
26. B
27. B
28. E
29. D
30. C
31. A
32. B
33. E
34. A
35. D
36. E
37. A
38. A
39. C
40. C
41. D
42. D
43. B
44. D
45. B

Once you have checked your answers, remember to return to page 4 and respond to the Reflect questions.

PRACTICE TEST 1 EXPLANATIONS

Multiple-Choice Questions

1. **B** To answer this question, think in terms of main idea. This is a fairly straightforward question that asks you to consider the type of material you are reading and what the author is saying within that context. In this piece of literary criticism, the author is making a connection between what Gulliver experienced and what an eighteenth-century Londoner might have seen exhibited in fairs and inns.

2. **C** The author describes Swift's achievement in *Gulliver's Travels* in generally positive terms, so (C) is correct. If the author were *cleverly subversive*, he would have attempted to undercut his generally positive portrayal of Swift in some way, but he never does; eliminate (A). Authors on the AP Exam are rarely only *halfheartedly engaged*, so (D) can also be eliminated. Both (B) and (E) are wrong and cannot be substantiated in the passage.

3. **E** This is a challenging question because the author provides no explicit definition for the *Scriblerians* in the passage. You know that they were *fascinated with popular entertainments* (line 16) and that they *satirized them in many of their works* (lines 17–18), which means they are authors, not book craftsmen, (A), or literary characters, (B). There is no evidence that they worked as either historians or politicians, so eliminate (C) and (D).

4. **C** In lines 18–19, you learn that Swift *shared this fascination with his fellow Scriblerians*, which makes him a member of the circle. Therefore, (C) is correct. While he does have a distinct interest in public entertainments, he is not necessarily a *producer* of one himself, so (B) can be eliminated. There is simply no evidence in the passage for any of the other answer choices.

5. **A** The first two paragraphs maintain a consistent tense and person, so (B) can be eliminated. The author does not invest time in drawing historical allusions or extended metaphors, so (C) and (D) can also be eliminated. He does make some claims that could be considered asides, but they are hardly for *didactic* (i.e., educational) purposes, and they are not the most *evident* stylistic feature, so eliminate (E) as well. The correct answer is (A) because the author uses a parallel, consistent syntactical structure throughout these paragraphs.

6. **D** The author wants readers to see the connection between miniature people and landscapes in *Gulliver's Travels* and the common public entertainments of Swift's London. Thus, he emphasizes their *commonness*, (D), over other features. This directly contradicts *obscurity* in (B), which can be eliminated. He does not emphasize merely the fact that they are small, so eliminate (A) as well. *Transience*, (E), which emphasizes their fleeting nature, is not discussed in the final paragraph; neither is *magnificence*, (C), so both answer choices can be ruled out.

7. **B** The series of quotes in the final paragraph substantiate the author's claim that *Gulliver's Travels* was at least somewhat based on the kinds of popular entertainments that people often saw in London. Therefore, (B) is the correct answer. The author does not really aim his argument at other scholars or at claims that *Gulliver's Travels was purely imaginative*, so eliminate (A) and (C). While he certainly does include information from other sources, his primary purpose is not to *inform the reader of the sources*, so eliminate (E).

8. **E** The first section of the essay introduces readers to the connection between *Gulliver's Travels* and popular entertainments, while the second section provides evidence to support that claim. Thus, (E) is correct. There really are no *series of questions*, (A), *positions of scholars*, (C), or *a technical definition*, (D), so those choices can be eliminated. It is not accurate at all that the second choice *challenges* claims made in the first, so (B) is wrong as well.

9. **C** Footnote questions were added to the test in response to concerns raised by colleges and universities. In these days of easy access to information via the Internet, colleges are becoming increasingly concerned that students do not take seriously the intellectual property of authors and end up plagiarizing, knowingly or not. Footnotes give information about authorship and publication place and date and can also provide hints as to the purpose of a piece of writing or its context. This particular footnote simply indicates that the quote about Lilliput does indeed come from *Gulliver's Travels*, part of a 14-volume set of works by Swift.

10. **D** This question asks you to analyze the citation in the footnote to assess the source of the cited information. Given the author, title, publisher and page numbers in the footnote, this was a book-length text written by John Ashton. The correct answer is (D).

11. **B** By paying attention to the title, author, subject matter, and footnotes, you can use POE to eliminate (D) and (E). And while the subject matter of this essay might be of interest to an *anthropologist*, (A), the writer is not impartial. Further, the content and format are inconsistent with literary criticism, (C). The correct answer is (B).

12. **B** The tone of this passage is scholarly and generally positive, which is somewhat more difficult to detect than more overtly negative tones. Therefore, (B) is correct. He does support his claims, but not frantically, so (A) is incorrect. He is not *dejected* (i.e., sad), so (C) is also incorrect. *Intransigent* basically means stubborn, so eliminate (E). And while this passage certainly is *erudite* (i.e., learned), he does not show any signs of cynicism, so (D) is incorrect.

13. **A** In the first two paragraphs, the author establishes that Jonathan Swift was a Scriblerian and that *All the Scriblerians were fascinated with popular entertainments; collectively and individually, they satirized them in many of their works.* Peepshows and moving pictures would be examples of this. Choice (C) may seem close, but since the passage is mainly about Swift and *Gulliver's Travels*, this choice is too broad.

14. **B** POE is the best way to approach this question. Choices (A), (C), (D), and (E) are all partially wrong (and therefore completely wrong). Take a look at (B). The author is being ironic when she says in the first line, *My own sex, I hope, will excuse me, if I treat them like rational creatures.* The second part of (B), *exposition*, is defined as *a setting forth of meaning or intent*, and that is exactly what the author is doing in this first paragraph. Choice (B) is correct. Note that in this context, *apology* has nothing to do with being sorry; it most nearly means *defense of an idea.*

15. **A** The author addresses women directly and pretends to excuse herself for addressing them as strong, confident people, instead of the weak, overly sentimental creatures that society wants (and expects) them to be. The correct answer is (A).

16. **E** Since men aren't mentioned anywhere in the first paragraph, your choice should boil down to (D) and (E). When the author says, *I wish to persuade women to endeavour to acquire strength, both of mind and body*, she means intellectual and physical strength, (E). Had she wanted to stress emotional strength, she would have replaced *mind* with *heart.*

17. **E** The roots *soft* and *weak* appear in both paragraphs and are used in both their adjective and verb forms. The connotations of these terms, and their use to describe negative stereotypes of women, unite the two paragraphs. The correct answer is (E).

18. **A** Narrow down your choices to (A) and (B). The best way to approach this type of question is to substitute each of the answer choices for the original word to see which one makes the most sense. Try (A): *supposed to be the sexual characteristics of the weaker sex.* This seems great, but try (B) too, just in case: *supposed to be the sexual characteristics of the weaker woman.* Not as good. Naturally, in this case, the weaker sex is woman, but you are asked to find the meaning for *vessel* only. Choice (A) is the best answer.

19. **C** Using Process of Elimination, get rid of (B), (D), and (E). Now you're down to (A) and (C). The author states that *the first object of laudable ambition is to obtain a character as a human being, regardless of the distinction of sex.* Thus, you should eliminate (A) because she is not suggesting that a comparison be made between a man and woman. This leaves (C) as the answer.

20. **A** The author wishes to convince the reader by the force of her cogent arguments and the sincerity of her emotions, so the answer is (A). If cogent is not on your vocabulary list, add it now. It means appealing to the intellect or powers of reasoning or convincing. You can eliminate the other choices because the author states unequivocally that she does not wish to polish her style, to employ the bombast and periodic sentences of a rhetorical style, to write elegantly, or to use flowery diction.

21. **C** The author points out that the *flowery* diction expected of women relegated them to a world outside that of men. The difference in the social level of men and women was reflected in the way they used language. Only men could use the crude words that attempt to express the harsh realities of life. Women were not supposed to know those same harsh realities and, therefore, could not use the crude words that fit with those realities.

22. **E** The sugary diction becomes associated with the taste of a cloyingly sweet delicacy. This is an extended metaphor, so Process of Elimination allows you to eliminate (A), (B), and (D); this is not a caricature of women, nor is it a critique of bombast (pompous speech or writing). If you do not know the meaning of *panegyric*, then add it to your list of vocabulary. A panegyric is a statement of high praise. It should be clear that the author does not sing the praises of *sugary writing.*

23. **E** In this passage, the author suggests that women have the capacity to be independent equals of men. She states this most plainly at the end of the second paragraph: *the first object of laudable ambition is to obtain a character as a human being, regardless of the distinction of sex.* Therefore, she is most likely to agree that if women were educated in the same manner as men, they would be more likely to be viewed as equal with men in the eyes of the world. The correct answer is (E).

24. **A** Use Process of Elimination, especially if you don't know what *sardonic* means (harsh, bitter, or caustic). *Lyrical* is far too positive, so rule out (B). *Frivolous,* (D), is a trap: the women are perceived as frivolous, but that is not the author's tone. The author is quite passionate and not at all reserved, so rule out (E). *Condescending,* (C), is a trap as well; lines 55–59 seem to convey this mood, but it directly contradicts the message of line 2 (*rational creatures*) as well as the main idea of the passage as a whole. The last line of the passage betrays the author's true purpose: to point out the illogic of assuming that women are helpless, useless creatures unfit for positions of responsibility.

25. **C** The writer's *exigence* is the motivation for the writer's effort in creating a piece of work. Here, the author is a feminist who wishes to argue that women should not be viewed as beings with inferior skills or rights in society. She must have been motivated by the observation that women were not viewed as equals in her era.

26. **B** The passage as a whole explores the legend that Dolly Pentreath was the last fluent, native speaker of Cornish before it went temporarily extinct. Choice (A) is lacking any reference to her language choices. Choice (C) cannot be true, since Dolly died in 1777. Choice (D) is out of sequence and seems to contradict sentence 1. Choice (E) is relevant to Cornish but does not mention Dolly. Sentence 1 states that Dolly *chose* to speak in Cornish, which implies that she rejected English. Choice (B) would establish this idea, as well as provide Dolly's full name, along with an entertaining start to the topic. Therefore, the answer is (B).

27. **B** The given sentence discusses her education. Look at the sequence of events in the paragraph. Since sentence 3 is about Dolly's birth, that should start the paragraph. Eliminate (A). It doesn't make sense to mention after any mention of her adult life (sentences 4–6). Eliminate (C), (D), and (E). The answer is (B).

28. **E** The controversy in the third paragraph is about whether Dolly Pentreath was, in fact, the last fluent native speaker of Cornish before the language went extinct. No one claims that she was the last speaker in *any* era (A), since the last paragraph mentions the revival of Cornish in the 20th century. Choice (B) would not necessarily exacerbate the controversy since Dolly died in 1777 and it's possible that the people William Bodinar knew were deceased before then. Choice (C) is irrelevant to the controversy, while (D) is consistent with the last paragraph rather than the third paragraph. Choice (E) mentions a native speaker who survived after Dolly's death. This expands on the controversy, so the answer is (E).

29. **D** The claim made by modern historians in the third paragraph is that Dolly Pentreath was *not* the last fluent speaker of Cornish. To rebut them, the author needs some additional evidence. Choices (A), (B), and (C) are all irrelevant to the issue of last fluent speaker. Choice (E) may look tempting, but you do not know whether the incompetent scholars are the ones making the claim in question. Choice (D) provides evidence that the people in Dolly's time believed her to be the last speaker of Cornish; it does not prove the historians wrong, but it weakens their case. The answer is (D).

30. **C** The main argument made in the fourth paragraph is that people who lived after Dolly Pentreath died did, in fact, speak some Cornish. Choice (C) is irrelevant to this claim, since this evidence would come from Dolly's own life. All the other choices provide evidence that there was interest in Cornish *after* the 18th century. The answer is (C).

31. **A** Choices (B) and (E) may show that there was an interest in Cornish, but do not prove that, in fact, people were actively speaking the language. Choice (C) does not support any particular argument, while (D) tends to weaken the author's argument. Choice (A) says that UNESCO does not consider Cornish to be an extinct language. If that is the case, then modern people must be speaking it, thus providing evidence of a successful revival. The answer is (A).

32. **B** Although Dolly is famous for being the "last" speaker of Cornish, the fourth and fifth paragraphs establish that there was a resurgence of interest in the language in the 20th century, and it is now spoken by around 600 people. Choice (A) is incorrect. Although her status as the last speaker of Cornish is disputable, it is what she was historically known as. Choice (C) is incorrect based on statements made about historians in sentence 8. Choice (D) is incorrect because the question of whether

she was a real historical figure is not posed. Although Dolly is famous for being the "last" speaker of Cornish, the fourth and fifth paragraph establishes that this was not the case, answering the question. Eliminate (E). The correct answer is (B).

33. **E** Sentences 11 and 12 are written with past tense verbs (*sparked, taught, published, coined*), but sentence 13 is written in the present tense (*speak*). The transition, therefore, must indicate this time shift. There is no example or contrast, so (B) and (D) are incorrect. Choices (A) and (C) are close, but do not communicate the time shift. The answer is (E).

34. **A** Sentence 4 mentions that *Anderson is still very much with us today* and contains the word *however*, so the sentence we insert before it must represent a contrasting idea. Choices (B), (C), and (E) contain details about Anderson's life that are irrelevant to any contrast in the perception of his work. Choice (D) may seem tempting, but it is not as effective as (A) since it merely refers to his past career and not his present influence. Only (A) represents the needed contrast, since it states that Anderson's influence often *appears* to be diminishing. The answer is (A).

35. **D** The claim made in sentence 8 is that *Winesburg, Ohio* was well-received by the reading public, but apparently it was difficult to obtain. Choices (C) and (E) are not as effective since they do not establish that the book was difficult to obtain. Choices (A) and (B) detract from the claim in sentence 8 by pointing out weaknesses in *Winesburg*'s success. Choice (D) adds detail to directly support both that it was well-received and that it was difficult to obtain. The answer is (D).

36. **E** Pay close attention to the years discussed in each of these paragraphs. The second paragraph discusses Anderson's death in *1941* and his influence *today*. It should be logically placed after the paragraph discussing the time period most directly before that. The fifth paragraph discusses the 1920s and the 1930s, the periods closest to 1941 in this passage. Therefore, the second paragraph would be best placed after the fifth paragraph. The other choices would put the timeline out of sequence. The answer is (E).

37. **A** This question asks you to identify something which harmonizes with the claim in sentence 4, which states that *much of what we understand about ourselves as Americans was made clear to us* by Sherwood Anderson. Choice (B) suggests that *Beyond Desire* had other influences and does not say whether Anderson was the first to incorporate these influences. Choices (C) and (D) discuss the reactions of critics and readers to the book, not the book itself. Choice (E) may seem close but is more relevant to other claims made in other parts of the passage, not in sentence 4. Choice (A) supports the idea that Anderson addressed an understanding of American culture that hadn't been written about by novelists previously. The answer is (A).

38. **A** The first paragraph states that Sherwood Anderson *helped to inaugurate an age of a truly homespun American Modernism* but never really explains what Modernism is or how Anderson made it *homespun* or *American.* Modernism is likewise referred to in the third and fifth paragraphs, so it is a major theme within the passage. All the other answers except for (A) mention things that are merely passing details in the passage, not crucial themes, so (A) is correct.

39. **C** The first paragraph makes the claim that Sherwood Anderson was part of a *new movement* in American literature and *helped to inaugurate an age of a truly homespun American Modernism.* The fifth paragraph provides much more detail about his role in Modernism and how his innovative style influenced other writers. Choice (B) gets this backward. Only (C) describes this relationship, so the answer is (C).

40. **C** Sentence 6 mentions *fragmentation and alienation* in Anderson's *uniquely American* characters. This is a good match for Fogel's quote, which mentions *frustration, loneliness, and longing* in *Midwestern small-town life*. Sentences 2, 4, 8, and 9 don't have the same clear connection, so the answer is (C).

41. **D** The main claims made in the essay are that a) Sherwood Anderson was part of a new literary movement, American Modernism, and that b) he influenced other writers. Choices (A), (B), (C), and (E) all refer to sentences that support these ideas. Sentence 10 is not directly connected to these claims, since you actually know nothing about *Beyond Desire* other than its time of publication, so the answer is (D).

42. **D** Choices (B) and (C) do not set up a contrast and, therefore, can be eliminated. Choice (A) and (E) do introduce contrasts but ones that are not supported by anything in the paragraph. Eliminate (A) and (E). Choice (D) is the best since it uses Even *though* to introduce two contrasting ideas.

43. **B** The best connecting statement should continue the previous idea that Siena has both ancient and modern elements, eliminating (A) and (D). The following sentence begins with *Another remnant*, which means the inserted sentence should already list specific examples and makes (B) better than (C) and (E). The answer is (B).

44. **D** Because the fourth paragraph introduces and defines the *contrada* discussed in sentence 7, the third paragraph cannot come before the fourth. Eliminate (A), (B), and (C). There is also a logical sequence from winning the *Palio* at the end of the third paragraph to the celebration in the beginning of the fifth paragraph, so it should not be deleted. Eliminate (E). The best location for the third paragraph is before the fifth paragraph, so (D) is correct.

45. **B** The main argument of the passage is that the Palio horse race is a significant tradition in the lives of the Sienese and remarkable for its long-lived popularity. Three of the answers mention *outsiders*, but there is no evidence within the text that those who do not live in Siena do not care about the race, (A), are suspicious to the Sienese, (C), or have tried to stop the tradition (D). There is also no evidence that the author has attended the race, (E). Choice (B) is the best answer.

HOW TO SCORE PRACTICE TEST 1

Section I: Multiple-Choice

__________ × 1.5000 = __________

Number of Correct (out of 45) — Weighted Section I Score (Do not round)

As of the printing of this book, there have been no official administrations of this test. Therefore, this scoring should only be used as an estimate.

Section II: Free Response

(See if you can find a teacher or classmate to score your essays using the guidelines in Chapter 4.)

Question 1 __________ (out of 6) × 4.5833 = __________ (Do not round)

Question 2 __________ (out of 6) × 4.5833 = __________ (Do not round)

Question 3 __________ (out of 6) × 4.5833 = __________ (Do not round)

Sum = __________

Weighted Section II Score (Do not round)

AP Score Conversion Chart English Language and Composition

Composite Score Range	AP Score
112–150	5
98–111	4
80–97	3
55–79	2
0–54	1

Composite Score

__________ + __________ = __________

Weighted Section I Score + Weighted Section II Score = Composite Score (Round to nearest whole number)

Part III
About the AP English Language and Composition Exam

- The Structure of the AP English Language and Composition Exam
- How the AP English Language and Composition Exam Is Scored
- Overview of Content Topics
- How AP Exams Are Used
- Other Resources
- Designing Your Study Plan

THE STRUCTURE OF THE AP ENGLISH LANGUAGE AND COMPOSITION EXAM

Below is a helpful outline that describes the basic format for the exam. The total time allotted for the completion of this exam is 3 hours and 15 minutes, or 195 minutes.

Section I: Multiple Choice (1 hour)—counts for 45 percent of your grade

Total number of questions: 45

Section II: Free Response (2 hours, 15 minutes; includes a 15-minute reading period)— counts for 55 percent of your grade

Composed of three essays, which the College Board describes as follows:

1. **Synthesis essay:** You will read several sources on a topic and create an argument that integrates information from at least three of the sources to support your thesis.
2. **Rhetorical analysis essay:** You will analyze a nonfiction text and discuss how the author's language choices contribute to the purpose and intended meaning.
3. **Argument essay:** You will create an evidence-based argument in response to a given topic.

HOW THE AP ENGLISH LANGUAGE AND COMPOSITION EXAM IS SCORED

Your Multiple-Choice Score

In the multiple-choice section of the test, you are awarded 1 point for each question that you answer correctly, and you receive no points for each question that you leave blank or answer incorrectly. So, even if you are completely unsure, guess. In Part IV, Chapter 1, we'll show you how to narrow down your choices and make educated guesses.

Your Free-Response Score

Each AP essay is scored on a scale from 0 to 6, with 6 being the best score. Essay readers (who are high school or university English instructors) will grade your three essays, and the scores for your three essays will be added together. The resulting total (which ranges from 0 to 18) constitutes your free-response score.

We will go into the details of essay scoring in Part IV, Chapter 4, but, in general, an essay that receives a 6 answers all facets of the question completely, making good use of specific examples to support its points, and is "well-written," which is a catch-all phrase that means its sentences are complete, properly punctuated, clear in meaning, and varied (that is, they exhibit a variety of structure and use a large academic vocabulary). Lower-scoring essays are considered to be deficient in these qualities to a greater or lesser degree, and students who receive a "0" have basically written gibberish. If you write an essay that is not on the topic, you will receive a blank ("—"). This is equivalent to a zero.

The essay readers do not award points according to a standardized, predetermined checklist. The essays are scored individually by individual readers, each of whom scores essays for only one prompt. Thus, you will have three different readers, and each reader will be able to see only the single essay that he or she reads. The readers do not know how you did on the other essays or what score you received on the multiple-choice section.

Your Final Score

Your final score of 1 to 5 is a combination of your scores from the two sections. Remember that the multiple-choice section counts for 45 percent of the total and the essay section counts for 55 percent. This makes them almost equal, and you must concentrate on doing your best on both parts.

You will have the opportunity to calculate your final score for each Practice Test in this book. The Answers and Explanations chapters include a worksheet to guide you through the scoring formula step by step. (Remember, this worksheet is meant to serve as a guideline only!)

What Your Final Score Means

After taking the test in early May, you will receive your scores sometime around the first week of July, which is probably when you'll have just started to forget about the entire harrowing experience. Your score will be, simply enough, a single number that will either be a 1, 2, 3, 4, or 5. Here is what those numbers mean.

Score meaning	Percentage of all test-takers receiving this score*	Roughly equivalent first-year college course grade	Will a student with this score receive credit?
5—Extremely qualified	10.1%	A	Usually
4—Well qualified	18.5%	A–, B+, B	Usually
3—Qualified	26.5%	B–, C+, C	Maybe
2—Possibly qualified	31.1%	N/A	Very Rarely
1—Not qualified	13.8%	N/A	No

*Percentages are based on the May 2019 administration of the exam, as reported in August 2019.

OVERVIEW OF CONTENT TOPICS

The AP English Language and Composition Exam tests your abilities to understand how authors use rhetoric and language to convey their purpose. Students are also expected to apply these techniques to their own writing and research projects. Some of the major skills tested include the ability to:

- identify an author's purpose and intended audience
- recognize rhetorical devices and strategies in an author's work
- demonstrate understanding of citations in research papers
- apply these skills and techniques to their own writing
- create and organize an argument defended with evidence and reasoning
- plan, write, and revise cogent, well-written essays

HOW AP EXAMS ARE USED

Colleges make their own decisions about the minimum AP score required to earn credit (points that count toward your college degree), the number of credit hours awarded, and whether advanced placement (the opportunity to skip introductory courses and enter higher-level courses) is offered.

Policies differ widely. Some colleges require a score of 3, while others require a 4, for instance. Some offer both credit and placement; some offer only credit, and some only placement.

The AP Exam administrators have created a helpful tool that lets you check the AP credit policy for most colleges. Go to apstudent.collegeboard.org/creditandplacement/search-credit-policies and enter the names of the colleges that interest you. The tool will give you the minimum score required for credit and/or placement. It will also give you a link to the college's website so you can check the most up-to-date policy information.

OTHER RESOURCES

There are many resources available to help you improve your score on the AP English Language and Composition Exam, not the least of which are your teachers. If you are taking an AP class, you may be able to get extra help from your teacher, such as obtaining feedback on your essays. If you are not in an AP course, reach out to an English teacher and ask if he or she will review your essays or otherwise help you review.

Another wonderful resource is **AP Students,** the official student site for the AP Exams. The scope of the information at this site is quite broad and includes:

- a Course Description, which provides details on what is covered and sample questions
- the 2001 and 2007 AP English Language and Composition Released Exams, available for purchase at the College Board Store
- essay prompts from previous years
- Frequently Asked Questions (FAQs)
- practice material for grammar, including a quiz and grammar guide
- tips for succeeding on the essays

The AP Students home page address is apstudent.collegeboard.org/home.

The AP English Language and Composition Course home page address is apcentral.collegeboard.org/courses/ap-english-language-and-composition/course.

Finally, **The Princeton Review** offers tutoring and small group instruction for the AP English Language and Composition Exam. Our expert instructors can help you refine your strategic approach and add to your content knowledge. For more information, call 1-800-2REVIEW or visit princetonreview.com/academic-tutoring/subjects/ap-english-language for AP English Language Homework Help.

Online Student Tools
Our online portal for the AP Exams, Student Tools, contains a bunch of helpful resources, including a study guide, printable bubble sheets, admissions advice, additional practice tests, and more. Follow the instructions on the Get More (Free) Content page at the front of this book to access this great content!

Break up your review into manageable portions. Download our helpful study guide for this book once you register online.

DESIGNING YOUR STUDY PLAN

In Part I, you identified some areas of potential improvement. Now let's delve further into your performance on Practice Test 1, with the goal of developing a study plan appropriate to your needs and time commitment.

Read the answers and explanations associated with the multiple-choice questions (starting on page 35). After you have done so, respond to the following questions:

- Review the Overview of Content Topics on page 46 and, next to each skill listed, indicate your rank as follows: "1" means "I need a lot of work on this," "2" means "I need some review of this," and "3" means "I have sufficiently mastered this."
- How many days/weeks/months away is your 2019 exam day?
- What time of day is your best, most focused study time?
- How much time per day/week/month will you devote to preparing for your exam?
- When will you do this preparation? (Be as specific as possible: Mondays and Wednesdays from 3:00 to 4:00 P.M., for example.)
- Based on the answers above, will you focus on strategy (Part IV) or the terms and modes review (Part V) or both?
- What are your overall goals in using this book?

Based on your answers to these questions, you should now have a better understanding of how to study for the exam. Use your answers to tailor the online study guide available for download when you register your book online.

Part IV
Test-Taking Strategies for the AP English Language and Composition Exam

- Preview

1. How to Approach Multiple-Choice Questions
2. Using Time Effectively to Maximize Points
3. Pacing Drills
4. How to Approach the Essays: Basic Principles
5. How to Approach the Synthesis Essay
6. How to Approach the Rhetorical Analysis Essay
7. How to Approach the Argument Essay

- Reflect

PREVIEW

Review your responses to the questions on page 2 of Part I and then answer the following questions:

- How many multiple-choice questions did you miss even though you knew the answer?
- On how many multiple-choice questions did you guess blindly?
- How many multiple-choice questions did you miss after eliminating some answers and guessing based on the remaining answers?
- Did you create an outline before you wrote each essay?
- Did you find any of the essays easier or harder than the others—and, if so, why?

Those answers will give you an idea of what you're doing now and where you could improve your performance on the multiple-choice section and the three essays.

- Did you miss too many multiple-choice questions when you knew (or think you should have known) the answer? Perhaps you're not working carefully enough, or you're letting test anxiety get the better of you.
- Did you guess blindly at more than a few questions? Maybe you didn't make your guesses in the most successful way.
- Did you use POE (Process of Elimination) to get rid of the obviously wrong answers, and still miss the correct response when you took a guess from the remaining answers? The "Letter of the Day" approach probably would have helped there too. You'll learn about this approach shortly.
- Did you simply start writing your essay without planning what you were going to say and organizing your points? A few minutes spent on an outline will save you from getting half an hour into your essay time and realizing you're seriously off track.
- If you found one essay more difficult than the others (typically the rhetorical analysis essay gives students the most grief), you know where to focus your efforts. The techniques and practice you'll find in the essay chapters will help you gain confidence in tackling all three of the essays on the exam.

HOW TO USE THE CHAPTERS IN THIS PART

Before you read the following strategy chapters, think about the previous strategies you learned and used for Practice Test 1. As you read on you'll start to recognize ways you can change your current approach in order to be more successful on each section of the exam. At the end of Part IV, you'll have the opportunity to reflect on the changes you plan to make.

Chapter 1
How to Approach Multiple-Choice Questions

WHAT TO EXPECT IN THE MULTIPLE-CHOICE SECTION

The multiple-choice section counts for 45 percent of your total score, but you're given only 31 percent (1 hour) of the total exam time to earn that large chunk of points. So how you spend that hour is extremely important.

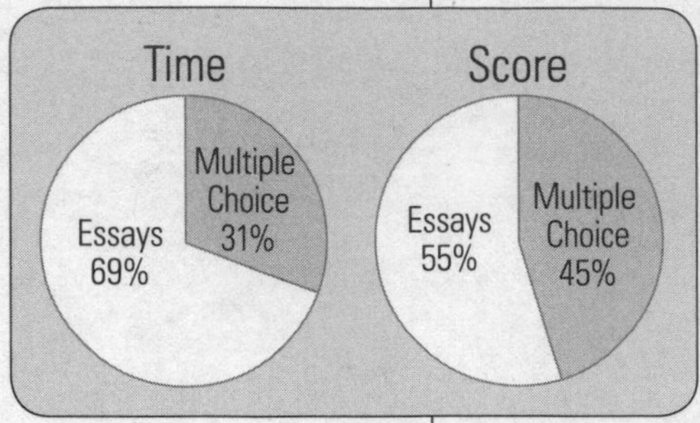

The multiple-choice portion of the exam consists of five passages and 45 questions. All five passages will be nonfiction. Two of them will be publication-quality passages and associated with Reading questions. These passages will range from the 19th, 20th, and 21st centuries. Three of the readings will be student-level passages and associated with Writing questions. These passages will be examples of contemporary, persuasive writing. Our practice tests include examples of each type of passage and style of question, just like the real exam, so that you will be ready by the time you get to the test. You will have one hour to complete 45 multiple choice questions. There will be 23–25 Reading questions and 20–22 Writing questions. All multiple-choice questions will be scored by computer.

"Nonfiction" is a very broad term, so you could find Reading passages taken from all sorts of works—essays, biographies, diary entries, speeches, letters, literary criticism, science and nature writing, and writings about politics or history. The passages will also run the gamut as far as types of diction (word choice), syntax (how words are combined into phrases and sentences), imagery, tone, style, point of view, and purpose.

The Reading questions emphasize not just *what* the author is saying, but especially *how* the author says it. The idea is to get you to focus on rhetorical devices, figures of speech and intended purposes, under rigid time constraints and with material you haven't seen before. You'll need to identify rhetorical devices and structures in a passage, and understand why and how the author used them. (Review Chapters 8–11 to learn more about rhetorical strategies. You'll find this helpful for the rhetorical analysis essay too.) The Reading questions are a challenging opportunity to demonstrate your ability to analyze how writers use language to achieve their purposes.

In at least one of the Reading passages, you'll also find several questions about citations, which are usually presented as footnotes to the passage. Citations often give credit to sources from which the passage author drew ideas or information. The citation could state a source's date and place of publication, which might be important in evaluating that source. (For example, a very old source might be questionable if there have been more recent discoveries about a topic.) Citations can also supplement information in the passage without cluttering up the main text with details that might distract readers.

The Writing questions will ask you to evaluate passages of student-level, persuasive writing. The questions are likely similar to peer-review exercises you've done in English classes over the course of your high school experience. Questions might ask you to select an ideal introductory sentence, revised thesis statement, or a piece of evidence that would enhance the writer's argument. Questions will also ask you to consider concessions, counterarguments, and rebuttals. Though the writing in these passages is simpler than in the Reading passages, you'll have to think critically about the argument being presented and any potential flaws therein.

So where do you start preparing to get that much done in such a short time? In this chapter, you'll find techniques for reading the passages and answering multiple-choice questions under the conditions that will confront you in the exam.

Active Reading

The passages on the exam are often heavy reading, particularly the older nonfiction, with the long sentences and sometimes obscure words that were common at the time. You need to read quickly but with understanding. If you just skim through the passage, you will have wasted much of your precious two or three minutes of reading time and will likely have to keep rereading parts just to gain a sense of what the author is talking about.

The solution? Active reading. That means you take control of the passage instead of simply letting it pour sentences and paragraphs into your head. Engage with it.

As you read each paragraph, ask yourself these questions:

- What is the author's main point in this paragraph?
- How does it connect to the paragraph that came before it?
- Where is it likely to lead in the next paragraph?

Active Reading

Look for the main point of the passage, the author's purpose, and the rhetorical strategies used to achieve that purpose.

At the end of the passage, ask yourself the following questions:

- What is the author's "big picture" purpose and main point in this passage as a whole?
- Did the author convince me? Interest me? Lead me to disagree strongly? How did the author achieve that effect on me as a reader?
- What impact would this passage likely have had on readers who lived when it was written? What techniques did the author use to achieve that effect?

You can practice this type of active reading with any written material—textbooks, printed ads, or product descriptions, for example. Once you get into the habit, you'll find that your reading comprehension increases considerably, along with your critical thinking skills. With enough practice, active reading will be second nature to you by the time you encounter the AP English Language and Composition Exam passages, where it's a necessity if you're to wade through most, if not all, of the questions and answer them successfully.

Words in Context

Guess the meaning of an unfamiliar word from its context.

Words in Context

Chances are you'll encounter some unfamiliar words on the exam, particularly in the nonfiction Reading passages. Another active reading technique can take you over that hurdle too: guessing the meaning of a word from its context. For example, let's say the passage is describing a politician who is trying to sell an unpopular new law to the voters in his constituency.

The speaker's passion and ebullience began to cut through the dour mood of the audience that confronted him.

If you have no idea what "ebullience" and "dour" mean, you can still figure them out from the context. The speaker is passionate about this law he's trying to promote, so—paired with "passion"—"ebullience" must have something to do with enthusiasm and excitement. The voters, on the other hand, don't like it at all, so "dour" must signify something opposite—gloomy, unreceptive. The word even sounds dark and unfriendly.

Guessing a word's meaning from its context is something you can practice on material you encounter in your daily life. Then you can check a dictionary or thesaurus to see how your skill is improving.

Attack the Questions and Go Back to the Passage

Each question is setting a specific task for you. Make sure you understand exactly what it's telling you to do. Read the question stem carefully, word for word.

Don't Play Mind Games

Your memory will fool you. Always go back to the passage.

When a question refers to specific lines in the passage, always go back to the passage and reread them. You should also read a few lines before and after the specified lines; context is often critical in determining the correct answer.

Relying on your memory—particularly in the dense, nonfiction works you'll encounter on the exam—can easily lead you astray. Sometimes a sneaky answer choice will start out partly correct, but then make a U-turn into something that is not supported by the passage. But if you're relying on your memory and get a glimmer of recognition from the first part, you might pick the wrong answer and miss out on scoring a point. Remember, half wrong is all wrong.

POE—Process of Elimination

After you understand the question task and have gone back to the passage to review the lines it specifies, look at the answer choices. Your active reading, careful analysis of the question task, and rereading of specific lines will most likely show you at least a couple of answer choices that are clearly wrong. Now instead of five possible answers, you have only three or perhaps two, and your chances of choosing—or even guessing at—the correct answer just went up substantially.

Main Steps of POE

First, eliminate the answers you know are wrong.

Then look for the right answer within the remaining choices.

So start there—by quickly getting rid of choices that are obviously wrong—instead of starting by puzzling through five possible answers looking for the one right choice. That's the Process of Elimination approach, and it will increase your success rate on multiple-choice questions significantly.

Guessing and the Letter of the Day

So you've tossed out two clearly wrong answers using POE, and narrowed five possible choices down to three. Suppose you still can't tell *which of* those three is the correct answer, though.

What do you do? Two things: guess and use the Letter of the Day.

Guessing

You get no points for a question that isn't answered at all. The good news with this exam, though, is that you don't lose any points for incorrect answers. So answer every single question, even if your answer is a guess. By using POE, you've raised your chances of guessing correctly within a smaller number of possible answers. There's another technique you can add that will increase your guessing success rate even more.

Letter of the Day

If you make a random guess for each question you can't answer—(A) for one and (D) for another and maybe (E) for this one—you've just made an excellent start at getting every one wrong. The solution? Pick one letter—any letter—and use it for every single guess. That's the Letter of the Day approach.

Proven Techniques
Use POE, Letter of the Day, and the Two-Pass System to help boost your score.

Let's say there are 10 questions you can't answer. If you pick, for example, (B) as your Letter of the Day and answer (B) on every one of those 10 questions, what are the chances that (B) really is the correct answer to at least one of them, possibly more? Pretty good. On the other hand, if you jump around with a different random letter for each guess, you stand a good chance of missing the correct answer on every one.

The Two-Pass System

With around 45 questions and 5 passages, you have roughly 1 minute and 30 seconds to answer each question, which is about 12 minutes for each passage and accompanying set of questions. The Two-Pass System will help you use that time most efficiently. Here are the steps to take:

On your first pass through the questions:

- Answer all the easy questions first. If you can answer a question as you come to it, do so.
- Each time you come to a hard question that you can't answer, fill in a "guess" answer using your Letter of the Day and circle the question.

The Two-Pass System

Pass 1: Answer the easy questions and guess at the hard ones, using the Letter of the Day.

Pass 2: Tackle as many of the hard ones as you can during the time left for that passage.

On your second pass through:

- Look at your watch to see how much time you have left for this passage. Go back to the hard questions you circled and tackle as many as you can before the chunk of time available for that passage runs out.

This system works well since all the questions are worth the same number of points, regardless of whether you think they're easy or hard, and since the order in which you answer the questions doesn't matter.

Now let's examine a sample passage.

SAMPLE READING PASSAGE—HERE'S HOW IT'S DONE

The following passage is excerpted from *A Technical Guide for Monitoring Wildlife Habitat* by the United States Department of Agriculture Forest Service.

The publication that includes this excerpt is intended as a guide for professionals involved in forest planning and wildlife habitat monitoring. It was published in 2013 by the USDA Forest Service, which aims to balance the use of public resources with the protection of those resources. The authors are professionals in such fields as ecology, biology, and forestry.

Management Considerations

Management objectives will differ substantially among species and, thus, influence habitat monitoring objectives. Emphasis species for which habitat may be monitored may come from a wide spectrum of conservation categories from taxa listed under the Federal Endangered Species Act to ubiquitous species that may be hunted or trapped.

The process of identifying monitoring priorities begins with a review of pertinent laws, regulations, policies, regional and forest management objectives, and priorities set through partnerships and agreements to determine those emphasis species for which monitoring of populations is required. Recovery plans for threatened or endangered species often require that cooperating agencies monitor population parameters for the species.[1] Others commit the Forest Service to monitor habitat.[2] Memoranda of understanding with State wildlife agencies obligate the Forest Service to assist with monitoring populations of important game species.[3]

Regional and forest management objectives also influence whether habitat is monitored for an emphasis species. If a land and resource management plan specifies management activities in ecological systems that also provide habitat for an emphasis species, it may be advisable to monitor habitat for that species.[4] Conversely, an emphasis species associated with habitat that is not likely to be influenced by planned management actions may be a poor candidate for habitat monitoring.[5]

Biological Considerations

Habitat monitoring should focus primarily on species that are most likely to respond to changes in habitat condition because of management actions, disturbances, or climate change. In particular, management actions may impact systems in ways that are detrimental or positive but remain uncertain and require monitoring. Thus, selecting emphasis species should include not only those that are associated with forest plan objectives or desired conditions, but also those that have the potential to be affected by management actions that modify habitat.

In addition, developing a successful habitat monitoring program requires making a clear distinction between habitat and population monitoring.[6] In some cases, the monitoring objective for a species at risk will specify the detection of relatively small changes in population size (especially decreases) or occupancy. Depending on the management concern, monitoring objective, detectability, demography, and ecological relationships of a species, it may be prudent to monitor only populations, rather than to also track habitat. Under some limited circumstances, behavioral and spatial relationships may exist that allow populations to be closely linked to specific habitat attributes.[7] If strong evidence indicates that habitat features are directly associated with population size of an emphasis species, then habitat monitoring, with the objective of indirectly monitoring populations may be an acceptable approach under a limited range of management circumstances.[8] Species that are difficult to detect and, therefore, difficult to monitor for population abundance are good candidates for habitat monitoring if strong habitat relationships have been documented and if information on annual population fluctuations are not needed. Under these circumstances, compare habitat monitoring results periodically with population data to ensure that the assumed relationship between habitat and population remains.[9] The indirect nature of the monitoring program relative to the link between habitat and populations must always be considered when the resulting monitoring data are used.

---

1 e.g., red-cockaded woodpecker *[Picoides borealis]* USDI USFWS. 2003. Recovery plan for the red-cockaded woodpecker (Picoides borealis). 2nd rev. Atlanta, GA: U.S. Department of the Interior, U.S. Fish and Wildlife Service, Southeast Region. 296 p.

2 e.g., Mexican spotted owl *[Strix occidentalis lucida]* USDI U.S. Fish and Wildlife Service (USFWS). 1995. Recovery plan for the Mexican spotted owl (Strix occidentalis lucida). Albuquerque, NM: U.S. Department of the Interior, U.S. Fish and Wildlife Service, Southwest Region. 172 p.

3 e.g., Sitka black-tailed deer *[Odocoileus hemionus sitkensis]* in the Alaska Region

4 e.g., woodland caribou. *[Rangifer tarandus caribou]*. USDA Forest Service. 1987. Forest plan Idaho Panhandle National Forests. Missoula, MT: U.S. Department of Agriculture, Forest Service, Northern Region. Irregular pagination.

5 e.g., gray-crowned rosy finch *[Leucosticte tephrocotis]* in alpine habitats relative to timber management activities

6 i.e., habitat monitoring should not be confused with population monitoring (See chapter 1).

7 e.g., amount of recently burned conifer forest is directly related to populations of black-backed woodpeckers *[Picoides arcticus]*. Hutto, R.L. 1995. Composition of bird communities following stand-replacement fires in northern Rocky Mountain (U.S.A.) conifer forests. Conservation Biology. 9: 1041–1058.

8 Haufler, J.B.; Mehl, C.A.; Roloff, G.J. 1999. Conserving biological diversity using a coarse-filter approach with a species assessment. In: Baydack, R.K.; Campa, H., III; Haufler, J.B., eds. Practical approaches to the conservation of biological diversity. Washington DC: Island Press: 107–125. Molina, R.; Marcot, B.G.; Lesher, R. 2006. Protecting rare, old-growth, forest-associated species under the survey and manage program guidelines of the Northwest Forest Plan. Conservation Biology. 20: 306–318.

9 See chapter 1.

Approaching Reading Questions

In active reading mode, you should be looking for and writing down the main point of each paragraph in the margins before you move on to the next. From those building blocks, you can identify the main point of the excerpt and the author's purpose.

The first section focuses on forest or other environment management programs. The first paragraph stresses flexibility: objectives and species can encompass a broad range. The authors are providing guidance that can be applied to just about any situation readers face. The second paragraph outlines a framework of requirements and partnerships for undertaking monitoring programs—again, within a broad range of situations. The third paragraph positions habitat monitoring within larger management programs, and gives examples of when it may or may not be appropriate to monitor habitats.

The excerpt then looks at selecting species for habitat monitoring. The fourth paragraph specifies that species likely to be affected by a change in habitat should be selected. The long fifth paragraph then makes a point the authors want to emphasize: habitat monitoring should be distinguished from population monitoring. The paragraph gives examples of when both types of information could be considered, or even when population monitoring could be carried out on its own. However, the two types of monitoring are always considered as distinct activities.

The introductory comments provide context that helps identify the authors' purpose and the rhetorical strategies they use. The excerpt is part of a guide written by nature management professionals for professionals. In order to influence readers to follow their recommendations and practices, the authors need to gain trust and build credibility. Rhetorical techniques they use include formal language, drawing on authorities, and providing examples. The authors do have a clear bias for distinguishing habitat monitoring from population monitoring; however, their tone is neutral and unemotional. They allow for exceptions, and they use qualified language such as "may be prudent" and "may be an acceptable approach." They avoid complex industry jargon, making their information accessible to readers from a broad spectrum of disciplines and with varying degrees of expertise. As a result of these techniques, the authors sound like trustworthy, experienced scientists who are making sound recommendations but not alienating readers by being authoritarian.

Let's look at a typical "big-picture" question.

1. The authors' main purpose in this excerpt is to
   - (A) encourage professionals to adopt a monitoring approach that is similar to the Forestry Service's approach
   - (B) influence habitat monitoring professionals to monitor populations too
   - (C) concentrate wildlife monitoring efforts on bird populations
   - (D) educate readers about how to monitor wildlife habitats
   - (E) direct resources toward protecting endangered species

Through active reading, you should have identified not only the main point of each paragraph, but also the authors' overall purpose. The correct answer is (A). The excerpt outlines the Forestry Service's approach and, through the frequent use of "should," encourages readers to follow a similar approach. The guide specifies that habitat and population monitoring should be distinct activities, and that they should be combined in only limited circumstances, so (B) is clearly wrong and could have been eliminated right away using POE. Although the footnote comments give several examples of birds, they also mention deer and caribou, (C). The intended audience is made up of professionals in the field, so they would not need to be educated about how to monitor wildlife habitats, (D). The authors specify that habitat can be monitored for any species, from the endangered and at risk to the thriving, so they intend to cover a broad spectrum of situations, making (E) incorrect.

Here's another "big picture" question, focused on only one paragraph this time.

2. Paragraph 4 implies that
   (A) resources available for habitat monitoring are limited
   (B) forest management programs focus only on the physical environment
   (C) the impact of forest management programs cannot be predicted
   (D) forest management programs include climate change
   (E) habitat monitoring should not be confined to species that are part of forest management programs

The answer is (E). The authors recommend also monitoring species that aren't part of the forest plan but which could be affected by any resulting changes to their habitat. This recommendation makes (A) incorrect; resources do not appear to be limited when the scope of the monitoring could be expanded beyond the original plan. The paragraph discusses both the physical environment and the species that inhabit it, so (B) is incorrect. In addition to being wrong, though, (B) is also too extreme ("focus only on"). On the AP Exam, it's unusual for an "all or nothing" response such as this to be correct. Extreme choices can usually be eliminated right away using POE. While the authors acknowledge that the impact of forest management actions may be uncertain, they don't claim that it's not possible to predict the impact in every case, so eliminate (C). Forest management programs are planned and run by humans; climate change is not, so (D) is incorrect.

Here's another question in which you're asked to make an inference from something stated in the passage.

3. The last sentence of paragraph 2 suggests that
   (A) readers must consult the Forest Service if they want to monitor habitats for endangered species
   (B) the Forest Service requires State wildlife agencies to include it in monitoring game species populations
   (C) the Forest Service must be involved in population monitoring programs for certain game species
   (D) permission must be obtained from the Forest Service before game populations are monitored
   (E) the Forest Service demands control of game species population monitoring programs

A set of relatively close answers such as this one demonstrates the importance of going back to the passage instead of relying on your memory. You need to review exactly what the sentence says to avoid being tripped up by a choice that sounds close but has something wrong with it. Reread only as much as you need to, though. If you can't answer a question without spending too much time rereading, then guess at the answer (using your Letter of the Day) and, if you have time, return to it on your second pass through the questions for that passage.

The correct answer is (C). As you found when you identified the main point of paragraph 2, the authors are cautioning that a framework of requirements governs monitoring programs. Readers can't necessarily just set off on their own. In the last sentence of paragraph 2, the authors state—in a gentle, non-threatening way —that the Forest Service is "obligated" to "assist" with population monitoring programs for important game species. Choice (A) can be eliminated immediately because the sentence mentions game species, not endangered species. The authors don't specify which organization initiated the agreements with State wildlife agencies, so we can't say for sure whether (B) is true. Choice (D) would suggest getting permission and then going off and conducting the monitoring program without any further involvement by the Forest Services, which is incorrect. Choice (E) is too extreme ("demands control") and can be eliminated on that basis.

Here are a couple of questions dealing with rhetorical strategies—*how* the authors say what they say in order to achieve their purpose with a specific audience in a particular context.

4. In the rhetorical strategies they use, the authors are trying to convince readers that they are
   (A) expert authorities in the field
   (B) a trustworthy source
   (C) a benign enforcement mechanism
   (D) independent thinkers
   (E) set in their ways as a result of extensive experience

The correct answer is (B). Through their formal language, objective tone, supporting citations, and flexibility in acknowledging exceptions, the authors position themselves as a source whose recommendations can be trusted by professionals in the field. While the authors do cite some other U.S. environmental agencies in the footnotes, they also give references to nongovernment research results. They position themselves as experienced guides, not as expert authorities, (A). The authors do not suggest that they can or will enforce compliance with the monitoring practices they describe, so (C) is incorrect. Even when they outline "laws, regulations, policies," they don't specify penalties for noncompliance. There is no suggestion that the authors are advocating an approach that differs markedly from established monitoring practices, (D). At several points, the authors demonstrate flexibility by acknowledging that there may be exceptions to their recommendations, demonstrating an openness that makes (E) wrong.

5. One rhetorical strategy the authors use in order to achieve their purpose with their professional audience is
   (A) examples of the negative results of combining population and habitat monitoring
   (B) appeals to authority
   (C) specialized technical language
   (D) understatement
   (E) appeals to logical reasoning

Choice (B) is the correct answer. In several of the footnotes, the authors draw on published works and authorities in the field to support their points. The citations in the footnotes become part of the authors' rhetorical strategy. The authors actually acknowledge that the two types of monitoring can be combined in certain circumstances. They do not give any examples of negative results from combining them in the wrong circumstances, (A). The authors do give the correct scientific classification for certain species, and they use the term "emphasis species" to signify a monitoring target. However, their use of technical language is not extensive. The authors are aiming at a diverse range of industry participants, so in general they use formal language to signify their professionalism while not excluding readers by using highly technical language from one specific field, so (C) is incorrect. The authors' tone is objective and neutral. They do not understate, (D), or overstate the impact of not following their general practice of distinguishing habitat monitoring from population monitoring. The authors don't rely on logical arguments, (E), such as "X and Y are the case; therefore, you should do Z or else *this* will happen because of *this*."

This next question shows the type of detail some questions can cover.

6. The term "taxa" in paragraph 1 refers to
   (A) characteristics of a group of organisms that distinguish them from other groups
   (B) criteria used to determine whether a species is endangered
   (C) a grouping of certain species of organism
   (D) the unusually frail members of a larger group of animals who likely would not survive without habitat support
   (E) any group of widespread and thriving organisms

This question demonstrates the importance of context in guessing the meaning of an unfamiliar word, and the need to go back to the passage to find the answer. Remember to read a line or two above and below the word specified, too, so you won't miss any important information from the context.

Here, the correct answer is (C). The paragraph states that habitat monitoring is appropriate for a full range of organisms, from those on the endangered species list to those that are so numerous and widespread ("ubiquitous") that they can be hunted. It sets up a contrast between species on both extreme ends of the range. Using the technical term "taxa" allows the authors to avoid repeating the word "species" three times in the same sentence. However, "taxa" could accurately be replaced by "species" in this sentence. Choice (A) is incorrect because "taxa" (the plural of "taxon," which would indicate a single species) refers to the groups themselves, not to the characteristics of those groups. Both (B) and (E) are incorrect as meanings for "taxa" because species could be either endangered or thriving. Choice (D) is incorrect because "taxa" refers to entire groups, not to individual members of those groups.

Here are some typical questions about citations, which are shown as footnotes. That means you'll need to read the footnote as well as go back to the corresponding place in the passage (indicated by the superscript number of the footnote). Read a couple of lines above and below the footnote number so you understand the context in which the authors cite a particular source or make a supplementary comment.

7. The primary function of footnote 9 is most likely to
   (A) give readers a method for carrying out a procedure
   (B) explain the reason for the authors' recommendation
   (C) provide an additional source for readers who are interested in more information
   (D) convince readers that they need more information before they can follow the authors' recommendations successfully
   (E) provide an authority to support the authors' point

Choice (A) is correct. The excerpt doesn't say what is in Chapter 1, so you'll need to guess at the most likely primary reason for referring readers to it. Since the footnote occurs at the end of a sentence that describes a procedure (comparing habitat monitoring results with population data to confirm an assumed relationship between the two), (A) is the best choice. The footnote is simply a side comment, not an integral part of the text, where the authors would likely have explained their reasoning, (B), or made a convincing case, (D), if they felt the need to do so. Choice (C) is too vague when the footnote follows the description of a specific procedure. Since the footnote sends readers to another spot in the same publication, it is not providing a supporting authority, (E).

8. The most unique aspect of footnote 8 in paragraph 5 is its

   (A) support for the separation of habitat and population monitoring
   (B) seven-year time span of support for the program objective of monitoring populations
   (C) geographical diversity of the resources cited
   (D) additional support for the authors' acknowledgement of a situation that would favor incorporating some population monitoring into a habitat monitoring program
   (E) acknowledgement of an opposing position

The answer is (D). Footnote 8 is the only one that cites two sources of support for the same point (indirect population monitoring as an objective of habitat monitoring). The sources are cited as support for a condition in which habitat and population monitoring could be combined, not separated. Going back to the passage should have allowed you to eliminate (A) immediately using POE. While there is a seven-year time span between the two references, the two sources are not cited as support for only monitoring populations. Choice (B) is half wrong; therefore, it's all wrong. Although the second study in the footnote specifies the northwest, the first study doesn't indicate which geographical area it covers; eliminate (C). The sources are cited in support of, not in opposition to, the authors' position; eliminate (E). Again, going back to the passage should have eliminated this choice right away.

9. The main effect of footnote 7 is to

   (A) support the authors' point
   (B) convince readers who might be skeptical about the authors' point
   (C) illustrate and support the authors' point
   (D) explain the authors' point
   (E) support and qualify the authors' point

Choice (C) is correct. The example of the impact of forest fires on woodpecker populations illustrates the authors' point, and the citation from published research supports it. While this footnote supports the authors' point with a reference to published research, that's not the only thing it does, eliminating (A). It's possible that an example and citation might convince skeptical readers, but the question asks for the *main* effect. The footnote is not worded as if its main objective were to convince skeptical readers, so you can get rid of (B). The footnote gives an example; it doesn't explain what the authors mean, so (D) can be eliminated. This footnote does support the authors' point. However, they already qualified their point in the main text ("Under some limited circumstances..."), not in the footnote. Remember, half wrong is all wrong. Eliminate (E).

Incidentally, if you had guessed at every one of these answers and had chosen (C) as your Letter of the Day, you would have gotten three correct answers on this passage. No, of course you can't know in advance which letter is best, but this example shows the results that are possible with the Letter of the Day technique.

SAMPLE WRITING PASSAGE—HERE'S HOW IT'S DONE

This is an example of the student quality persuasive writing you that will be associated with Writing questions on the exam. Begin by reading the passage carefully and using the same active reading techniques you used on Reading passages. Look for and write down the main point of each paragraph in the margins as you go. Remember that this passage will be imperfect; Many of the Writing questions will provide you options to make it better.

The passage below is a draft.

(1) Bottled water comprises 67.3% of plastic bottle use in the United States, a leading cause of waste that threatens our oceans and our air quality. (2) Many cities, venues, colleges, and recreational areas have decided to ban single-use plastic water bottles.

(3) Upwards of 70% of plastic water bottles in the U.S. never see the inside of a recycling bin, which is why many Americans are upset. (4) Plastic bottle production takes a dramatic toll on the environment, and the Pacific Institute estimates that it took 17 million barrels of oil to produce single-use plastic bottles consumed in the U.S. in 2006. (5) Those numbers have only increased since: bottled water consumption in the U.S. increased 65% between 2006 and 2017, necessitating 13.7 billion barrels of oil that year.

(6) Concord, Massachusetts, San Francisco, California, the Detroit Zoo, the University of Vermont, and the Grand Canyon National Park have all banned single-use water bottles. (7) Not only will banning water bottles protect the environment, it will also be good for our health. (8) This is because bottled water isn't well regulated. (9) Banning single-use plastic bottles will also reduce pollution associated with plastic bottle creation; communities living near plastic bottle manufacturers report higher levels of chronic illness and birth defects than those that don't.

(10) Banning single-use plastic water bottles may seem like an unpopular idea, but tap water is less expensive than you might realize, particularly considering that bottled water costs between 400 and 2,000 times as much as tap water. (11) It's time for the United States to make the choice that is best for the environment and our pocket books and ban single-use plastic water bottles.

Approaching Writing Questions

The first paragraph acts as an introduction. The introduction has a few different goals: to hook the reader's attention, to introduce the topic of the essay, and, perhaps, to state the writer's thesis (though, be careful, in some essays, the thesis will develop over the course of the essay).

The introduction is followed by body paragraphs. Though there's no set formula for the construction of the body paragraphs, most will start with a clearly stated claim that will be developed in the paragraph. Usually, that claim is substantiated through the use of evidence. Evidence could consist of concrete data, expert opinion, or personal anecdotes. Body paragraphs may also include a concession, an acknowledgment of a plausible argument held by the opposing view. Similarly, body paragraphs may rebut that concession, providing an explanation as to why the writer's argument remains the better viewpoint, despite the concession.

Because Writing paragraphs are drafts, they may or may not contain a formal conclusion. In a conclusion, the writer usually summarizes their main points and/or restates their thesis. In more complex examples, the conclusion may include the fully-realized form of a thesis that has developed over the course of the essay.

Let's take a look at questions that commonly pertain to the introductory segment of the passage:

1. Which of the following sentences, if placed before sentence 1, would both engage the audience's attention and introduce the topic of the paragraph?

   (A) In 2017, Americans consumed nearly 17 billion gallons of bottled water.
   (B) Every second, 20,000 plastic bottles are bought around the world, most of which contain only drinking water.
   (C) Bottled water manufacturers have been known to deplete water supplies in local communities.
   (D) Cities that have already banned single-use plastic bottles are planning to increase the numbers of public drinking fountains.
   (E) Residents of Flint, Michigan, were exposed to unsafe tap water when private companies bottled their water supply.

Using active reading, you should have identified the subject matter of this essay: the effects of bottled water consumption and the need to ban it. Reading the question closely, you know that you're looking for a response that is both interesting and relevant to the passage. Using POE, you can eliminate (B) and (D). Choice (B) pertains to water consumption around the world, whereas the information provided pertaining to water consumption is limited to the United States. Choice (D) describes drinking fountain access, which is irrelevant to the rest of the paragraph as well.

While response (E) is interesting and reflects a negative aspect of bottled water, it also describes a danger of tap water, which is contrary to the purpose of the paragraph and essay. Choice (C) is plausible but reads as a random factoid as opposed to an engaging introductory sentence. Choice (A) is the best answer, as many readers will be surprised by the quantity of bottled water Americans consume. It also introduces the topic of the paragraph: bottled water consumption.

Here's another questions that addresses the use of transitions in an introductory paragraph:

2. In sentence 2 (reproduced below) the author wants a more fluid transition between the introductory sentences and the thesis of the passage:

   Many cities, venues, colleges, and recreational areas have decided to ban single-use plastic water bottles.

   Which of the following versions of the underlined text achieves this purpose?

   (A) (as it is now)
   (B) In order to reduce waste and protect the environment, many cities
   (C) Angering corporate interests, many cities
   (D) To protect developing communities abroad, many cities
   (E) Seeing it as an ethical imperative, many cities

The goal of transitional phrases is to bridge ideas between sentences, so look for a phrase that captures, or even summarizes, the content of the previous sentences and explains the relationship between it and the subsequent sentence. As it is, the sentences are two independent ideas in sequence: the waste produced and environmental consequences of plastic water bottle, and the fact that certain entities have already banned their use. No transition is made, so eliminate (A). Choices (C) and (D) can be eliminated because the ideas they use to transition—angry corporate interests, protecting developing communities abroad—are irrelevant to the sentence that precedes them. While (E) is a plausible response, (B) is significantly more specific to the ideas presented in the previous sentence. As such, (B) creates a better transition than leaving the text as is. Therefore, (B) is the best answer.

This question focuses on the thesis of the passage:

3. In sentence 3 (reproduced below), which version of the underlined statement most clearly states the author's thesis?

Upwards of 70% of plastic water bottles in the U.S. never see the inside of a recycling bin, which is why many Americans are upset.

(A) (as it is now)
(B) which is just one reason the United States needs to ban single-use plastic bottles.
(C) which is why consumers need to stop buying bottled water.
(D) which is why plastic bottles threaten future generations.
(E) which causes unnecessary environmental degradation.

This sentence comes at the start of the second paragraph, where the writer begins to develop the argument of the essay. For any questions that pertain to a thesis or the author's argument, it's important to consider the essay as a whole and not just the context of the surrounding sentences. Though the essay is imperfect, each paragraph builds on the idea that banning plastic water bottles has positive effects. Choice (C) presents the idea that consumers need to stop buying plastic water bottles. While this is perhaps a valid point, it is too specific to be described as the thesis of the essay. Choice (E), on the other hand, is too general. Unnecessary environmental degradation may be accurate and relevant, but it doesn't create an argumentative focus (or thesis) for the essay. Choice (D) has similar flaws, it is too broad, and it is somewhat off topic from the points presented in subsequent paragraphs. The current draft, reflected by (A), is weak because it is unsubstantiated; nowhere does the writer present evidence to support the idea that many Americans are upset. Choice (B) is the best answer, because the idea that *the United States needs to ban single-use plastic bottles* is a specific argument that is substantiated over the course of the essay.

The following questions pertain to the body paragraphs of the essay:

4. The writer wants to emphasize the surprising increase in plastic bottle use between 2006 and 2017, described in sentences 4 and 5. Adjusting for capitalization as needed, which phrase best accomplishes this goal at the start of sentence 5 (below)?

   Those numbers have only increased since: bottled water consumption in the U.S. increased 65% between 2006 and 2017, necessitating 13.7 billion barrels of oil that year.

   (A) (as it is now)
   (B) Actually,
   (C) By contrast,
   (D) Shockingly,
   (E) As a matter of fact,

This is another question that's asking you to consider the relationship between sequential sentences. However, in this question, you're asked to consider which question emphasizes the surprising relationship between the two ideas. Choice (A) can be eliminated because, as the draft currently stands, there is no transitional phrase. Choices (C) and (E) can be eliminated because they are illogical. By contrast introduces a different, or even contradictory, piece of information. While the use of water bottles does in 2017 does contrast the use of water bottles in 2006, it is an increasing trend, and not the best use of this transitional phrase. As a matter of fact is used to introduce a piece of evidence that substantiates a claim. Choice (B) is plausible, through (D) does more to emphasize the surprising information. Therefore, (D) is the best answer.

5. The writer wants to add evidence to the second paragraph (sentences 3–5) to support the main idea of the paragraph. All of the following sentences accomplish this goal EXCEPT:

   (A) Plastic bottles are usually made from polyethylene terephthalate, a material derived from crude oil.
   (B) Plastic bottle consumption is directly linked to American consumption of crude oil.
   (C) As plastic bottles are rarely recycled, they end up polluting land and oceans.
   (D) Due to not being recycled, plastic bottles are one of the top three kinds of trash found in ocean clean ups.
   (E) Banning plastic bottles could save a family of four up to $5,000 per year.

This question is unique in its structure. You have to select the one answer that doesn't work, as opposed to the one answer that does. The first step to answering this question is identifying the main idea of the passage: the environmental costs of water bottle production. Choices (A) and (B) further develop the relationship between plastic water bottle production and oil consumption. Choices (C) and (D) further develop the negative implications of plastic bottles that aren't recycled. The economic benefits of banning plastic bottles are irrelevant to the topic of the paragraph. Therefore, (E) is the best answer.

6. In sentence 8, the writer wants to provide convincing evidence as to why banning plastic water bottles would be good for Americans' health.

   This is because bottled water isn't well regulated.

   Which sentence below best replaces sentence 8 to achieve this goal?

   (A) (as it is now)
   (B) Tap water is more strictly regulated than bottled water.
   (C) The Environmental Protection Agency monitors tap water (multiple tests per day) more closely than the Food and Drug Administration monitors bottled water (weekly tests).
   (D) The Environmental Protection Agency monitors tap water, and the Food and Drug Administration monitors bottled water.
   (E) Both tap water and bottled water are regulated by government agencies.

This question seeks to assess your understanding of what makes high-quality, persuasive evidence. Good evidence is relevant, specific, and detailed. Choice (A) can be immediately eliminated because it is overly general. They tricky aspect of assessing the remaining options is that they are all accurate and in agreement with each other, so your task is figuring out which evidence is best. Putting them in order of most general to most specific, (E) is the weakest because it is a vague statement stating that both tap water and bottled water are regulated by the government. Choice (B) adds the detail that tap water is more strictly regulated than bottled water. Choice (D) falls somewhere in between, naming the agencies that are responsible for regulation but providing no comparison between bottled and tap water. Choice (C) provides the highest quality evidence, naming both the agencies responsible for regulation and the frequency with which the water quality is tested. Therefore, (C) is the best answer.

7. The writer wants to add the following sentence to the third paragraph (sentences 6–9):

   This illustrates that there is already public support for banning single-use plastic bottles.

   Where is this sentence best placed?

   (A) Before sentence 6
   (B) After sentence 6
   (C) After sentence 7
   (D) After sentence 8
   (E) After sentence 9

This is a difficult question in which to use POE, because it asks you to insert the sentence in the question into the existing paragraph and assess it for logical flow and clarity. The key to this question is that the sentence starts with *This illustrates.* Therefore, the best strategy is to return to the paragraph in question, asking yourself what illustrates that there is already public support for banning single-use plastic bottles. Placing this sentence after sentence 7 or sentence 8 would not flow logically, since neither sentence gives any indication of public support. Eliminate (C) and (D). It would also create an illogical flow to start the paragraph with this sentence as the sentence's claim is unsubstantiated by the previous paragraph, so eliminate (A). While this sentence could potentially function as a conclusion, it doesn't quite make logical sense to follow sentence 9. Just because people living near water plants experience greater rates of illness doesn't necessarily mean they want plastic water bottles banned. Eliminate (E). Sentence 6, however, by describing that water bottles have already been banned in certain places, does suggest that there is already support to ban water bottles. Therefore, (B) is the best answer.

Here are a couple of questions pertaining to the final, or concluding, paragraph of the essay.

8. In the fourth paragraph (sentences 10–11), the writer wants to develop the counterargument that banning plastic water bottles might be unpopular. Which of the following sentences best achieves this goal?

   (A) Some argue that banning single-use plastic water bottles limits consumer choice.
   (B) Some turn to bottled water when their tap water proves toxic; however, this is often linked to industrial pollution.
   (C) Plastic water bottles require fewer crude resources than plastic bottles used for soft drinks.
   (D) Residents of some American cities have already voted to ban plastic bottles.
   (E) American politics often favor unpopular ideas that grow in popularity with time.

The key to understanding this question is grasping the phrase that develops the counterargument. This usually means providing reasoning or evidence for the counterargument presented. In this case, the counterargument is that banning plastic water bottles might be unpopular. Choices (D) and (E) can be eliminated. Choice (D) supports the original argument and refutes the counter argument. Choice (E) introduces a new claim pertaining to American politics. Choice (C) can be eliminated because it supports an environmental argument that describes water bottles as beneficial to soft drink bottles but doesn't necessarily pertain directly to the popularity of water bottle ban. Choice (B) begins by developing a counterargument, but also points out that tap water toxicity can be caused by industrial pollution. Choice (A) best develops the counterargument as it describes an argument against a ban, thus directly showing a negative public opinion. Therefore, (A) is the best response to the question.

9. In the fourth paragraph (sentences 10–11), the writer wants to include evidence to counter the claim that banning single-use plastic bottles may be unpopular. Which of the following best achieves this aim?

   (A) Residents of some American cities have already voted to ban plastic bags.

   (B) When tap water is undrinkable, bottled water becomes a necessity.

   (C) Banning bottled water often eliminates a healthy beverage choice at restaurants.

   (D) Citizens of a number of cities in the United States have already chosen to eliminate single-use plastic bottles.

   (E) Research completed at the State University of New York found that there were fewer plastic micro-particles in tap water than in bottled water.

This question asks you to consider a claim—that banning single-use plastic bottles might be unpopular—and consider evidence that refutes this claim. In other words, you're looking for a piece of evidence that supports the idea that banning single-use plastic bottles *is* popular. Choices (B) and (C) can be eliminated because they describe benefits of bottled water. Choice (E) can be eliminated because it doesn't speak to the popularity of banning plastic water bottles, despite describing a negative aspect of plastic water bottle use. Choice (A) is plausible, but support for banning plastic bags doesn't necessarily translate to support for plastic bottles. Choice (D) is the best answer as it describes the popularity the idea has already had in cities in the United States.

You'll have the opportunity to practice what you've learned in the drills in Chapter 3. First, let's look a bit more closely at some approaches to two essential aspects of doing well on the multiple-choice questions: timing and pacing.

Summary

- The multiple-choice test consists of five passages and 45 questions. Two passages will be associated with Reading questions; Three passages will be associated with Writing questions. You will have 60 minutes to complete this portion of the exam.
- Passages for Reading questions will be publication quality and could be from the 19th, 20th, or 21st centuries.
- Passages for Writing questions will be contemporary, argumentative, student-quality writing.
- Use active reading to identify the main point of each paragraph (or chunk) of the passage; then see how they connect to form the main point of the passage as a whole.
- Concentrate on the author's purpose, tone, and point of view.
- Look for the rhetorical strategies the author uses to achieve that purpose.
- Always go back to the passage when multiple-choice questions refer you to specific lines. Relying on your memory can easily lead you to select a close—but incorrect—answer.
- Read a couple of lines above and below the lines specified in the question. The context of the lines is almost always critical in determining the correct answer.
- Pace yourself. Divide the multiple-choice section into 12-minute chunks for each passage.
- Use the Two-Pass System. On your first pass, answer the questions you can and guess at the rest, using your Letter of the Day. Circle the questions you guessed on, and go back to them later if time remains in your 12-minute chunk.
- Use POE to eliminate wrong answers instead of looking for the right answer among five alternatives.

Chapter 2
Using Time Effectively to Maximize Points

STUDYING ISN'T EVERYTHING

Very few students stop to think about how to improve their test-taking skills. Most assume that if they study hard, they will get a high score, and if they do not study, they will do poorly.

Have you ever studied really hard for an exam and then blown it on test day? Have you ever aced an exam for which you thought you probably hadn't studied enough? Most students have had one, if not both, of these experiences. The lesson should be clear: factors other than how much you've studied influence your final test score, particularly on a test such as the AP English Language and Composition Exam, where timing and pacing are important aspects of thorough preparation.

This chapter will provide you with some insights that will help you perform better on the multiple-choice section of the AP English Language and Composition Exam, and on other exams as well.

Pacing and Timing

A big part of scoring well on an exam is sharpening your awareness of time. Another is working at a consistent pace.

Don't Waste Your Time

If you can't answer a question, make an educated guess and move on to the next question. Although you don't lose any points for wrong answers in the multiple-choice section, you don't want to waste time on a question you're unsure of because you will take away time from questions you're more likely to get correct.

The worst mistake made by inexperienced test-takers is that when they come to a question that stumps them, rather than just skipping it, they panic and stall. Time stands still when you're working on a question you can't answer, and it is not unusual for students to waste five minutes on a single multiple-choice question (especially a question involving a long selection from the passage or the word EXCEPT) instead of cutting their losses and moving on to questions they *can* answer.

Every question is worth the same one point, whether it's a hard question or an easy one. The computer that scores your responses doesn't know whether you agonized for three minutes over a hard question or breezed through an easy one in a few seconds; it only knows whether your answer is right or wrong.

It is important to be aware of how much time you have spent on a given question or section. There are several ways to improve your pacing and timing for the test.

- **Know your average pace.** While you prepare for your test, gauge how long you take on a passage with 11 or so questions. Knowing how long you spend on average per passage (and per question) will help you identify how many passages you can read (and questions you can answer) effectively in 60 minutes, and how best to pace yourself for the test.
- **Have a watch or clock nearby.** You are permitted to have a watch or clock nearby to help you keep track of time. However, constantly checking the clock is in itself a waste of time and can be distracting and stressful. Devise a plan. Try checking the clock after every passage or two to see whether you are keeping the correct pace or need to speed up. This will ensure that you're managing your time but won't permit you to fall into the trap of dwelling on it.

- **Know when to move on.** Because all of the multiple-choice questions are scored equally, and you are not penalized for wrong answers, investing long stretches of time on a single question is inefficient and can potentially deprive you of the chance to answer easier questions later on. If you can eliminate answer choices with POE, do so, but on your first pass through the questions, just guess from among the remaining choices (using your Letter of the Day) and move on if you can't find the correct answer. Remember, tests are like marathons: you do best when you work through them at a steady pace.
- **Be selective.** You don't have to do the multiple-choice questions in order. If you are stumped by a question, guess, skip it, and choose a different one. You might not have to answer every question correctly to achieve the score you need for your first choice of college. Select the questions you can answer and work on them first. This will boost your confidence, make you more efficient, and give you the greatest chance of getting the most questions correct.
- **Use Process of Elimination on every question.** Every answer choice that can be eliminated increases the odds that you will answer the question correctly.

Remember, when all the questions on a test are of equal value, and you don't lose any points for incorrect answers, no one question is that important. Your overall goal for pacing is to get the most questions correct.

Getting the Score You Need

Depending on the score you need, it may be in your best interest *not* to try to work through every multiple-choice question. Check with the schools to which you are applying. If you're aiming for credit hours and need to score a 5, it's best to find out as early in your preparation as possible. On the other hand, if you're simply aiming for placement and you find out your first choice of college sets the cut-off point at a score of 3, some of the pressure is off and you can prepare without feeling crushed by anxiety.

Lit Lover?
Are you taking AP English Literature and Composition as well? Check out our *Cracking the AP English Literature and Composition Exam!*

Reducing Test Anxiety

No matter what score you need, everybody experiences anxiety before and during an exam. To a certain extent, test anxiety *can* be helpful. Some people find that they perform more quickly and efficiently under stress. If you have ever pulled an all-nighter to write a paper and ended up doing good work, you know the feeling.

However, too much stress is definitely a bad thing. If you find that your stress level prevents you from doing your best work during exams, here are a few actions you can take to stop excessive stress in its tracks.

- **Take a reality check.** Evaluate your situation before the test begins. If you have understood and practiced all of the techniques we give for success on the exam, remind yourself that you are well prepared. Remember that many others taking the test are not as well prepared as you are, and you're being graded against them, so you have an advantage.

- **Don't fixate on how much you don't know.** Your job is to score as high as you can by maximizing the benefits of what you do know. Think of a test as a game. How can you get the most points in the time allotted?

- **Try to relax.** Slow, deep breathing works for almost everyone. Close your eyes, take a few slow, deep breaths, and concentrate on nothing but your inhalation and exhalation for a few seconds. This is a basic form of meditation, and it should help clear your mind of stress and, as a result, concentrate better on the test. If you have ever taken yoga classes, you probably know some other good relaxation techniques you could use in the test setting.

- **Visualize.** Imagine your favorite park, beach, hiking trail, or room, and visualize yourself sitting there taking the exam—all alone, calm and relaxed, and enjoying your surroundings. You're still taking the test, but in a pleasant place instead of in a stress-filled atmosphere. Most likely you'll need to practice this technique in advance in order to be able to slip into another place mentally while you're taking the test. Try it while you're having breakfast, or riding the bus, or walking down a noisy, chaotic street.

Remember...
Your purchase of this book comes with access to online Student Tools, a resource hub filled with bonus material like study guides and college advice. Follow the instructions on the Get More (Free) Content page to start using your online Student Tools.

- **Eliminate as many surprises as you can.** Make sure you know the testing location, how long it will take you to get there, and where to park if you're driving. Take a "dry run" trip to the test center before the day of the exam. Know when the exam room will open, when the actual exam starts, what type of questions you will be asked, and how long each section of the test will take. You don't want to be worrying about any of these things on the test day.

- **Plan to reward yourself.** After all, you deserve a reward for all of your hard work. Make a plan for doing something enjoyable right after the test is over. While you're preparing, keep thinking of the reward you've promised yourself.

The best way to avoid stress is to become familiar with the test material and practice doing exam questions under actual time constraints. (By reading this book, you are taking a major step toward a stress-free AP English Language and Composition Exam.)

In the next chapter, you'll have an opportunity to practice the strategies you've learned.

Chapter 3
Pacing Drills

DRILL 1

Questions 1–8. Read the following passage carefully before you choose your answers.

This passage is excerpted from the British Prime Minister's 1846 speech about the repeal of the Corn Laws.

Sir, believe me, to conduct the Government of this country is a most arduous duty; I may say it without irreverence, that these ancient institutions, like our physical frames, are "fearfully and wonderfully made." It is no easy task to ensure the united action of an ancient monarchy, a proud aristocracy, and a reformed constituency. I have done everything I could do, and have thought it consistent with true Conservative policy to reconcile these three branches of the State. I have thought it consistent with true Conservative policy to promote so much of happiness and contentment among the people that the voice of disaffection should be no longer heard, and that thoughts of the dissolution of our institutions should be forgotten in the midst of physical enjoyment. These were my attempts, and I thought them not inconsistent with true and enlarged Conservative policy. These were my objects in accepting office—it is a burden too great for my physical, and far beyond my intellectual structure; and to be relieved from it with perfect honour would be the greatest favour that could be conferred on me. But as a feeling of honour and strong sense of duty require me to undertake those responsible functions, I declare, Sir, that I am ready to incur these risks, to bear these burdens, and to front all these honourable dangers. But, Sir, I will not take the step with mutilated power and shackled authority. I will not stand at the helm during, such tempestuous nights as I have seen, if the vessel be not allowed fairly to pursue the course which I think she ought to take. I will not, Sir, undertake to direct the course of the vessel by the observations which have been taken in 1842. I will reserve to myself the marking out of that course; and I must, for the public interest, claim for myself the unfettered power of judging of those measures which I conceive will be better for the country to propose.

Sir, I do not wish to be the Minister of England; but while I have the high honour of holding that Office, I am determined to hold it by no servile tenure. I will only hold that office upon the condition of being unshackled by any other obligations than those of consulting the public interests, and of providing for the public safety.

1. The opening sentence of the passage contains
   (A) an expression of fear
   (B) an appeal to authority
   (C) a humorous simile
   (D) an irreverent attack
   (E) equivocation

2. The speaker is addressing
   (A) a friend
   (B) a group of his peers
   (C) a king
   (D) a crowd of voters
   (E) his political adversaries

3. The most significant transition takes place in
   (A) line 9 ("I have thought it consistent…")
   (B) line 16 ("These were my objects…")
   (C) line 20 ("But as a feeling of honour…")
   (D) line 24 ("But, Sir, I will not…")
   (E) line 28 ("I will not, Sir, undertake…")

4. All of the following are part of the same extended metaphor EXCEPT
   (A) "helm" (line 26)
   (B) "vessel" (line 27)
   (C) "fairly" (line 27)
   (D) "course" (line 29)
   (E) "unshackled" (line 38)

5. Which term in the first paragraph serves to prepare the dominant point of the final paragraph?
   (A) "disaffection" (lines 11–12)
   (B) "enjoyment" (line 14)
   (C) "dangers" (line 24)
   (D) "tempestuous" (line 26)
   (E) "unfettered" (line 32)

6. Based on the passage, the speaker's motivation to serve as prime minister is dictated mostly by

(A) greed
(B) political ambition
(C) sense of honor
(D) political power
(E) youthful exuberance

7. The tone of the entire passage

(A) remains consistently cynical
(B) shifts according to the speaker's mood
(C) shifts from light to serious
(D) becomes more frivolous in the final paragraph
(E) remains consistently lighthearted

8. Which of the following best describes the rhetorical function of lines 17–20 ("it is a burden too great… the greatest favor that could be conferred upon me")?

(A) It makes an appeal to emotion.
(B) It states the overall thesis of the passage.
(C) It expresses a causal relationship between events in the past and events in the present.
(D) It provides a specific example for the preceding argument.
(E) It reinforces the author's claim of responsibility in the following sentence.

DRILL 2

Questions 9–16. Read the following passage carefully before you choose your answers.

This passage is excerpted from an influential work published in 1839.

This archipelago consists of ten principal islands, of which five exceed the others in size. They are situated under the Equator, and between five and six hundred miles westward of the coast of America. They are all formed of volcanic rocks; a few fragments of granite curiously glazed and altered by the heat, can hardly be considered as an exception. Some of the craters, surmounting the larger islands, are of immense size, and they rise to a height of between three and four thousand feet. Their flanks are studded by innumerable smaller orifices. I scarcely hesitate to affirm, that there must be in the whole archipelago at least two thousand craters. These consist either of lava or scoriae, or of finely-stratified, sandstone-like tuff. Most of the latter are beautifully symmetrical; they owe their origin to eruptions of volcanic mud without any lava: it is a remarkable circumstance that every one of the twenty-eight tuff-craters which were examined had their southern sides either much lower than the other sides, or quite broken down and removed. As all these craters apparently have been formed when standing in the sea, and as the waves from the trade wind and the swell from the open Pacific here unite their forces on the southern coasts of all the islands, this singular uniformity in the broken state of the craters, composed of the soft and yielding tuff, is easily explained.

The *Beagle* sailed round Chatham Island, and anchored in several bays. One night I slept on shore on a part of the island, where black truncated cones were extraordinarily numerous: from one small eminence I counted sixty of them, all surmounted by craters more or less perfect. The greater number consisted merely of a ring of red scoriae or slags, cemented together: and their height above the plain of lava was not more than from fifty to a hundred feet; none had been very lately active. The entire surface of this part of the island seems to have been permeated, like a sieve, by the subterranean vapours: here and there the lava, whilst soft, has been blown into great bubbles; and in other parts, the tops of caverns similarly formed have fallen in, leaving circular pits with steep sides. From the regular form of the many craters, they gave to the country an artificial appearance, which vividly reminded me of those parts of Staffordshire, where the great iron-foundries are most numerous. The day was glowing hot, and the scrambling over the rough surface and through the intricate thickets, was very fatiguing; but I was well repaid by the strange Cyclopean scene. As I was walking along I met two large tortoises, each of which must have weighed at least two hundred pounds: one was eating a piece of cactus, and as I approached, it stared at me and slowly walked away; the other gave a deep hiss, and drew in its head. These huge reptiles, surrounded by the black lava, the leafless shrubs, and large cacti, seemed to my fancy like some antediluvian animals. The few dull-coloured birds cared no more for me than they did for the great tortoises.

9. This passage is most notable for its
   (A) meticulous classification
   (B) unusual point of view
   (C) precise description
   (D) resourceful analogies
   (E) lyrical prose

10. The speaker in the passage can best be described as
   (A) a scientist making entries in a nature journal
   (B) a professional sailor touring a remote island
   (C) a fiction writer on holiday
   (D) a surveyor measuring land for future development
   (E) a volcanologist studying the site of a recent eruption

11. In context, one can infer that "tuff" (line 13) is
    (A) an alternate spelling for "tough"
    (B) a kind of sand
    (C) made up principally of grass
    (D) volcanic rock
    (E) dense and resistant

12. In this passage, the speaker is most notably impressed by
    (A) the flora on the islands
    (B) the force of the Pacific Ocean
    (C) the fragments of granite
    (D) the symmetrical craters on the islands
    (E) the topography of the smaller islands

13. Which of the following phrases represents a literary allusion?
    (A) "parts of Staffordshire" (lines 41–42)
    (B) "the strange Cyclopean scene" (lines 45–46)
    (C) "situated under the Equator (lines 2–3)
    (D) "the coast of America" (line 4)
    (E) "the swell from the open Pacific" (line 21)

14. Which of the following landscape features are described throughout the entire passage?
    (A) Craters and lava
    (B) Craters and tortoises
    (C) Tortoises and birds
    (D) Islands and bays
    (E) Tuff and volcanic mud

15. In line 52, "antediluvian" most nearly means
    (A) artificial
    (B) lifeless
    (C) prehistoric
    (D) volcanic
    (E) enormous

16. Which of the following are virtually synonymous as presented in the author's description?
    (A) "ten principal islands" (line 1) and "two thousand craters" (line 12)
    (B) "tuff" (line 13) and "volcanic mud" (line 15)
    (C) "iron-foundries" (line 42) and "intricate thickets" (line 44)
    (D) "craters" (line 40) and "caverns" (line 38)
    (E) "tortoises" (line 47) and "birds" (line 53)

DRILL 3

Questions 17–25. Read the following passage carefully before you choose your answers.

This passage is excerpted from an essay by a nineteenth-century British writer.

Art begins with abstract decoration, with purely imaginative and pleasurable work dealing with what is unreal and non-existent. This is the first stage. Then Life becomes fascinated with this new wonder, and asks to be admitted into the charmed circle. Art takes Life as part of her rough material, re-creates it, and refashions it in fresh forms, is absolutely indifferent to fact, invents, imagines, dreams, and keeps between herself and reality the impenetrable barrier of beautiful style, of decorative or ideal treatment. The third stage is when Life gets the upper hand, and drives Art out into the wilderness. That is the true decadence, and it is from this that we are now suffering.

Take the case of the English drama. At first in the hands of the monks Dramatic Art was abstract, decorative and mythological. Then she enlisted Life in her service, and using some of life's external forms, she created an entirely new race of beings, whose sorrows were more terrible than any sorrow man has ever felt, whose joys were keener than lover's joys, who had the rage of the Titans and the calm of the gods, who had monstrous and marvelous sins, monstrous and marvelous virtues. To them she gave a language different from that of actual use, a language full of resonant music and sweet rhythm, made stately by solemn cadence, or made delicate by fanciful rhyme, jeweled with wonderful words, and enriched with lofty diction. She clothed her children in strange raiment and gave them masks, and at her bidding the antique world rose from its marble tomb. A new Caesar stalked through the streets of risen Rome, and with purple sail and flute-led oars another Cleopatra passed up the river to Antioch. Old myth and legend and dream took shape and substance. History was entirely rewritten, and there was hardly one of the dramatists who did not recognize that the object of Art is not simple truth but complex beauty. In this they were perfectly right. Art itself is really a form of exaggeration; and selection, which is the very spirit of art, is nothing more than an intensified mode of over-emphasis.

But Life soon shattered the perfection of the form. Even in Shakespeare we can see the beginning of the end. It shows itself by the gradual breaking-up of the blank-verse in the later plays, by the predominance given to prose, and by the overimportance assigned to characterization. The passages in Shakespeare—and they are many—where the language is uncouth, vulgar, exaggerated, fantastic, obscene even, are entirely due to Life calling for an echo of her own voice, and rejecting the intervention of beautiful style, through which alone should life be suffered to find expression. Shakespeare is not by any means a flawless artist. He is too fond of going directly to Life, and borrowing Life's natural utterance. He forgets that when Art surrenders her imaginative medium she surrenders everything.

17. The author of this passage is most likely

 (A) a poet
 (B) a novelist
 (C) an art critic
 (D) a journalist
 (E) an actor

18. The author relies principally on which of the following to substantiate his thesis?

 (A) A faulty analogy
 (B) Process analysis
 (C) Deductive reasoning
 (D) An accumulation of facts
 (E) Illustration by example

19. "...when Art surrenders her imaginative medium she surrenders everything" (lines 50–52) is in the form of

 (A) a fundamental principle
 (B) an inverted sentence structure
 (C) an antithesis
 (D) an understatement
 (E) an analogy

20. Above all else, the author reveres

    (A) beauty
    (B) life
    (C) Shakespeare
    (D) Caesar
    (E) English drama

21. In the context of the entire passage, "Life gets the upper hand" (line 10) is best interpreted as having which of the following meanings?

    (A) Art is favored over Life in English drama.
    (B) Life rewrites history.
    (C) Life drives Art out of English drama.
    (D) Life is uncouth, vulgar, and unsophisticated.
    (E) Life dominates Art in English drama.

22. The quality discussed in lines 22–26 is most directly the antithesis of which of the following?

    (A) "marble tomb" (line 28)
    (B) "The passages in Shakespeare" (line 43)
    (C) "to find expression" (line 47–48)
    (D) "her imaginative medium" (line 51)
    (E) "a flawless artist" (lines 48–49)

23. The author's observation in the first three sentences (lines 1–5) is best described as an example of which of the following?

    (A) Personification
    (B) Linguistic paradox
    (C) First-person narrative
    (D) Dramatic irony
    (E) Authorial intrusion

24. In line 26, "She" refers to which of the following?

    I. "Dramatic Art" (line 14)
    II. "English drama" (line 13)
    III. "Life" (line 15)

    (A) I only
    (B) II only
    (C) I and III only
    (D) II and III only
    (E) I, II, and III

25. The author's tone in the passage as a whole is best described as

    (A) harsh and strident
    (B) informal and analytical
    (C) rueful and expository
    (D) superficial and capricious
    (E) enthusiastic and optimistic

DRILL 1 EXPLANATIONS

1. **C** The simile in this first sentence compares the great and ancient parliamentary institutions with the august, but somewhat ancient, bodies of the members of Parliament. The speaker is warming up his audience with a bit of humor before launching into what amounts to a very serious ultimatum: that the speaker will continue to serve as prime minister, but only if they concede to him much greater authority than before (1842). The answer is (C).

2. **B** The speaker is addressing a group of his peers, (B), who are the other members of Parliament. The tricky part here is, of course, the repetition of *Sir*, a political convention in Great Britain—it is as if the prime minister were addressing each member of Parliament as an individual. There is evidence that he is the British prime minister in the final sentences, and these sentences also reveal definitively that he is speaking to peers: *Sir, I do not wish to be the Minister of England; but while I have the high honour of holding that Office, I am determined to hold it by no servile tenure. I will only hold that office upon the condition of being unshackled by any other obligations than those of consulting the public interests, and of providing for the public safety.*

3. **D** Everything before this line is an introduction to the prime minister's real message; until this point, he has joked, given a general review of his former motivations and actions as the leader of the Conservative party, and explained his reasons for accepting to serve again as prime minister (*feeling of honour*) in spite of his failing health and aged mind (*a burden too great for my physical, and far beyond my intellectual structure*). The transition comes with *But, Sir, I will not take the step with mutilated power and shackled authority*. He will do the country and his peers a favor, but only if he is granted much more authority to rule. Choice (D) is the answer.

4. **E** Eliminate (A), (B), and (D) so you're left with (C) and (E), which do not fit neatly into the nautical terminology. Choice (C) is the one to eliminate. All the other terms fit neatly into the nautical terminology. However, one could stretch a point and claim that *fairly* is related to fair weather, whereas *unshackled* is clearly unrelated to this metaphor. The answer is (E).

5. **E** The first step is to determine the *dominant point* of the final paragraph. Thankfully, the second paragraph is short—it is the rhetorical summation of his ultimatum. The key phrases are *servile tenure* and *unshackled by any other obligations.* Of course, *unfettered* and *unshackled* are synonyms, so the best answer is (E), *unfettered.*

6. **C** The prime minister states unequivocally that honor is his motivation, in the following passage in particular: *and to be relieved from it [the position] with perfect honour would be the greatest favour that could be conferred on me. But as a feeling of honour and strong sense of duty require me to undertake those responsible functions, I declare, Sir, that I am ready to incur these risks, to bear these burdens, and to front all these honourable dangers*. The word *honor* comes up numerous times in this excerpt. Choice (C) is correct.

7. **C** You should be able to narrow your options to (B) and (C). But be careful! Do you think that the speaker, the most powerful man in Great Britain, allowed his mood to shift or to affect his tone? The speech was carefully constructed, and the tone was coolly calculated when the author wrote it. The prime minister begins with a light tone because he is looking to set up his audience, not because he starts his speech in a good mood. In fact, his real mood never shifts: he manipulates tone for maximum effect.

8. **E** In lines 17–20, the prime minister describes his time in office as a *burden* and how he wishes to be *relieved of it*. But in the following sentence, lines 21–24, he states that *a strong sense of duty* requires him to *incur these risks, bear these burdens, and to front all these honourable dangers*. So he is burdened but feels a sense of responsibility. This aligns with (E). Although readers may feel sympathy with the prime minister, an appeal to emotion is not the primary goal, so eliminate (A). The overall thesis of the passage has more to do with duty than burden, so (B) can be eliminated as well. The author's sense of burden did not cause anything to happen, which eliminates (C), and there is no specific example, so rule out (D).

DRILL 2 EXPLANATIONS

9. **C** This is a scientifically precise description of the Galapagos Islands. Choice (A) is incorrect because nothing is being classified in this passage. Choice (B) is also wrong—no point of view is presented here, just facts. The passage is not dominated by analogies, so (D) is incorrect. Finally, you know that (E) is also incorrect because *lyrical* pertains to personal sentiment, and there are practically no personal feelings expressed at all; the closest we get to personal sentiment is the statement that some of the craters are *beautifully symmetrical.*

10. **A** You can use POE to answer this question. Choice (C) is the easiest to eliminate; the passage is factual, not fictional. The passage is about the islands themselves, not about volcanoes as (E) suggests, and, according to the second paragraph, *none had very lately been active*. Choices (B) and (D) are somewhat plausible; however, there is no evidence that the author is a *professional* sailor, nor that he has done any formal *surveying*. The passage contains a detailed description of nature, so (A) is the best match.

11. **D** In this case, the answer is made clear from the passage; the craters have a border of soft stone (tuff) that has worn away on the southern side. The specific line from the passage that allows you to answer this question is this: *These consist either of lava or scoriae, or of finely stratified, sandstone-like tuff*. Sandstone is a type of rock. Tuff is actually a rock composed of compacted volcanic ash varying in size from fine sand to coarse gravel. Choice (D) is correct.

12. **D** The author doesn't address (A) or (E), so you can eliminate those and look more closely at the middle three choices. Although the author mentions the Pacific Ocean and the fragments of granite, he incorporates these elements in his overarching discussion of the symmetrical craters.

13. **B** A literary allusion is a reference, usually to a character from art, literature, or mythology, which requires the reader to have some outside knowledge of the topic. Staffordshire, (A), is a place, but not a feature of literature or mythology. The Cyclops, (B), is a character from Greek mythology, so this is the best match. Choices (C), (D), and (E) are geographical references, not literary or mythological.

14. **A** Check BOTH paragraphs. Tortoises are mentioned only toward the end of the passage and are not landscape features, so eliminate (B) and (C). Tuff is mentioned only in the first paragraph, so eliminate (E). Bays are mentioned only at the beginning of paragraph 2, so eliminate (D). Craters and lava are mentioned throughout the passage, making (A) the best answer.

15. **C** If you know the definition of *antediluvian*, then you have a distinct advantage here; if not, you can get clues from the context of the passage. Since the word is describing animals, they would not be *artificial* or *volcanic*, so eliminate (A) and (D). The tortoises are not *lifeless*, (B), since one of them hisses at the author. *Enormous*, (E), is tempting, since the tortoises are described as *huge,* but that would ignore the middle phrase in that sentence and create a redundancy. *Black lava*, *leafless shrubs*, and *large cacti* are not features of many modern landscapes, and the tortoises are larger than normal, so *old* or *primordial* is the meaning you're looking for here. Choice (C) is the closest choice.

16. **D** Synonymous phrases would represent virtually the same idea. The islands have craters, but they are not, in themselves, actual craters, so eliminate (A). *Tuff* and *volcanic mud,* (B), may be associated together in the first paragraph, but you don't know for sure whether they are the same substance. *Iron-foundries* are more closely aligned to craters, not *thickets*, (C). And the *tortoises* and *birds*, (E), are in opposition, according to the author, because they react to him in different ways. That leaves you with (D): both *craters* and *caverns* are holes in the landscape.

DRILL 3 EXPLANATIONS

17. **A** In reality, the author is both a poet and a novelist, but you are asked to make a judgment based on the passage. To answer this question correctly, you need to use POE and your best judgment to eliminate all of the least likely answer choices. The passage is an attack against the intrusion of prosaic life into the realm of art. The panegyric (high praise) of classical language is a key to understanding the author's point of view: *a language different from that of actual use, a language full of resonant music and sweet rhythm, made stately by solemn cadence, or made delicate by fanciful rhyme, jeweled with wonderful words, and enriched with lofty diction.* In a word, this is poetry. Choice (A) is correct.

The writing is far too lyrical for the author of the passage to be a journalist, (D), or an actor, (E); the latter choice is thrown in for readers who assume that a passage dealing with English drama should be somehow related to a theatrical term. The same may be said for (C). The author capitalizes *art* because he is not discussing painting specifically, but the general realm of artistic creation that encompasses all the arts.

18. **E** The example is stated rhetorically—*Take the case of the English drama*—and lasts for most of the passage. *Illustration by example*, (E), is definitely the defining rhetorical mode of this passage.

19. **A** The sentence provides a fundamental principle on when Art fails, so (A) is the best answer. POE can help you narrow down your choices. Clearly, the statement does not compare Art to something else, so you can eliminate (E). If anything, the statement is overstatement (hyperbole), and for that reason (D) can be discarded. For the statement to be an antithesis, the author would have needed to put two things or concepts in opposition, but you have only one element (Art); thus, you can eliminate (C). At this point, your chances are fifty-fifty, so you could guess and move on. But look at (B). There is a parallel structure in the two halves of the sentence, so there is no reversal.

20. **A** The author does not revere life above everything else—for example, he clearly states that he doesn't like life as an intrusion on Art, at the very least, or as it appears in certain parts of William Shakespeare's work. He includes these examples of Caesar and English drama for rhetorical reasons, and while he admires English drama, he does not appear to revere it. (By the way, to *revere* something is to regard it with awe, deference, and devotion.) Beauty is held up as an ideal, and this is clear when the author says, *the object of Art is not simple truth but complex beauty.* The answer is (A).

21. **E** The idiom *getting the upper hand* means having an advantage over something or someone. If *Life gets the upper hand*, then (A) is wrong. Choice (D) is a trap, since it sounds like a direct quote from line 45 and does not connote having an advantage. Choice (B) is likewise irrelevant to *getting the upper hand.* Choices (C) and (E) have very close meanings, but (C) is too extreme, since you can't say for sure that Art is absent from all English drama. Choice (E) is the best choice.

22. **B** The quality in lines 22–26 is *a language full of resonant music and sweet rhythm.* This is the antithesis (direct opposite) of the author's description on Shakespeare's writing in line 43. Choice (B) is the best answer.

23. **A** Throughout the first paragraph, the author refers to Life and Art as though they were people: *Life becomes fascinated* (lines 3–4), *Art takes life as part of her rough material* (lines 5–6). This is known as personification, (A). Although Life and Art are in opposition to each other, there is no inherent confusion or contradiction, (B). The passage is not written in first-person narration ("I," "me," etc.), so eliminate (C). And there is no sense that circumstances are the opposite of how one might anticipate, so eliminate (D). Authorial intrusion is an interruption in the narrative, so rule out (E).

24. **A** Check the beginning of the paragraph. In line 14, *Dramatic Art* is mentioned. In line 15, *she enlisted Life.* So the *she* used throughout this paragraph is *Dramatic Art*, not *Life*, and certainly not *English drama* as a whole.

25. **C** First, eliminate the extreme answers: (A) and (E). *Informal*, (B), is not a good match, since the passage is written in a rather lofty style. Choice (D) would make the author seem petty or unpredictable. Overall, the author laments the *takeover* of Art by Life. This is especially obvious in the last line of the passage. Thus, he is *rueful*, (C). *Expository* simply means that the author is *exposing* the supposed problem with English drama.

Chapter 4
How to Approach the Essays: Basic Principles

ESSAY SECTION TASKS

Yes, that's right—tasks. You'll need to write three different essays: synthesis, rhetorical analysis, and argument.

In the **synthesis essay**, you'll be given a scenario and tasked with writing a response using at least three of six or seven short accompanying sources for support. You'll need to cite the sources you use (in a simple format such as "Source A"), and incorporate them into your own position (instead of simply quoting them). At least one of the sources will be a visual (such as a picture, drawing, or graph) rather than text.

The **rhetorical analysis essay** asks you to analyze the techniques (such as choice of language or organization of points) an author uses, and discuss how those techniques contribute to the author's purpose. The passage you'll be asked to analyze is typically about a page long.

Three Rules for Successful Essay Preparation

1. Do plenty of TIMED practice on all three essay types.

2. Hand-write your practice essays; don't use a computer.

3. Ask for feedback on your essays from a trusted source (such as an English teacher or Princeton Review tutor).

The **argument essay** presents a claim or assertion in the prompt and then asks you to argue a position based on your own knowledge, experience, or reading. You can choose to agree with the claim, disagree with it, or give it qualified support (for example, arguing that the claim is true only in certain circumstances).

In Chapters 5–7, you'll learn more about the approach and expectations for each type of essay.

For all three essays, you will be writing cold on a prompt or passage you read just two minutes ago for the first time. You have to come up with good ideas and get them written down efficiently—on the very first try.

Writing a clear, effective, well-organized essay under rigid time constraints is a learned skill; writing three consecutive essays under such conditions requires special techniques and lots of practice. Fortunately, this book provides you with both of those.

Time Crunch

You'll have 2 hours to write all three essays, which allows about 40 minutes for each. Before you even start working on the essays, though, you'll have 15 minutes to read all three prompts and the source documents for the synthesis essay. While we suggest you use all 15 minutes, if you finish reading the prompts and the documents early, you may start writing your response.

This 15-minute period is crucial for building a solid foundation in understanding the prompts and the source documents. You'll need to put your active reading skills in high gear to get the best possible head start from the reading time available.

Why *Three* Essays?

The AP English Language and Composition Exam is designed to predict your ability to perform college-level work on such assignments as research papers and on-demand essay questions on tests. The AP Exam's three types of essays essentially give you an opportunity to demonstrate some of the important skills required for those types of college assignments:

- using research sources to support your own position
- examining sources critically in order to assess credible or faulty support
- arguing your own position persuasively

The three essays simply separate—and highlight—these skills. In college work, you'll often be combining them.

HOW ARE THE ESSAYS SCORED?

The essays are scored separately on a scale of 0–6; then the three scores are combined. Each essay has equal weight in that combined score, which is then combined with the result of the multiple-choice section to yield a final AP score of 1–5.

Together, the essays count for 55 percent of your final score. However, they take up 69 percent of the exam time, so it's easy to lose perspective and feel as if the essay section is more crucial to your success than it actually is. Doing well on the multiple-choice section is almost as important, even though it's only an hour long.

The grading is analytical, meaning that the reader will assess using a point-by-point checklist to arrive at a score. This includes major errors, such as using fewer than three sources in the synthesis essay or consistently expressing ideas in such a confused way that the reader has great difficulty following the argument. Such lapses automatically knock an essay down to a lower point on the scoring scale.

Essays are graded analytically, based on:

- your ability to state a clear thesis
- your ability to present concrete evidence and link it to your thesis
- your skillful use of sophisticated language to develop your argument

Who Does the Scoring?

The readers are college English professors and AP course teachers who come together in June for an intense week of scoring. Thousands of readers go through thousands of essays in a few short days. A different person will read each of your essays.

Before the scoring starts, though, readers are trained in assessing that particular year's group of essays. The College Board, the nonprofit organization that develops the exam, combs through the current crop of essays looking for work that represents a top-level 6 synthesis essay, a mediocre 3 rhetorical analysis essay, and so on, from that year's group. These sample essays are used to train the readers so the scoring will be as standardized as possible, given that the readers are still human beings who make subjective decisions.

So what? Well, the readers are your audience—the people you're addressing in your essays—and this scoring process tells you a few important things about them.

- First, they're buried in student essays, most of them mundane and mind-numbingly similar, and are just hoping for that one brilliant piece of writing that breaks the monotony and is a pleasure to read.
- Second, the readers have been trained to score your essays in relation to the work of the other students who took the exam that year. They're not judging your work in relation to some ideal standard of what a "perfect" essay should be.
- Third, these are teachers who guide students through English composition for a living. They know that polished essays require time, draft after draft, revision after revision. They don't expect an essay written in 40 minutes to be polished or perfect—they couldn't produce a flawless essay themselves in 40 minutes.

The essay section is the only place in this exam where your personality—at least to a limited degree—will shine through to test graders. Use it as an opportunity to show off what an exceptional thinker and writer you are.

What Are the Characteristics of Each Score Level?

The scale breaks down into four categories: effective, adequate, inadequate, and little success.

Effective. These are the essays with thorough and convincing discussions, perceptive analyses, well-developed positions, smooth organization, and sophisticated control of expression. They demonstrate that the writer has understood and thought about the prompt and created an original response.

Adequate. They address the prompt with appropriate explanations and evidence, do an adequate job of organizing and developing points, and express the writer's ideas clearly.

Inadequate. In these essays, the writer may have misunderstood the prompt or (in the case of the synthesis essay) the sources. Evidence and explanations are limited or simplistic, or even flat-out inappropriate. The organization does not flow smoothly, and the writer has less control of English language conventions in expressing ideas.

Little Success. Here the writer has oversimplified or completely misunderstood the prompt, and presented evidence that is inappropriate or just plain unrelated. These essays show a consistent weakness in expressing ideas in a clear, organized, and grammatically correct way.

Essays fall within one of those four categories based on the general characteristics of that category. The specific score within the two higher bands reflects more or less skill and depth in demonstrating those characteristics. Within the two lower bands, the number score reflects varying degrees of problems.

In Chapters 5–7, you'll learn some more details about how these score levels apply to each type of essay.

WHAT ARE THE KEYS TO REACHING THE "EFFECTIVE" BAND?

Your goal is to rise above the vast middle bulge of essays. You're aiming for the "effective" band. How do you get there? By familiarizing yourself with the types of essays you'll have to write and by following a few basic tips.

Understand the Prompt

Use your active reading skills to tear the prompt apart.

- What is the prompt *really* asking you to do? Understanding your task and maintaining a laser focus on it will keep you out of the swamp of inappropriate examples and unrelated arguments that populate the lower levels of the scoring scale.
- Does the prompt have broader implications? For example, if a quote in the argument essay prompt states that a government has a duty to protect its citizens, could carrying out that duty lead to undesirable limits on people's freedom? And protect citizens from what? Who says that's a government's duty? The key here is to demonstrate some depth of thought instead of simply taking the prompt at face value. Where does it lead you?
- Does the prompt contain any terms that you should define in order to keep your discussion on target? Broad, "fuzzy" concepts such as "justice" or "education" are prime examples. They mean different things to different people. Giving a precise explanation of how you understand the term *as it's used in the prompt* and how you intend to discuss it will help you avoid producing a vague, rambling essay.

Take a Position

No fence-sitting, no ambiguity, no neutral descriptive essays. The highest scoring essays take a definite position on the prompt topic and argue it convincingly. They use strong, relevant evidence to support the position and leave no doubt about where the essay writer stands.

Even in the rhetorical analysis essay you're expected to take a position: "This is the author's purpose, these are the three (or four, or five) most important techniques the author uses to achieve that purpose, and (very important) this is *how* each technique makes the purpose more effective." Another student might see a different purpose or highlight other techniques in the passage, but then that student would be taking a different position.

Manage Your Time

No one is going to tell you that your first 40 minutes are up and it's time to move on to the next essay. That's up to you. Since each essay has equal weight in the combined score, you should devote about the same amount of time to each one. A slightly better score on one essay will not make up for a bad score on another. Aim for the following breakdown within each 40-minute period:

- 3–5 minutes to think through the prompt and plan your essay
- 30–35 minutes to write
- 1–2 minutes to proofread

BC UR 2 GOOD 4 THIS

Even though you're under tremendous time pressure, don't use shorthand symbols such as "&" or "w/" or "tho." Get into the habit of using a relatively high level of discourse on AP Exam essays. Writing in the style of a casual email or text message won't impress the reader who is scoring your essay.

The more you practice writing each type of essay within 40 minutes, the more you'll gain a sense of how that block of time "feels" and the better you'll get at making occasional time checks to stay on track instead of engaging in distracting clock-watching that might only increase your anxiety.

Your school has likely given you sample essay prompts for practice. You can also find example prompts from several previous years on the AP website at https://apcentral.collegeboard.org/courses/ap-english-language-and-composition/exam.

Plan Your Response

Just getting into the car and starting to drive could land you anywhere, at a great waste of time and fuel. It's the same with just starting to write—you could easily spend 20 minutes and then realize you're seriously off track.

To make the best use of your 30–35 minutes of writing time, you first need to spend a few minutes planning where you want to end up and how you'll get there.

- Exactly what do you want to conclude about the topic of the synthesis prompt? Which three sources best support the points you want to make? In which order should you incorporate them into your discussion? Does one of the sources present a significant opposing argument that you should mention and then refute?

- In the rhetorical analysis passage, what is the writer's purpose? What techniques make that purpose clear and effective to you? In which order should you explain them?
- What position do you want to take about the topic presented for the argument essay? What evidence from your own experiences or reading could you use to support your position? How can you make your argument persuasive?

Organize Your Points

You're likely familiar with the five-paragraph essay model. While it's not the only method of organizing an essay, there's nothing wrong with using it on this exam if it's already a comfortable model for you. It goes like this:

Paragraph 1:

- An introductory sentence or two that capture the reader and announce, "This is going to be a great essay within your pile of boring, mediocre essays."
- The thesis that you intend to argue in your essay. A good thesis is debatable (that is, someone could possibly have a different opinion) and narrow enough to be covered adequately in a short essay.
- A brief list of the three pieces of evidence you'll use in the essay to prove your thesis
- A transition to the body of your essay

Paragraphs 2–4:

- One paragraph for each piece of evidence you listed in the first paragraph, in the same order as you listed them. Each piece of evidence should be linked directly to your thesis, with a clear explanation of *why* it supports your thesis. One of these paragraphs might describe a conflicting view which you then shoot down, or which supports an "only in certain circumstances" position in your thesis.

Paragraph 5:

- A conclusion that doesn't simply restate your thesis. You've developed your argument throughout the body of your essay, so it's now meatier and more convincing. The conclusion should remind the reader of your now-stronger position.

Of course, there's no rule that says you have to stop at three pieces of evidence; you might have four. Just don't take on more complexity and length than you can handle well in 40 minutes. And if you're familiar with another method of organizing an essay and feel more comfortable with it, then use it, as long as it provides a clear organizational framework for your points.

Get Off to a Strong Start

A great first impression goes a long way. Remember your audience of bored readers mired in stacks of mediocre essays? If you can wow them right off the top, you'll create an expectation that the rest of your essay belongs in the "effective" band too. That initial glow of "finally—*finally*—a good essay!" can diminish the impact of later lapses in greatness.

Suppose the prompt for a rhetorical analysis essay quotes from a speech by Mayor Nellie Smith attributing her election victory to the many volunteers who worked on her campaign. You could clearly announce, "This is going to be a mediocre essay" by starting out with a sentence like, "This essay will describe how Mayor Nellie Smith uses rhetorical strategies to communicate the main point of her speech." Yawn. And do you have any clue what her main point is or what rhetorical strategies she uses? Even if you eventually do get to an insightful point later in the essay, chances are your opening has already caused the reader to tune out and miss it.

On the other hand, you could grab the reader's attention with an opening like, "Dedicated volunteers are the bricks and mortar of successful political campaigns. That's the overriding message of Mayor Nellie Smith's speech thanking them for their passionate support and acknowledging the key role they played. Through the skillful use of parallelism, repetition, and analogy, she makes her listeners feel that the victory is really theirs, likely winning their support after she takes office too."

That stronger start doesn't take a lot of extra effort or time, but it shows the reader that you understand the mayor's purpose and rhetorical strategies, and can express your ideas with style and sophistication. You've just raised the reader's impression of your abilities, even if your essay tapers off to a more routine effort later on.

Express Your Ideas Clearly, Specifically, Concisely, Correctly, Smoothly, Persuasively, and with Flair

Oh yes, you *can* do that.

Be clear. You should know exactly what you want to say as a result of your initial planning and organizing. Imagine yourself on a clear path instead of stumbling around in the underbrush. If you find you're getting tangled up in long sentences or overlapping ideas, pause for a minute and think of *telling* someone right beside you what you mean to say. This strategy usually helps clarify your thoughts and language in your own mind. Now write down what you just "said."

Be precise. Making a vague statement such as, "The demand for subsidized housing increased a lot during the past few years (Source A)" isn't good enough if Source A actually referred to a study that proved demand grew by 65 percent between 2000 and 2010. Being as specific and concrete as possible will add credibility and impact to your words. Your argument will be clearer and more persuasive.

Be concise. That doesn't mean leaving out details that are essential to your argument. It means leaving out pointless repetition and padding. Say it once, precisely and with punch, and then move on.

Say it correctly. Use proper grammar. Essays with so many errors that the reader can't follow the argument are consigned to the bottom of the scoring scale.

Create correct paragraphs too. Have you ever opened a book and seen nothing but very long paragraphs? Your next thought is probably, "Do I *really* have to read all of this?" That's exactly what readers think when they see an essay without paragraphs.

So create proper paragraphs—one main idea per paragraph, beginning with a topic sentence and ending with a smooth transition to the next paragraph—and make them obvious by leaving a space between or indenting them.

Create a great first impression before the person scoring your essay even reads a word.

- Write legibly.
- Make sure readers can see the paragraphs at first glance.
- Don't strike out too many things.
- Make sure your work looks neat, organized, and clear.

Say it smoothly. Lead the reader through your argument with seamless transitions between your points and paragraphs. Transition words and phrases such as "on the other hand," "in addition," "therefore," and "nevertheless" will do the job.

The reader expects you to write like someone who is suffering through a tedious, nerve-racking exercise. If you write like someone who enjoys writing, the reader will enjoy reading your essay and reward you.

Say it persuasively. These essays are all evidence-based writing, so you need strong evidence that supports each of your main points. Connect each piece of evidence clearly to the point it supports, and explain exactly how or why the evidence is relevant. Unrelated evidence and vague, weak explanations won't persuade anyone.

Say it with flair. Is there a punchier, more descriptive word you could use? Perhaps "shack" or "cabin" or "mansion" instead of "house." Can you make the phrasing of a sentence slicker? For example, instead of "The candidate's appearance was neat, and the boss gave him the job right away," let yourself get carried away and say, "The candidate's Armani suit and sleek silk tie captivated the boss, who slipped a contract across the table without comment or hesitation."

It doesn't take long to think of a more forceful word or a stronger way of saying something if you put your mind on that track, and even a few of these sprinkled throughout your essay can impress the reader with your ability to control language and use it to achieve your desired effect.

Make it easy for the reader to give you a high score.

- Understand the task in the prompt.
- Think about where the prompt takes you.
- Stake out a definite position.
- Plan and organize your points before you start to write.
- Be clear and specific.
- Link each piece of evidence directly to your thesis.
- Use correct grammar and paragraph construction.
- Vary sentence length and structure.
- Write legibly.

Proofread

You won't have time to revise, but leaving a couple of minutes to proofread allows you to fix minor errors you probably would not have made if you weren't writing in such a rush. And that, in turn, might just knock your essay up a notch on the scoring scale. You'll have to write your essay in dark blue or black pen—no pencils allowed on this section of the exam. However, you can strike out any errors you want the readers to ignore (they will) and then write in (neatly) your correction.

In Chapters 5–7, you'll get a closer look at the types of prompts on the exam, and find additional suggestions for responding to the three different types.

Summary

General Essay Information

- There are three essays: synthesis, rhetorical analysis, and argument.
- You have a total of 2 hours, 15 minutes—40 minutes for each essay plus 15 minutes to read the prompts and the sources for the synthesis essay.
- The three essays count for 55 percent of your total score. Each essay is worth an equal amount.

Essay Scoring

- Each essay is scored by a different reader on a scale from 0 to 6.
- Essays are awarded up to one point for the thesis statement, four points for evidence and commentary, and one point for sophistication.
- The reader wants good essays that are easy to score.
- Essays that earn high scores show that the writer has thought deeply about the prompt, taken a clear position, supported that position with appropriate examples, and argued that position persuasively with sophisticated control of the language.
- Boring essays that do only an adequate job earn mid-range scores.
- Students who misunderstand the prompt, use inappropriate examples, and can't express their ideas clearly can expect low scores.

Presentation

- Make your essay look neat, clear, and well organized with legible writing, obvious breaks between paragraphs, and few strike-outs, if any.

Expression

- Capture the reader and create a great first impression with your opening paragraph.
- Vary your choice of words and sentence structure. A little extra effort will pay great dividends.
- Use correct grammar and paragraph construction.

Content

- Plan and organize your points before you start writing.
- Address the prompt. If you write a great essay that doesn't address the prompt, you will receive a low score.
- Develop your argument based on strong, relevant evidence. Connect each piece of evidence directly to the point it supports.

Chapter 5
How to Approach the Synthesis Essay

SYNTHESIZE WHAT?

By "synthesis," the AP Exam writers mean two things:

1. Using sources to develop your own position
2. Citing those sources accurately

High-scoring synthesis essays draw a clear connection between a source and a particular point in the writer's argument. The sources chosen are appropriate; the explanations are thorough and convincing. By the time you get down to a score of 5 (the bottom of the "adequate" band), the link is still apparent but "strained."

Also at the higher score levels, the essay writer cites the specific source being used (with a simple reference such as "Source A"; you're not expected to remember formal citation formats for this exam). Writers who score in the lower bands merely summarize a jumbled collection of points they've read in various sources, without citing a specific source and linking it to a particular point in their argument.

Your performance on the synthesis essay will help the readers (and yourself) predict how well you'll be able to handle college research assignments. In particular, your essay will show whether you can:

- judge the best sources to back up your position
- incorporate other writers' claims or explanations into your *own* argument
- draw on sources in the order that develops your argument in the most logical, persuasive way

Steps to Choosing Sources

1. Analyze the prompt.
2. Decide which position you want to take.
3. Use active reading—what is the main point of each source?
4. Select three sources that provide the best support for your position.

How Many Sources?

The prompt will instruct you to use at least three sources, and in most cases that's a safe choice. Trying to use more than three might lead you into an unnecessarily complicated essay at best, and at worst, a pyramid of similar, superficially treated points piled up on top of one another. Using fewer than three will definitely knock your essay down into the "inadequate" scoring band.

Three sources are enough to show progress in your argument (for example, a more general or older source of support followed by increasingly specific or more recent claims, each one building upon the previous one). If you choose to argue a qualified position, three sources will give you, for instance, two authors who argue against something and one who is in favor of it in particular circumstances, supporting your qualified rejection of the claim.

Having a Conversation with Your Sources

Since your aim is synthesis, you need to weave the three sources into your own discussion of the prompt, using them to support and develop the position you've chosen to take. The exam writers offer a helpful image of how to do that. They call it having a conversation with your sources.

Imagine the creators of your chosen sources are sitting together in a living room discussing the topic of the prompt. Now you walk in and join the conversation. You wouldn't simply record each author's (or artist's) comments. That's the equivalent of just copying and pasting chunks from each source into your essay and stringing them together.

You would respond to each person's comments, build on them, and use them to enrich your own views about the topic. You would add something to the discussion your three authors are having, and they would add something to your own understanding of the topic. Then, if you had a conversation with each author individually, you would try to understand that author's position and add your own ideas to the discussion. That's what the test-writers mean. They call the result a "source-informed" argument.

Direct Quote vs. Paraphrase

When you're drawing a source into your argument, you have a choice of paraphrasing (summarizing in your own words) what the author says, or quoting some of his or her words directly (within quotation marks, of course).

In many cases, paraphrasing makes it easier to incorporate someone else's ideas smoothly into your own. Several quotes, too, could make your essay appear to be more of a copy-and-paste exercise than a synthesis. However, if an author uses a particularly striking phrase or unusual wording that would be difficult to paraphrase accurately, then an occasional direct quote could make your essay more vivid.

SAMPLE ESSAY—HERE'S HOW IT'S DONE

Here's an example of a synthesis essay prompt. As you go through it, use your active reading skills to make sure you understand exactly what it's asking you to do.

The Directions

Question 1
Suggested reading and writing time—55 minutes.
It is suggested that you spend 15 minutes reading the question, analyzing and evaluating the sources, and 40 minutes writing your response.
Note: You may begin writing your response before the reading period is over.

(This question counts for one-third of the total essay section score.)

Artificial intelligence (AI) is hyped as the magic bullet for every challenge—from easing traffic congestion to providing medical care in remote locations, from protecting endangered species to rescuing hostages in dangerous settings. The common foundation is a conviction that AI operations will be faster, more effective, more accurate and sometimes cheaper than human operations, and—critically—will avoid human errors. But with their functional superiority and machine learning capabilities, will AI implementations also be able to evolve beyond human control? And is that necessarily a bad thing?

Carefully read the following seven sources, including the introductory information for each source. Then synthesize information from at least three of the sources and incorporate it into a coherent, well-written essay that addresses this question: Is artificial intelligence to be feared because of its potential independence from human control, or is it to be embraced due to its superior ability to deliver benefits that enhance our lives?

Use the sources to develop and explain your argument. Avoid merely summarizing the sources. Indicate clearly which sources you are drawing from, whether through direct quotation, paraphrase, or summary. You may cite the sources as Source A, Source B, and so forth, or by using the descriptions in parentheses.

Source A (Future)

Source B (Letter)

Source C (Frankenstein)

Source D (slides)

Source E (Third Offset)

Source F (Robots)

Source G (graph)

It's Time to Read

There's quite a lot of reading as you go through the sources for a synthesis essay question. In order to use your 15 minutes of reading time effectively, before you start you should already be clear on what the prompt is asking you to do and have some idea which position you want to take on the question you need to address. Do you want to argue that we should fear Artificial Intelligence (AI)? Welcome it? Or do you want to give a qualified answer? For example, "we should fear it unless…" or "we should welcome it except when..."

To show the depth of thought that pulls an essay up into the "effective" score band, you also need to consider implications that extend beyond the question in the prompt. In other words, use your active reading skills on the prompt. For instance, are fearing and embracing AI our only choices? Can we modify its current course of development? Stop it entirely? If AI is beyond our control, can we make sure we don't need to fear it?

Now you're ready to read through the sources with a fairly clear idea of what you're looking for. You want three sources that will enrich the position you've chosen, and will help you develop your own argument in a logical way. If two sources say essentially the same thing, you probably don't need both—which one is stronger? Which sources deal with the "beyond the prompt" questions you asked during your active reading? If you've chosen to take a qualified position, which source presents an opposing viewpoint that will support your "only in these circumstances" argument?

To help you locate supporting points later on while you're writing, underline a few key words and put a stroke through sources you don't want to use.

Then plan your essay: jot down a quick outline of the points you want to make, the order in which you'll explain them as you develop your argument, and the source you'll use (and cite) to support each of your points. A few minutes of planning will prevent you from going off track while you're writing.

Linear Graffiti

Underlining, circling, and making brief notes in the margins of the sources are all good practices, but don't get too carried away. The purpose of marking the passage is to make information easy to retrieve. A good rule of thumb is to underline no more than five words at a time. Anything longer should be marked with simple brackets.

Source A

"Preparing for the Future of Artificial Intelligence," *The National Science and Technology Council.* Office of Science and Technology Policy, October 2016. Web. 21 January 2018.

The following is an excerpt from The Office of Science and Technology Policy's 2016 federal government report on the future of artificial intelligence in the U.S.

One area of great optimism about AI and machine learning is their potential to improve people's lives by helping to solve some of the world's greatest challenges and inefficiencies.... Public- and private-sector investments in basic and applied R&D on AI have already begun reaping major benefits for the public in fields as diverse as health care, transportation, the environment, criminal justice, and economic inclusion.

At Walter Reed Medical Center, the Department of Veteran Affairs is using AI to better predict medical complications and improve treatment of severe combat wounds, leading to better patient outcomes, faster healing, and lower costs.... Given the current transition to electronic health records, predictive analysis of health data may play a key role across many health domains like precision medicine and cancer research.

In transportation, AI-enabled smarter traffic management applications are reducing wait times, energy use, and emissions by as much as 25 percent in some places....

Some researchers are leveraging AI to improve animal migration tracking by using AI image classification software to analyze tourist photos from public social media sites. The software can identify individual animals in the photos and build a database of their migration using the data and location stamps on the photos.... Other speakers described uses of AI to optimize the patrol strategy of anti-poaching agents, and to design habitat preservation strategies to maximize the genetic diversity of endangered populations.

Autonomous sailboats and watercraft are already patrolling the oceans carrying sophisticated sensor instruments, collecting data on changes in Arctic ice and sensitive ocean ecosystems in operations that would be too expensive or dangerous for crewed vessels....

The Administration is exploring how AI can responsibly benefit current initiatives such as Data Driven Justice and the Police Data Initiative that seek to provide law enforcement and the public with data that can better inform decision-making in the criminal justice system, while also taking care to minimize the possibility that AI might introduce bias or inaccuracies due to deficiencies in the available data.

Several U.S. academic institutions have launched initiatives to use AI to tackle economic and social challenges. For example, the University of Chicago created an academic program that uses data science and AI to address public challenges such as unemployment and school dropouts. The University of Southern California launched the Center for Artificial Intelligence in Society, an institute dedicated to studying how computational game theory, machine learning, automated planning and multi-agent reasoning techniques can help to solve socially relevant problems like homelessness. Meanwhile, researchers at Stanford University are using machine learning in efforts to address global poverty by using AI to analyze satellite images of likely poverty zones to identify where help is needed most.

Source B

"An Open Letter: Research Priorities for Robust and Beneficial Artificial Intelligence." *Future of Life Institute.* January 2015. Web. 21 January 2018.

The following open letter is an initiative of the Future of Life Institute in collaboration with the AI research community.

Artificial intelligence (AI) research has explored a variety of problems and approaches since its inception, but for the last 20 years or so has been focused on the problems surrounding the construction of intelligent agents—systems that perceive and act in some environment. In this context, "intelligence" is related to statistical and economic notions of rationality—colloquially, the ability to make good decisions, plans, or inferences. The adoption of probabilistic and decision-theoretic representations and statistical learning methods has led to a large degree of integration and cross-fertilization among AI, machine learning, statistics, control theory, neuroscience, and other fields. The establishment of shared theoretical frameworks, combined with the availability of data and processing power, has yielded remarkable successes in various component tasks such as speech recognition, image classification, autonomous vehicles, machine translation, legged locomotion, and question-answering systems.

As capabilities in these areas and others cross the threshold from laboratory research to economically valuable technologies, a virtuous cycle takes hold whereby even small improvements in performance are worth large sums of money, prompting greater investments in research. There is now a broad consensus that AI research is progressing steadily, and that its impact on society is likely to increase. The potential benefits are huge, since everything that civilization has to offer is a product of human intelligence; we cannot predict what we might achieve when this intelligence is magnified by the tools AI may provide, but the eradication of disease and poverty are not unfathomable. Because of the great potential of AI, it is important to research how to reap its benefits while avoiding potential pitfalls.

The progress in AI research makes it timely to focus research not only on making AI more capable, but also on maximizing the societal benefit of AI. Such considerations motivated the AAAI 2008–09 Presidential Panel on Long-Term AI Futures and other projects on AI impacts, and constitute a significant expansion of the field of AI itself, which up to now has focused largely on techniques that are neutral with respect to purpose. We recommend expanded research aimed at ensuring that increasingly capable AI systems are robust and beneficial: our AI systems must do what we want them to do. The attached research priorities document gives many examples of such research directions that can help maximize the societal benefit of AI. This research is by necessity interdisciplinary, because it involves both society and AI. It ranges from economics, law and philosophy to computer security, formal methods and, of course, various branches of AI itself.

In summary, we believe that research on how to make AI systems robust and beneficial is both important and timely, and that there are concrete research directions that can be pursued today.

Source C

Shelley, Mary. *Frankenstein, or, The Modern Prometheus.* 1818.

The following is an excerpt from Mary Shelley's 1818 novel.

I trembled and my heart failed within me, when, on looking up, I saw by the light of the moon the dæmon at the casement. A ghastly grin wrinkled his lips as he gazed on me, where I sat fulfilling the task which he had allotted to me. Yes, he had followed me in my travels; …and he now came to mark my progress and claim the fulfilment of my promise.

As I looked on him, his countenance expressed the utmost extent of malice and treachery. I thought with a sensation of madness on my promise of creating another like to him, and trembling with passion, tore to pieces the thing on which I was engaged. The wretch saw me destroy the creature on whose future existence he depended for happiness, and with a howl of devilish despair and revenge, withdrew.…

Several hours passed, and I remained near my window gazing on the sea;…I felt the silence, although I was hardly conscious of its extreme profundity, until my ear was suddenly arrested by the paddling of oars near the shore, and a person landed close to my house.…

Presently I heard the sound of footsteps along the passage; the door opened, and the wretch whom I dreaded appeared. Shutting the door, he approached me and said in a smothered voice,

"You have destroyed the work which you began; what is it that you intend? Do you dare to break your promise? I have endured toil and misery; I left Switzerland with you;…I have endured incalculable fatigue, and cold, and hunger; do you dare destroy my hopes?"

"Begone! I do break my promise; never will I create another like yourself, equal in deformity and wickedness."

"Slave, I before reasoned with you, but you have proved yourself unworthy of my condescension. Remember that I have power; you believe yourself miserable, but I can make you so wretched that the light of day will be hateful to you. You are my creator, but I am your master; obey!"

"The hour of my irresolution is past, and the period of your power is arrived. Your threats cannot move me to do an act of wickedness; but they confirm me in a determination of not creating you a companion in vice.…"

The monster saw my determination in my face and gnashed his teeth in the impotence of anger. "Shall each man," cried he, "find a wife for his bosom, and each beast have his mate, and I be alone?…Beware, for I am fearless and therefore powerful. I will watch with the wiliness of a snake, that I may sting with its venom. Man, you shall repent of the injuries you inflict."

Source D

"High Profile NITRD Technical Activities." *Federal R&D Agency Workshop.* The Networking and Information Technology Research and Development (NITRD) Program, 29 September 2016. Web. 21 January 2018.

The following slides were used in a workshop presentation about Networking and Information Technology Research and Development Program's (NITRD) High Profile Technical Activities.

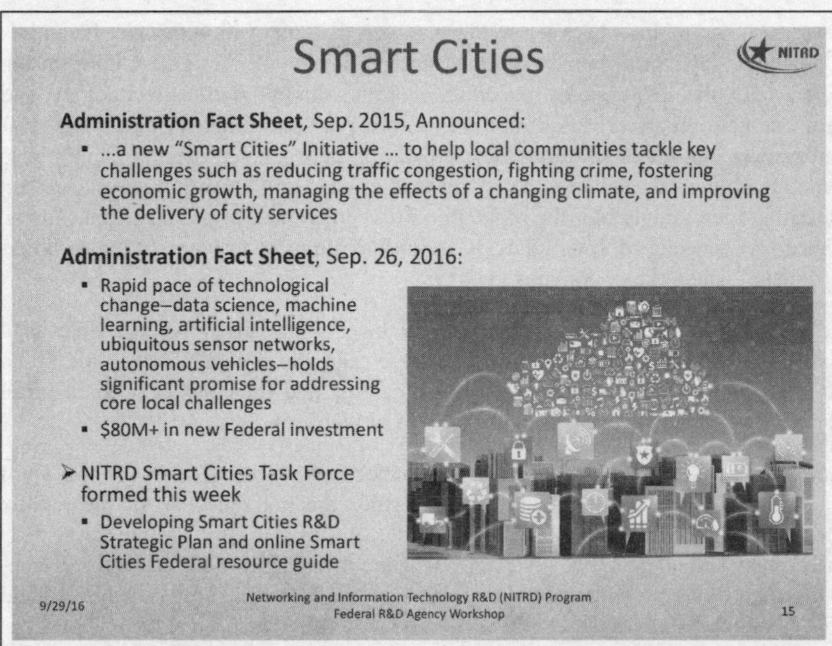

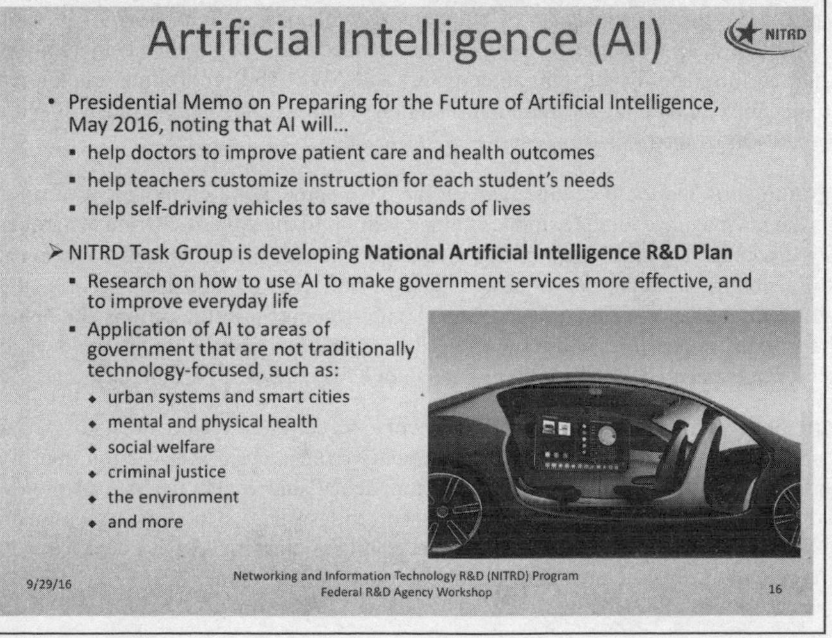

Source E

"Closer than you think: The Implications of the Third Offset Strategy for the U.S. Army." *U.S. Army Strategic Studies Institute and U.S. Army War College Press*, October 2017. Web. 21 January 2018.

This is an excerpt from a publication by the U.S. Army Strategic Studies Institute. Note: "Third Offset" refers to "leap-ahead technologies and capabilities" that could give an advantage over an otherwise-equal opponent.

...There is a natural symbiosis between military and civilian innovation that, in the end, is driven by a need to solve problems and gain advantage. The challenges and realities of big data, complex networks and systems, uncertain environments, ubiquitous technology, and intense peer competition are drivers in both the commercial and military spaces and steer each toward a common set of solutions. The separation between self-driving automobiles and autonomous military air and ground systems is thin—and will grow thinner as deep and machine learning increasingly blur the separation between civilian or military applications. Once advanced AI is achieved, it will quickly spiral into almost every area of the commercial, governmental, and military domains.

The allure of science fiction-like capabilities will be a strong incentive for states and nonstates to pursue Third Offset technologies. These leap-ahead capabilities could be so game changing that the difference between finishing first and finishing next could mean years of decisive advantage in every meaningful area of warfare.

...The United States is rightfully concerned about the implications of many of the Third Offset technologies—but current policies and priorities are not reflective of the rapidly evolving technologies or the operational environment. As a result, the United States risks falling dangerously behind potential adversaries who are investing heavily in advanced technologies—and are doing so without self-imposed constraints which limit capabilities and fail to allow full exploitation of these technologies.

The DoD Directive 3000.09, *Autonomy in Weapons Systems*, establishes requirements and parameters for development and use of autonomous weapons systems (AWS). In short, Directive 3000.09 seeks to minimize the risk of unintended lethal engagements by requiring positive human interface for all semi-autonomous and AWS, and prohibiting autonomous lethal force against human targets. While this caution is understandable, the policy is out of step with the evolving battlefield.

Placing a "human in the loop" requirement on the development and employment of future weapons systems may inadvertently induce vulnerability into the system. Swarm technology has already exceeded the capability for any meaningful human control of individual agents and, as the technologies advance, swarms of tens or hundreds of thousands of individual agents will make human control—or even human understanding—of the actions and behaviors of the swarms impossible. In the future vague and uncertain environment, the decision to engage or not engage—to kill or not kill—may not be best made by a human.

...The battlefield of the next 30 years will likely evolve far differently (and much faster) than over the past 30 years. The legacy "big five" combat systems, even with version improvements and upgrades, may well be rendered outmatched and ineffective by AI-enabled unmanned autonomous systems, cyber dominance, and swarms. Continued incremental upgrades to current systems may address current readiness challenges, but could leave the Army ill-prepared to contend on a far different battlefield in the future.

Source F

Yong, Ed. "A Swarm of a Thousand Cooperative Self Organising Robots," *Not Exactly Rocket Science: A Blog* by Ed Yong. Phenomena on National Geographic Magazine, 14 August 2014. Web. 21 January 2018.

The following is an excerpt from a blog post on the growing population of self-organizing "kilorobots."

In a lab at Harvard's Wyss Institute, the world's largest swarm of cooperative robots is building a star…out of themselves. There are 1024 of these inch-wide "Kilobots," and they can arrange themselves into different shapes, from a letter to a wrench. They are slow and comically jerky in their movements, but they are also autonomous. Once they're given a shape, they can recreate it without any further instructions, simply by cooperating with their neighbours and organising themselves.

The Kilobots are the work of Mike Rubenstein, Alejandro Cornejo and Radhika Nagpal, who were inspired by natural swarms, where simple and limited units can cooperate to do great things. Thousands of fire ants can unite into living bridges, rafts and buildings.…

"This is a staggering work," adds Iain Couzin, who studies collective animal behaviour at Princeton University. "It offers a vision of the future where robot groups could form structures on demand as, for example, in search-and-rescue in dangerous environments, or even the formation of miniature swarms within the body to detect and treat disease.…"

The tyranny of cost-efficiency meant that the team had to lose any sensors that might tell the robots their bearings or positions. They can't tell where they are, or if they're going straight.…

Fortunately, they have each other. A stuck Kilobot can't tell if it's stuck on its own, but it can communicate with its neighbors. If it thinks it's moving but the distances from its neighbors change, it can deduce that something is wrong.…

Every Kilobot runs on the same program. The team only has to give them a shape and nominate four of them as seeds. Once that's done, the rest slowly pour into the right pattern, in an endearingly life-like way. It takes them around 12 hours, but they do it all without any human intervention. And although the final shapes are always a little warped, that's life-like too. Fire ants don't have a Platonic ideal of what a bridge or raft should look like; they just work with their neighbours to get the job done.…

The next step will be to build robots that actually self-assemble by attaching to each other, says Marco Dorigo from the Free University of Brussels.…

Eventually, he also wants to get to a position where the robots can sense their environment and react accordingly, rather than just slide into some pre-determined shape. Like fire ants, when they get to a body of water, they wouldn't have to be fed the image of a bridge; they would just self-assemble into one. "That's a whole other level of intelligence, and it's not really understood how to do that in robotics," says Rubenstein. "But nature does it well."

Source G

"America's Wars Fact Sheet" and "American War and Military Operations Casualties: Lists and Statistics." *U.S. Department of Veterans Affairs and Congressional Research Service Report for Congress.* 13 July 2005 and May 2017. Web. 21 January 2018.

The following graph comparing battlefield fatalities in various historical conflicts is derived from reports by the U.S. Department of Veterans Affairs and the Naval History and Heritage Command. The timeline ends with the 1990–1991 Persian Gulf War. The graph shows battlefield fatalities as a percentage of the number serving in each conflict, so it offers an "apples-to-apples" comparison, even though the conflicts differed in size.

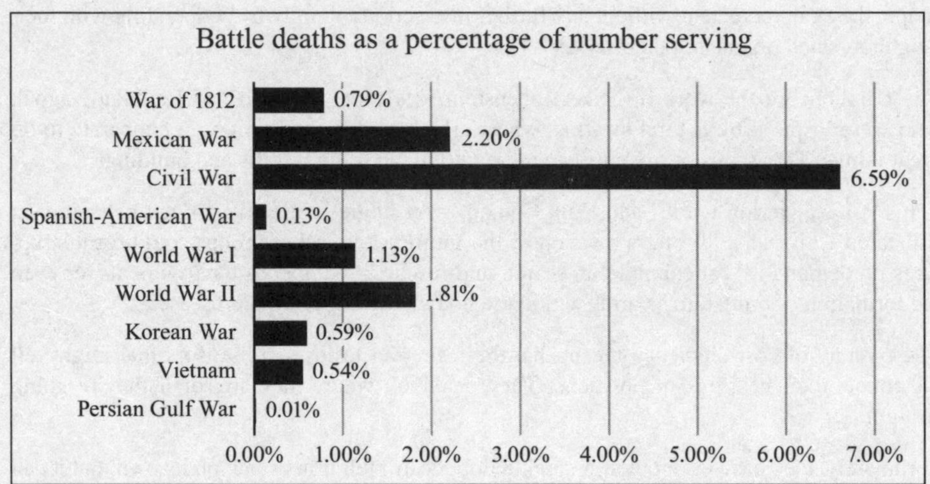

You Try It

Now you're ready to begin writing. Remember to plan your essay first and leave a couple of minutes at the end to proofread your work.

After you're finished writing your essay, take a look at the following page. This is a student essay that was written in the allotted 40 minutes. As you read it, evaluate how well it:

- addresses the prompt
- ties each source clearly to one of the writer's points
- integrates the sources smoothly into the progression of the argument
- develops the writer's *own* argument
- expresses the writer's ideas

Then read the discussion of the student essay from a grader's viewpoint.

It's Not Me

Your essay will seem more professional and credible if you use third-person narrative instead of first person ("I think...").

A Student Essay

Some people see advances in artificial intelligence as leading to a frightening scenario where we can no longer control AI and therefore can't ensure that it doesn't harm us. Others imagine grand possibilities of AI making our lives easier, safer and less complex.

We are just now discovering the potential benefits of AI applications. Source A lists several benefits: better medical treatment, less traffic congestion and ways to address social problems. The same source suggests environmental benefits, too: protecting animal habitats and monitoring climate change in the Arctic. In general, Source A is optimistic about how AI can "improve people's lives" and "solve some of the world's greatest challenges and efficiencies."

Source B also mentions social benefits, such as autonomous vehicles and speech recognition. This source is even more ambitious than Source A, predicting that AI might be able to end poverty and disease entirely.

Many of these benefits depend on AI's ability to collect and analyze vast amounts of data that would be beyond human capability. Others allow us to learn about locations that would be too expensive or dangerous for human agents to enter.

Such characteristics suggest that AI will make us capable of doing more than we could do on our own. We must also consider the other side of the debate, though. By being able to do things we can't do, does AI also have the potential to master us, and will it always use its superior capabilities to help us?

Source B, while optimistic about the benefits AI can deliver, does raise this question. AI systems are going to grow more and more capable as research progresses. Therefore, we must focus the different AI research projects on the same goal: "our AI systems must do what we want them to do." AI must enhance and remain a tool of human intelligence, even if its abilities are superior to ours.

Source E raises a frightening scenario of AI research that does not prioritize the social benefits the other two sources describe. AI weapons systems, it says, could become so complex that we wouldn't even be able to understand them, let alone control them. Weapons that don't require a human to make them work should deliver the benefit of reducing war casualties, Source G does indicate that would be true. From World War II, when radio-controlled bombs were first directed by humans far away from the danger, to the automatic air defense systems of the Gulf War, the percentage of battlefield fatalities has been decreasing. Still, Source E's prospect of an autonomous weapon that can make its own decision to kill is frightening, especially since that same source draws a close connection between military and civilian developments. AI killers could roam our cities as well as our battlefields.

> As Source B suggests, it's too late now to stop AI development. Many different disciplines are already collaborating on a vast array of applications. As research results reach commercial success, there is an economic incentive to do more research and develop even more commercially viable applications. The genie can't be put back in the bottle now.
>
> AI, if not to be feared in the light of its potential benefits, must at least be viewed with caution and closely monitored because of its capacity to do harm. If we are to tame AI to do our bidding and to deliver only benefits, then everyone involved in AI research and development must have that same objective. How realistic is that?

What did you think? This essay has some strong points:

- The essay stretches beyond the question posed in the prompt to ask, "under what condition(s) would we *not* need to fear AI?"
- The writer does a good job of maintaining the high-level discussion initiated in the prompt. AI is such a broad topic that it would be easy to fall off the main track into a distracting consideration of one particular type of AI application.
- The writer's argument progresses smoothly, with points building on previous points and smooth transitions between them. For the most part, he shows good control of the language, expressing his ideas clearly and concisely.
- The writer does a decent job of incorporating a fourth source (the battle casualties graph) and outside knowledge (advances in developing weapons that don't require a human operator right beside them). He mentions both only briefly, and in the context of discussing one of his main sources (Source E). In general, though, your essay will exhibit better focus and demonstrate your research skills more effectively if you stick to three of the sources provided and avoid outside knowledge.

Did you pick up the weaknesses in this essay, too? They're significant.

- The sources—often summarized—dominate the writer's argument. He integrates them into the essay smoothly, and the progression of his argument is orderly and logical. However, the reader is left with an impression of sources strung together rather than an original argument supported by sources.
- The writer's position isn't evident until the end. This is a legitimate structure for an essay: build evidence that leads to a conclusion at the end instead of the more traditional structure of stating a thesis at the beginning, followed by evidence that proves it. However, the conclusion isn't stated clearly even at the end. The writer describes the condition under which we wouldn't need to fear AI (if everyone is aiming at beneficial applications) and then suggests that condition couldn't be reached ("How realistic is that?"). By implication, his conclusion is that we *do* need to fear AI.

- The opening isn't a strong one that would grab readers and make them want to keep reading. Instead, it basically restates information in the prompt, giving the reader (remember, there is a human grader for the AP essays) a first impression of an unoriginal, uninteresting essay.

This essay does an adequate job of addressing the question in the prompt. The writer's ability to go beyond the prompt and his generally good control of the language elevate his score. However, the dominance of the sources over the writer's own original argument keep this essay from gaining a higher score.

By following our strategies and using the essays that you've seen as models, you can aim for—and achieve—higher scores.

Next, let's take a look at how to tackle the rhetorical analysis essay.

Chapter 6
How to Approach the Rhetorical Analysis Essay

FIRST THINGS FIRST: WHAT'S A RHETORICAL STRATEGY?

Authors use certain techniques, in both the language and the structure of the piece they're writing, to convey their messages effectively and to achieve the intended effect(s) on their audiences. Speakers use these techniques, too. Often they're trying to persuade their audiences to do something or to agree with their points of view.

In Chapters 8–11, you'll find explanations and examples of rhetorical strategies, plus questions so you can practice using them. Once you become familiar with rhetorical strategies and their effects, you'll probably start spotting them in your day-to-day life, too—in ads, in interviews given by politicians, or in instructions from your teachers, for instance.

YOUR TASKS IN THE RHETORICAL ANALYSIS ESSAY

The AP readers are looking for three main things in the rhetorical analysis essay:

- an understanding of the author's intended purpose
- the ability to identify the chief rhetorical strategies used to achieve that purpose effectively
- an analysis of *how* those strategies contribute to the development and effectiveness of the writer's argument, *supported by references to the text*

Of course, the readers are also assessing the usual skillful control of the language, clear expression, and smooth organization that they want to see in all three essays.

In the rhetorical analysis essay, the AP readers don't want a summary of the entire passage, or an argument for or against the author's main point. Your focus is strictly on what the author's purpose is, and what rhetorical strategies the author uses to achieve it effectively. Students typically find this essay the most challenging of the three, and straying from that focus is often where they go wrong.

Another common problem that lands essays in the lower score bands is being too general. An essay might describe the author's purpose right up front, in the first paragraph (a good idea, incidentally), and identify the three or four most important rhetorical strategies, but then fail to link each one to the author's purpose with a specific, thorough explanation of exactly how that strategy makes the message more effective. Direct references to the passage are a must, too, or the explanation runs the risk of being too general and oversimplified.

So your first task is to identify the author's purpose, which your active reading skills will enable you to do. After that, your task is to detect the main rhetorical strategies and build a convincing case for why and how each advances the author's purpose.

The Rhetorical Diamond

While you're reading the prompt and the passage, imagine—and try to flesh out—a baseball diamond with the following four points:

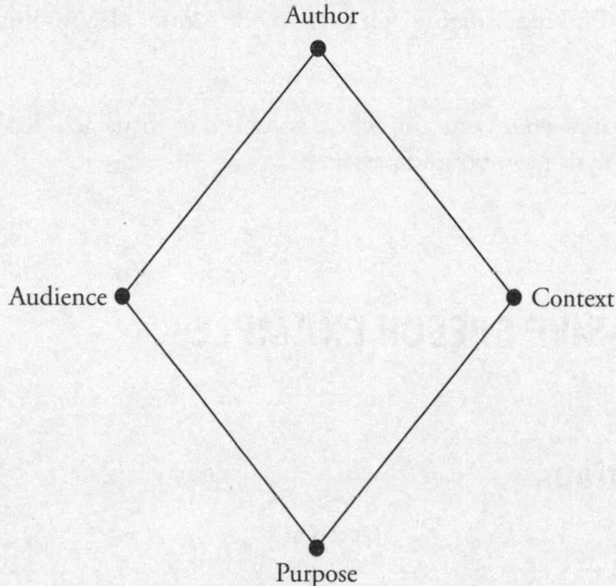

The passage represents an interaction among those points. Understanding them will help you recognize rhetorical strategies that an author might use to achieve his or her purpose for a specific audience and within a distinct context.

For example, you would expect a politician trying to win support from a mass audience at a rally to use different rhetorical techniques than a heart disease specialist writing the findings from a research study for publication in a professional, peer-reviewed journal. The politician, because of the verbal delivery and the diversity of the mass audience, would use simpler language, emotional appeals (pathos), and techniques such as repetition. The heart disease specialist, on the other hand, would use technical language and techniques to inspire respect for her qualifications and the thoroughness of her work (ethos).

The prompt will give you some of the information you need to describe the four points of the rhetorical baseball diamond. With a solid understanding of those points, you'll be able to predict at least some of the rhetorical strategies you can expect to find as you apply your active reading skills to the passage.

More Tips for Spotting Rhetorical Strategies

The author's main point will give you some clues about the rhetorical strategies you might find in the passage. Does it deal with a controversial topic, or with a "motherhood and apple pie" position that would create almost no opposition from anyone? Is it promoting a new, "fuzzy" concept that the audience would find hard to understand, or a topic that would be familiar to most people?

Diamonds Are an AP Student's Best Friend

Think of the four main aspects of a passage (author's message, context, purpose, and audience) in terms of a diamond. Understanding these main points will help you predict the rhetorical strategies being used in a text.

Trying to put yourself in the audience's shoes can also help you uncover rhetorical strategies. If you were part of that audience, at that time and in that context, would this piece of writing influence you? Why? Did it help you understand something through the use of examples, for instance? Did it make you feel the author sympathized with your concerns, perhaps through the use of anecdotes echoing your own experiences? Did it keep bringing you back to one central idea through the skillful use of repetition?

Now that you know your tasks and where you need to focus, let's look at a couple of rhetorical analysis prompts and passages.

A PERSUASIVE SPEECH EXAMPLE

The Directions

Question 2

Suggested time—40 minutes.

(This question counts for one-third of the total essay score.)

Susan B. Anthony delivered the speech below in 1873, after she was arrested for voting in the 1872 presidential election. She spoke throughout the county where her trial was to be held, aiming primarily at potential jurors and other women. Read the passages carefully. Then, in a well-developed essay, analyze the rhetorical strategies Anthony uses to persuade her audience that she did not commit a crime.

Analyzing the Prompt

As you're reading the prompt, look for how much it tells you about the four points on the rhetorical diamond.

- **Author**—Even if you've never heard of Susan B. Anthony (a leading 19th-century advocate for women's rights and co-founder of the National Woman Suffrage Association), the prompt gives you enough information to guess that she was an activist who deliberately defied a current law.
- **Purpose**—Sometimes the prompt will outline the author's purpose; sometimes it won't. In this case, you can guess that since Anthony is in conflict with legal authorities, she is probably giving a speech to present her side of the story in advance of her trial, and to convince her audience that her position is right.

- **Audience**—This prompt provides an unusual amount of information about the audience. Most of the time, you'll need to make inferences based on whatever details about the author and context you can squeeze from the prompt.

  In this case, since Anthony has been arrested but not yet tried, you could have guessed (even if the prompt didn't tell you) that the audience would include potential members of the jury pool. And since she felt strongly enough about her cause to risk arrest, you could guess that the audience would include a mix of supporters (who want to hear their champion) and people who are simply curious.

- **Context**—Anthony is giving a speech, so you can look for rhetorical strategies that you would expect to find in verbal delivery (such as simpler language, shorter sentences, repetition, and rhythm). And since she is facing a trial for following her beliefs, you could expect suggestions of urgency and passion.

Armed with the information you've gained from the prompt, you can now put your active reading skills into gear looking for Anthony's rhetorical strategies in the passage. Imagine you're in the audience listening to her speech. Does she convince you to agree with her? If so, how does she do it? If not, what would you need to hear in order to be convinced? As you identify each rhetorical strategy, keep asking yourself, "Why does she use this? How does it help her achieve her purpose?" because you'll need to answer those questions in your essay.

First, try writing your own essay in 40 minutes. Remember to spend a few minutes planning your essay and support your points with direct references to the passage. Then read the sample student essay and assessment that follow the passage.

The Passage

Woman's Rights to the Suffrage
by Susan B. Anthony (1820–1906)
1873
[abridged]

The terms "bill of attainder" and "ex post facto law" in paragraph 5 refer to the power of the legislature to declare someone guilty (often without a trial), and to change, retroactively, the legal status of an action that occurred before the law was passed. The three people mentioned in paragraph 6 all published dictionaries.

Friends and Fellow Citizens: I stand before you tonight under indictment for the alleged crime of having voted at the last presidential election, without having a lawful right to vote. It shall be my work this evening to prove to you that in thus voting, I not only committed no crime, but, instead, simply exercised my citizen's rights, guaranteed to me and all United States citizens by the National Constitution, beyond the power of any State to deny.

The preamble of the Federal Constitution says:

"We, the people of the United States, in order to form a more perfect union, establish justice, insure domestic tranquility, provide for the common defense, promote the general welfare, and secure the blessings of liberty to ourselves and our posterity, do ordain and establish this Constitution for the United States of America."

It was we, the people; not we, the white male citizens; nor yet we, the male citizens; but we, the whole people, who formed the Union. And we formed it, not to give the blessings of liberty, but to secure them; not to the half of ourselves and the half of our posterity, but to the whole people—women as well as men. And it is a downright mockery to talk to women of their enjoyment of the blessings of liberty while they are denied the use of the only means of securing them provided by this democratic-republican government—the ballot.

For any State to make sex a qualification that must ever result in the disfranchisement of one entire half of the people is to pass a bill of attainder, or an ex post facto law, and is therefore a violation of the supreme law of the land. By it the blessings of liberty are for ever withheld from women and their female posterity. To them this government has no just powers derived from the consent of the governed. To them this government is not a democracy. It is not a republic. It is an odious aristocracy; a hateful oligarchy of sex; the most hateful aristocracy ever established on the face of the globe; an oligarchy of wealth, where the right govern the poor. An oligarchy of learning, where the educated govern the ignorant, or even an oligarchy of race, where the Saxon rules the African, might be endured; but this oligarchy of sex, which makes father, brothers, husband, sons, the oligarchs over the mother and sisters, the wife and daughters of every household—which ordains all men sovereigns, all women subjects, carries dissension, discord and rebellion into every home of the nation.

Webster, Worcester and Bouvier all define a citizen to be a person in the United States, entitled to vote and hold office.

The only question left to be settled now is: Are women persons? And I hardly believe any of our opponents will have the hardihood to say they are not. Being persons, then, women are citizens; and no State has a right to make any law, or to enforce any old law, that shall abridge their privileges or immunities. Hence, every discrimination against women in the constitutions and laws of the several States is today null and void.

A Student Essay

Susan B. Anthony broke the law. For this, she was arrested and about to be tried. Before the trial took place, however, she wanted to prove that she didn't do anything wrong and to gain support for her innocence. So she gave this speech to convince people—potential jurors at her trial, other women and anyone who chose to listen—that it wasn't wrong for her to vote in the presidential election.

That would have been a radical assertion at the time. Anthony lived in an era when men and women had different rights, and the difference in their status was widely accepted as normal. While the audience likely included people who knew of Anthony and supported her position, others would have been shocked by the fact that she dared to challenge the accepted social order. She would have needed a strong argument to explain her action and win those people over.

Anthony bases her entire appeal on logos, or logic. "Are women persons?" she asks. If women are people, then they are also citizens and entitled to the "blessings of liberty" that the nation's Constitution guarantees, including the right to vote. She does not try to claim that she didn't break a state law. Instead, she argues that the law she broke is "null and void" because it denies her the status and the rights that the federal Constitution guarantees her.

In this appeal to reason and logic, Anthony is basically claiming that anyone who thinks she did something wrong by voting is also saying that she—or any woman—is not a person. In addition, anyone who thinks she committed a crime would also have to argue that a state law (which she did break by voting) outweighs the Constitution of the entire nation. Both positions would be hard to defend. By attributing these positions to her opponents, Anthony portrays people who don't agree with her—including everyone connected with her arrest and trial and with passing the law in the first place—as illogical, unreasonable idiots. Such people couldn't possibly be right.

Not only are her opponents fools; Anthony claims they are more dangerous than that. They have created a "hateful aristocracy" and ensured that every family in the country is plagued by "dissension, discord and rebellion." The government is not a democracy, as the Constitution intended, she claims, but is instead controlled by a privileged few who are depriving her—and all women—of liberty. Her passion and hyperbole come through even more when she describes the government as "the most hateful aristocracy ever established on the face of the globe."

After this tirade, Anthony comes full circle back to her original point: women are citizens too, and therefore no state law (like the one preventing them from voting) can deny them the rights guaranteed by the country's Constitution. Through this passionate appeal to logic, Anthony achieves the purpose she clearly stated at the beginning: "to prove to you that in thus voting, I... committed no crime." It is as if she were a lawyer arguing her case at her upcoming trial, rather than the accused trying to drum up support and influence potential jurors. How could anyone disagree with her after listening to the logic of her argument?

The Assessment

This student makes a common mistake in responding to the rhetorical analysis essay question. Can you identify it? He focuses on *what* the author says rather than on *how* the author says it in order to achieve her purpose.

His discussion of Anthony's logical argument is accurate, although rather superficial. The trouble is, that's not what the prompt asked. The prompt instructed him to identify and analyze the *rhetorical strategies* the author uses. That task requires a focus not just on the author's message, but on the interaction among message, purpose, audience, and context. Different elements—for example, if Anthony were creating a written submission to the judge at her trial—would require different rhetorical strategies in order to achieve the author's purpose effectively.

This confusion between *what* the author says and *how* the author says it is one of the main reasons why test-takers typically earn a lower score on the rhetorical analysis than on any of the other essay tasks. In this case, the essay would likely have received an inadequate score because the student misread the prompt and did not do an adequate job of analyzing Anthony's rhetorical strategies.

There are some good points in this essay. Although the first paragraph is simply an uninspiring restatement of the information provided in the prompt, the first sentence does turn out to be a good attention-getter. It makes the reader want to keep going to uncover more of the story, and creates a good first impression. The student also cites some evidence from the passage, which is essential to earning a good score. He conveys his thoughts clearly, leads the reader through his argument with transitions between points, and displays a good vocabulary and grasp of English language mechanics.

Let's look at some points this student could have covered in his essay to get a better score.

Although he correctly identifies Anthony's classical appeal to logos, or logic, the student doesn't catch her use of pathos—an appeal to the audience's values, to a sense of fairness in this case.

He does touch upon the likely makeup of the audience and the context of an era in which the restricted status of women was the norm. However, he connects these two elements only to the content of Anthony's message (the need for a strong argument), not to rhetorical strategies that would help her deliver that content more effectively to that audience in that era. For example, he could have discussed strategies such as identifying with the audience and establishing common ground (the wording of the Constitution, the desire for a peaceful home life) to make her action seem less alien to listeners who might initially find it shocking.

The student mentions "passion and hyperbole" but doesn't connect these rhetorical devices to Anthony's verbal delivery (can't you just hear the rising volume as she goes through that long "odious aristocracy" sentence?) or to her purpose of inflaming her audience to support her right to vote. And Anthony injects a bit of humour ("not we, the white male citizens") to give some relief to her impassioned plea for support.

He astutely notices that Anthony concludes her speech by returning to her starting point. However, again he fails to tie this rhetorical technique to the verbal delivery or to the mass audience she's addressing. Her listeners don't have a written version of her argument in front of them. In that context, she can achieve her purpose more effectively by reminding them of her main points and wrapping up her speech neatly by returning to the beginning.

The student also ignores some major rhetorical strategies used in speeches: repetition, cadence, and rhythm. Try to hear, for instance, the "...not to...but to..." rhythms of the fourth paragraph, or the repeated "an oligarchy of" descriptions in the fifth. Anthony also uses repetition in organizing her points, again in consideration of the verbal delivery and an audience that could well include people who are simply curious. She not only begins and ends with her main points (women are people, the nation's Constitution supersedes a state law, and therefore she did nothing wrong), but also refers to those points throughout the body of her speech.

The student misses the rhetorical technique of appeal to authority too. Anthony claims she has no less authority on her side than the founding Constitution of the entire nation, and in case that isn't enough, she invokes Webster (of dictionary fame), Worcester, and Bouvier (who also published dictionaries). That technique would enhance her stature and credibility with listeners who might have regarded her as just some minor figure who was silly enough to challenge a state law.

Anthony also uses the tried-and-true politician's technique of identifying with her listeners in order to get them on her side. She addresses them as "Friends and Fellow Citizens," and tells them that she is fighting for them because the injustice she wants to overturn affects "every household."

Keep this student's mistake in mind when you reach the rhetorical analysis essay on the test. Don't simply discuss what the author says. Discuss how the author delivers the message in order to achieve his or her purpose with this particular audience in this particular context.

Here's another example for you to try, this time from a written work.

More AP Info Online!
We have put together even more goodies for a handful of AP Exam subjects. For short quizzes, high level AP course and test information, and expert advice, head over to www.princetonreview.com/college-advice/advanced-placement-resources.

AN EDUCATIONAL BOOK EXAMPLE

The Directions

Question 2

Suggested time—40 minutes.

(This question counts for one-third of the total essay score.)

In1880, nine years after he created "The Greatest Show on Earth," circus promoter P.T. Barnum wrote a short book about making money. He became wealthy himself, and believed that anyone could do the same if they would only follow the simple rules he had learned. Read the passages carefully. Then, in a well-developed essay, analyze the rhetorical strategies Barnum uses to convey his point of view.

Analyzing the Prompt

As you're reading the prompt, look for how much it tells you about the four points on the rhetorical diamond.

- **Author**—You may have heard of P.T. Barnum and the Barnum and Bailey Circus. The prompt reveals something about this successful businessman and promoter that you might not expect, though. He wants to share his secrets for making money—to help ordinary people become wealthy, too. That suggests a philanthropic quality and empathy for the kind of people who come to see his circus (and who, in the process, have helped him become a millionaire).
- **Purpose**—This prompt reveals a lot of information about the author's purpose. Anyone can get rich, he believes, and he wants to teach them how. And incidentally, he will be able to sell a lot of books to a mass audience if he really does provide helpful information geared to ordinary people. Readers who find his rules useful will tell their friends and relatives, who will buy the book and tell their friends and relatives, and so on.

- **Audience**—Barnum says his rules apply to anyone, not just financiers or businessmen. He is addressing the laborers and housewives of the era—people who don't have much money now, and who don't have a lot of formal education but hope for a better future.

- **Context**—This is a book for the masses, so it has to be useful to ordinary people or it won't sell. Look for rhetorical strategies that make the author's points easy to understand and remember. You can also expect efforts to identify with the audience; they won't listen to someone who thinks he is better than them and who "talks down" to them. He will want to convince his readers that he genuinely wants to help them get rich, and that they really can succeed if they follow his rules.

Armed with the information you've gained from the prompt, you can now use your active reading skills to look for Barnum's rhetorical strategies. In this excerpt, does he teach you any lessons that would help you improve your own financial situation? How does he do it? Does he explain his rules in a way that will help you remember them? Does he make you believe that his desire to help you is genuine, and that you, too, can become wealthy? As you identify each rhetorical strategy, keep asking yourself, "Why does he use this? How does it help him achieve his purpose?" because you'll need to answer those questions in your essay.

First, try writing your own essay in 40 minutes. Remember to spend a few minutes planning your essay and support your points with direct references to the passage. Then read the sample student essay and assessment that follow the passage.

The Passage

Excerpt from
The Art of Money Getting
or
Golden Rules for Making Money
by P.T. Barnum
1880

In paragraph 2, "Dr. Franklin" refers to Benjamin Franklin, the Founding Father who promoted the virtues of thrift and frugal living. "Mr. Micawber" is the chronic debtor in Charles Dickens' novel, David Copperfield. "Furbelows" signifies showy, basically useless ruffles on women's dresses. In paragraph 4, a "bung-hole" is a hole in a barrel (which might hold beer or whisky) capped with a cork called a bung. Punch was a popular satire magazine at the time.

In the United States, where we have more land than people, it is not at all difficult for persons in good health to make money. In this comparatively new field there are so many avenues of success open, so many vocations which are not crowded, that any person of either sex who is willing, at least for the time being, to engage in any respectable occupation that offers, may find lucrative employment.

Those who really desire to attain an independence, have only to set their minds upon it, and adopt the proper means, as they do in regard to any other object which they wish to accomplish, and the thing is easily done. But however easy it may be found to make money, I have no doubt many of my hearers will agree it is the most difficult thing in the world to keep it. The road to wealth is, as Dr. Franklin truly says, "as plain as the road to the mill." It consists simply in expending less than we earn; that seems to be a very simple problem. Mr. Micawber, one of those happy creations of the genial Dickens, puts the case in a strong light when he says that to have annual income of twenty pounds per annum, and spend twenty pounds and sixpence, is to be the most miserable of men; whereas, to have an income of only twenty pounds, and spend but nineteen pounds and sixpence is to be the happiest of mortals. Many of my readers may say, "we understand this: this is economy, and we know economy is wealth; we know we can't eat our cake and keep it also." Yet I beg to say that perhaps more cases of failure arise from mistakes on this point than almost any other. The fact is, many people think they understand economy when they really do not.

True economy is misapprehended, and people go through life without properly comprehending what that principle is. One says, "I have an income of so much, and here is my neighbor who has the same; yet every year he gets something ahead and I fall short; why is it? I know all about economy." He thinks he does, but he does not. There are men who think that economy consists in saving cheese-parings and candle-ends, in cutting off two pence from the laundress' bill and doing all sorts of little, mean, dirty things. Economy is not meanness. The misfortune is, also, that this class of persons let their economy apply in only one direction. They fancy they are so wonderfully economical in saving a half-penny where they ought to spend twopence, that they think they can afford to squander in other directions. A few years ago, before kerosene oil was discovered or thought of, one might stop overnight at almost any farmer's house in the agricultural districts and get a very good supper, but after supper he might attempt to read in the sitting-room, and would find it impossible with the inefficient light of one candle. The hostess, seeing his dilemma, would say: "It is rather difficult to read here evenings; the proverb says 'you must have a ship at sea in order to be able to burn two candles at once;' we never have an extra candle except on extra occasions." These extra occasions occur, perhaps, twice a year. In this way the good woman saves five, six, or ten dollars in that time: but the information which might be derived from having the extra light would, of course, far outweigh a ton of candles.

But the trouble does not end here. Feeling that she is so economical in tallow candles, she thinks she can afford to go frequently to the village and spend twenty or thirty dollars for ribbons and furbelows, many of which are not necessary. This false connote may frequently be seen in men of business, and in those instances it often runs to writing-paper. You find good businessmen who save all the old envelopes and scraps, and would not tear a new sheet of paper, if they could avoid it, for the world. This is all very well; they may in this way save five or ten dollars a year, but being so economical (only in note paper), they think they can afford to waste time; to have expensive parties, and to drive their carriages. This is an illustration of Dr. Franklin's "saving at the spigot and wasting at the bung-hole;" "penny wise and pound foolish." Punch in speaking of this "one idea" class of people says "they are like the man who bought a penny herring for his family's dinner and then hired a coach and four to take it home." I never knew a man to succeed by practising this kind of economy.

True economy consists in always making the income exceed the out-go.

A Student Essay

Circus promoter P.T. Barnum wanted to do more than entertain people at the Greatest Show on Earth. He wants to teach them how to make money and become wealthy, too. To do this, he uses some effective rhetorical strategies. He tells stories, he gives examples, he uses a comparison/contrast structure, he mentions authorities, he identifies with his readers, he uses the tone of a cheerleader and he uses simple language.

Telling stories is a good way to teach lessons. Barnum's readers are ordinary people, without much formal education. They will remember stories much more easily than if the author ordered them to follow a list of rules. For example, Barnum tells the story of the woman with the candle so vividly that readers could likely see her guest squinting, then finally giving up on trying to read

Simon Says

Try to use more varied verbs in your essay. Instead of constantly writing "The author says," how about "The author... claims, suggests, implies, states..."?

with such inadequate lighting. Then they could imagine the woman dashing around the village buying ribbons with the money she saved by only burning one candle.

Readers would also be more accepting of a lesson told in a story than they would of a rule ordered by a successful businessman. If Barnum just told them not to save money for buying foolish things, but to invest the money instead (in this case, in the knowledge she would gain by reading), readers might resent being ordered around. A story conveys the same rule in a friendlier way to this audience. They are reading Barnum's book because they want to learn, not be ordered around.

The author gives other examples so he can avoid delivering his lessons as rules and so readers will remember them better. He tells the story of the businessman who saves scraps of paper, but wastes the money he saved on parties and carriages. He gives the example of Mr. Micawber, who always spent more than he earned and therefore couldn't become wealthy. The author compares Mr. Micawber's practice with a contrasting habit of spending less than one earns, which leads to the ability to accumulate wealth.

Citing authorities that would be familiar to readers gives Barnum more credibility with his audience, and also strengthens his position as "one of them" rather than a remote, successful businessman they could never hope to become. Barnum reads Charles Dickens and the satire magazine Punch, too, just like his readers do. His statement, "many of my hearers will agree," reinforces his connection with the audience so they will accept his rules as advice from a friend rather than a route to something they could never achieve (wealth). The author needs to convince his readers that he really wants to help them become wealthy. Making them feel that he is "one of them" helps him achieve that goal.

He cheers them on and encourages them to follow his advice. It's "not at all difficult for persons in good health to make money," he assures them. Anyone can do it, even women (which would have been unusual at the time).

Barnum used simple language to convey simple lessons. There are no complex financial terms or concepts that would make his readers feel the book or Barnum's lessons were beyond their abilities. Spend less than you earn, and invest wisely instead of spending foolishly are his two main messages in this excerpt. The rhetorical strategies he chooses ensure that these important lessons are understood and remembered by ordinary readers.

The Assessment

In terms of the task given in the prompt, this student gets it to a large extent. Instead of simply rehashing the author's message, she focuses on the rhetorical strategies the author uses to help readers understand, remember, and accept his rules for gaining wealth. She gives evidence from the passage to support her points. It's obvious that she planned her response before she started writing, since her first paragraph contains a laundry list of rhetorical strategies that she then checks off in the following paragraphs.

That sense of checking items off a list makes her discussion adequate, landing this essay at an adequate score. It's the "analyze" part of the task where this student's essay falls short of a top score. Her explanations don't have the depth, sophistication, or conviction to elevate her work into the higher score range. A more effective, thorough analysis would explain how each of the author's rhetorical strategies fits into the interplay among purpose, audience, and context.

For example, plenty of authorities counsel thrift. Why was Benjamin Franklin a particularly good one for Barnum to cite? The student doesn't explore what the author gains with a mass audience by drawing on a trusted Founding Father: Barnum gains credibility for his message, legitimacy for his subject (the pursuit of wealth), and a connection to the concept of helping people build something.

As another example, the student misses the fact that Barnum uses different rhetorical strategies to achieve different purposes. Before he can successfully teach readers how to become wealthy, Barnum needs to convince them that his desire to help them is genuine and that they will benefit from his book. In order to achieve that initial purpose, he first gets his readers on his side with a rousing, encouraging "land of opportunity" opening. It's easy to make money in a country where there is so much land and so many jobs, he claims. An ordinary reader would likely feel, "I can actually do this, too, just like the famous Barnum did, and he really wants me to succeed." Next, the author identifies with his readers and demonstrates that he understands them: "I have no doubt many of my hearers will agree it is the most difficult thing in the world to keep it." Only then does he turn to his main purpose, launching into the stories that teach the difference between false economy (which does not lead to wealth) and true economy (which does).

In addition to the superficial analysis, another weakness in this essay occurs in the way the student expresses her ideas. No one expects a polished essay from a 40-minute effort. However, there is a choppy, disjointed quality to the way the student develops her points, and a weakness in her ability to control English mechanics (such as some confusion in verb tenses and some unclear pronoun antecedents). As a result, it's difficult to follow her argument in spots. A more in-depth analysis of the author's rhetorical strategies would have raised her score another notch, but effective essays demonstrate a smoother, more controlled prose style than this student achieves. Understanding the task and citing evidence from the passage are both important in the rhetorical analysis essay, but so is the ability to express ideas clearly and effectively, with smooth transitions to guide the reader through the discussion.

In the next chapter, we move on to the argument essay.

Chapter 7
How to Approach the Argument Essay

WHERE YOUR OPINION COUNTS

At last—a chance to make your own argument, without being limited by the source documents you're given and without having to focus on rhetorical strategies instead of the merits of what an author says. Here you get to take a stand and present your point of view on the topic in the prompt. This should be an essay you look forward to!

Even better, there is no "right" or "wrong" answer. All that matters is how effectively you argue and back up your position. If you like to debate, this is the part of the essay section where you can really shine.

Argument Essay Checklist

Be sure to accomplish these three tasks in your argument essay!

The argument essay isn't a license to ramble on about your own personal views, though. To get a high score, you need to do three things.

1. Take a definite position, so no one would question where you stand on the topic of the prompt.
2. Develop an argument that builds and moves forward instead of simply repeating the same point several times in different ways.
3. Support the points in your argument with evidence drawn from your own knowledge, reading, experiences, and observations.

Lower-scoring essays tend to simply summarize what the author says in the passage, or wander aimlessly through an impassioned list of the student's own beliefs without giving any evidence to support them. As in the synthesis essay, the concept of a conversation with the author is helpful. If you were talking with this author and either agreeing, disagreeing, or giving a "yes, but" (qualifying) opinion, how would you argue your position? What evidence would you offer to back it up?

Let's look at an example. We'll work through an analysis of the prompt and passage before you try writing your own essay in 40 minutes. Then read the student essay and evaluation that follow.

SAMPLE ESSAY #1—HERE'S HOW IT'S DONE

Here's a sample argument essay prompt.

The Prompt

Question 3

Suggested time—40 minutes.

(This question counts for one-third of the total essay section score.)

In Utilitarianism, John Stuart Mill promoted a theory of morality that postulated: "The creed which accepts as the foundation of morals, Utility, or the Greatest Happiness Principle, holds that actions are right in proportion as they tend to promote happiness, wrong as they tend to produce the reverse of happiness. By happiness is intended pleasure, and the absence of pain; by unhappiness, pain, and the privation of pleasure."

Mill argues that happiness is the foundation of morality, and that pursuing one's own happiness will necessarily lead to an ethical society for all. Write an essay that argues your position on the extent to which Mill's claims are valid. Use appropriate examples from your reading, experience, or observations to support your argument.

Analyzing the Prompt

If you've taken a lot of history courses, then you may have studied John Stuart Mill, and this would give you some information about context. If not, then the prompt still gives you rich material for a thoughtful argumentative essay.

Whatever you decide to argue, make your position perfectly clear in the first paragraph of your essay.

Your first task is to identify the author's main point, so you can decide what position you want to argue. In this case, the author's main point is clearly stated: "actions are right in proportion as they tend to promote happiness, wrong as they tend to produce the reverse of happiness." In the next sentence, Mill defines happiness ("pleasure") and unhappiness ("pain or the privation of pleasure").

You still have terms to define when you write your own essay, though. Happiness may equal pleasure, but one person's pleasure may be a matter of complete indifference to another person. What does Mill mean by "pleasure"? How will you define it?

You can see why this particular example is tailor-made to take you beyond the prompt. Here you can really demonstrate that you've thought deeply about the topic. Is "pleasure" the same thing for everyone? What are the consequences of individuals pursuing a "pleasure" that doesn't mean the same thing to all of them? If everyone pursued pleasure, what consequences might result for society? Does one person pursuing pleasure mean someone else has to experience pain?

As you think through those questions, what kind of evidence from your own experiences or reading pops into your mind? Which would be the strongest and the easiest to develop? That evidence should determine what stand you take on the argument. Remember that no reader knows or cares what you really think about an issue. You'll want to take the stand that's easiest for you to defend at that particular moment, based on the ideas that come to you. The most important things are that you have clearly decided how you feel about the issue and that you have the examples to back up your position.

I Remember When...

If you're describing your own experience or observation in the argument essay, you can use first-person narration.

Let's look at an essay that was written by a student under actual testing conditions.

A Student Essay

In John Stuart Mill's work Utilitarianism, the author advances a theory of morality that associates "the promotion of pleasure and the prevention of pain" with ethical correctness. While the pursuit of happiness can sometimes lead to a path of moral righteousness, Mill's claim is flawed in that it assumes hedonism will inherently bring positive results. By championing any action that produces pleasure, Mill condones humanity's greed, lust, and selfishness; three traits that are clearly immoral. As history and literature have demonstrated, pursuing goals motivated purely by self-interest does not lead to ethically responsible outcomes. Furthermore, the greatest achievements often arise when people readily eschew pleasure to attain a nobler end.

During the second half of the nineteenth century, a number of technological advances made the American economy blossom and helped to make the nation a world power. Eager to enjoy the pleasures made possible by great wealth, entrepreneurs and businessmen sought to increase profits and lower costs in any possible way. Workers were paid abysmally low wages, conditions were highly unsafe, and monopolies were commonplace. Though the heads of "Big Business" clearly adhered to Mill's "Greatest Happiness Principle," their actions were highly unethical. Their pleasure came at the expense of the poor and created a polarized society. In contrast, patriots seeking independence from England a century before, gladly relinquished the "absence of pain" afforded by accepting the status quo. Despite the great "privation of pleasure" brought about by the Revolutionary War, the patriots achieved their lofty goal of freedom, a morally desirable outcome. Evidently, seeking happiness does not necessarily entail finding "what is right and good."

F. Scott Fitzgerald's portrait of the Roaring Twenties, The Great Gatsby, examines hedonism and reaches a conclusion much different than Mill's. Jay Gatsby pursues pleasure in the form of rekindling a relationship with a former love, Daisy. Following utilitarian principles, seeking the desirable outcome should be an ethically sound choice. However, it instead leads Gatsby to engage in questionable business and to court a married woman, two clear violations of ethical standards. Clearly, morality based on pleasure is an unsound principle.

This essay is rather short. An additional example—perhaps from the student's own experience—would have made it stronger. However, it does the job quite well, and would likely earn a score at the bottom of the "effective" band.

The introduction is slightly long, but notice how well this student addresses the two tasks set forth. Right away, the student states the author's claim ("the author advances a theory of morality that associates the 'promotion of pleasure and the prevention of pain' with ethical correctness") and takes a firm stand against it: "As history and literature have demonstrated, pursuing goals motivated by mere self-interest does not lead to ethically responsible outcomes." The student's clear definition of pleasure ("humanity's greed, lust, and selfishness") both explains and reinforces this stand.

The student gives the reader a roadmap for the rest of the essay by first mentioning history and then literature, and follows that roadmap in the same order.

Write in the Present Tense

This student does an excellent job of handling verb tenses. Particularly important is the use of the present tense when addressing the author, text and claim: "the author advances," "it assumes," "achievements often arise," and so on. The student uses the past tense only when presenting historical facts in the second paragraph.

One of the most common grammatical errors that students make in AP essays is using improper verb-tense shifts.

The conclusion is weak and seems tacked on. It would have been stronger if it reminded the reader of the evidence brought in to support the student's stand against Mill's claim.

What keeps this essay from scoring in the effectve range is the student's failure to follow the prompt where it leads. This essay simply takes the prompt at face value and doesn't examine the broader ethical questions it raises.

SAMPLE ESSAY #2—GIVING IT ANOTHER TRY

Let's try another one. Again, now that you're comfortable with the process for writing the argument essay, try writing this one on your own before you look at the student's essay.

The Prompt

Question 3

Suggested time—40 minutes.

(This question counts for one-third of the total essay section score.)

The former slave and abolitionist Frederick Douglass (1818–1895) wrote, "Once you learn to read, you will be forever free."

Write an essay that argues your position on the relationship between literacy and freedom in the world today. Use appropriate examples from your reading, experience, or observations to support your argument.

A Student Essay

Frederick Douglass once wrote, "Once you learn to read, you will be forever free" and this is true of the modern world. Though everyone in America can read, alot of people in the world can't read today and that's a serious problem for them. There are too many people in places like India and China who can't read and this iliteracy is holding them back. If we would have more programs to teach literacy to people in these Third World countries, then we would have more literacy and therefore more freedom for all.

One reason I think there should be more literacy is that you need to educate children early on in their educational experience, otherwise, they will not learn what they need to succeed. Once the children in a given country achieve literacy, then the country can also improve the quality of life and the children can teach there parents how to read when they return home from school. This would help the parents to find better jobs and allow for more financial freedom for the family. Also, if the people in China and India learned English, they could get jobs using their new skills in English.

Short, But Not Sweet

Shorter essays usually indicate a less successful effort. It's difficult to examine a prompt thoroughly and present enough strong evidence to support your position if the essay is too short.

Another reason why I think literacy increases freedom is because literacy is the key concept to the development of political freedom. When Frederick Douglass was a slave in America, black people were enslaved and deprived of literacy. When the slave owners didn't teach their slaves to read, they were holding them back from the freedoms they deserved; including the right to read. If the slaves learned to read, though, they would have been more free and this would have threatened the slave

> masters. So with slaves having been deprived of literacy, the owners could keep control of them.
>
> In conclusion, literacy is the key to freedom around the world. As the examples of India and slavery have demonstrated, freedom is possible for people who have a chance to read the way we do.

This essay has significant flaws in both content and style and would not score above adequate. The most serious problem is the absence of a strong connection between literacy and freedom. This is not an easy concept and many students would struggle to find good, specific examples to bridge a connection between these ideas. While literacy in the Third World and in American slavery could be excellent examples, they are not made specific or relevant in this essay. In the discussion of slavery, for example, the student wrote

> If the slaves learned to read, though, they would have been more free and this would have threatened the slave masters. So with the slaves having been deprived of literacy, the owners could keep control of them.

What does this mean? How would literacy have made slaves "more free"? How did illiteracy help slave owners "keep control of them"? Good essays on the AP English Language and Composition Exam develop specific examples and then carefully connect them to the issue at hand. They also demonstrate a depth of thought and complexity that is mostly absent in this essay. As you write your own essays, be sure to have a clear, stable definition of the essential terms (in this case, "literacy" and "freedom") in mind and don't be afraid to talk about how complex the terms can be.

The style of this essay did not help. It is not necessary, for example, to repeat the quote verbatim in the first sentence: the grader already knows what Frederick Douglass said. Also, the first paragraph does not really contain a thesis or any clear statement about how literacy allows people to be more free. Throughout, the student makes some awkward errors in style and diction, which detract from the overall effect.

But, in spite of these flaws, the essay does provide some examples and at least attempted to address the relationship between literacy and freedom, so it would receive an inadequate.

Now let's take a look at a more successful essay, which was also written by a student under time constraints.

A Student Essay

Literacy is something we take for granted in America. Most children learn to read at an early age and receive formal education until they are eighteen years old. During this time, they develop a deep understanding of their own language, both in its written and spoken forms. I remember when I first learned to read and how it made me feel so empowered over my younger sister, who hadn't learned yet. As my teachers encouraged me in elementary school, I grew to enjoy reading adventure stories and then much harder books. In my AP English class this year, my teacher Mrs. Lasko assigned extremely challenging books, such as Paradise Lost, Gulliver's Travels, and Lord of the Flies. In all these cases, literacy empowered me to feel more and more intellectually free and to explore new ideas through reading.

But literacy does more than just free our minds: it is the key to bringing about political and economic freedom for ordinary people. There are many times in history when increasing literacy allowed people to experience a new kind of political freedom. For example, during the Protestant Reformation, ordinary people began to read because the printing press allowed books to be printed quickly rather than copied by hand. As the people began to read the Bible for themselves, they developed their own interpretations about theology and they challenged the teachings of the Catholic Church. People also read political pamphlets and were empowered to overthrow the leaders in power during that time. These kinds of political pamphlets, which only work when the majority of the population can read, have formed the basis of many political movements in the modern era.

In women's history, too, increasing literacy has brought about an increase in political freedoms. For centuries, few women could read or write and thus they were denied freedoms we now consider basic: the freedom to vote, the freedom to hold political office, the freedom to represent oneself in court. When we think of the movement for women's suffrage a century ago, how could the suffragettes have succeeded if they did not have a largely literate population of women to support them. As women learned to read in large numbers, they began to develop the political tools necessary to fight for their own freedom. In this way, literacy was a prerequisite to real political freedom for millions of women around the world.

When Frederick Douglass wrote of literacy and freedom, he was speaking of real freedom from the bondage of slavery. For him, the power to read and write played a role in his abolitionist activities. But as I have discussed in this essay, literacy can bring about more than just freedom from slavery: it can free us to think for ourselves, determine our own theologies, and fight for real political freedom. And whether it is African Americans, children, the poor, or just ordinary people, reading can transform the lives of those with less power. Literacy is thus a direct cause of freedom, both in the distant historical past and in the future of our constantly evolving world.

This essay is an obvious success and would earn an effective score on the real AP. Not only did the student specifically answer the question at hand, she offered a nuanced assessment of the relationship between literacy and freedom. In fact, she took pains to define multiple senses of the word freedom (intellectual, political, etc.) throughout the paper. The examples were specific, detailed, and relevant to the topic at hand.

The student begins by briefly recounting her own history of literacy and how it empowered her as she developed her reading skills. The first body paragraph then explicitly connects increasing literacy with newfound political and religious freedom during the Protestant Reformation. Notice how the student takes her time in introducing each example and then adds as much relevant, specific information as possible. The next body paragraph is equally effective and shows yet another dimension of the complex link between literacy and freedom.

The student also helped her score by creating fluid prose and elegant transitions from one paragraph to the next. The range of vocabulary was good, but not exceptional—it never needs to be to get a high score on this test. Offer the readers as wide a range of vocabulary as you can, but focus on writing a good essay as you design, develop, and execute your response.

Study Break!
You're about halfway through your review! Before you dive into Part V, be sure to give yourself some downtime to let your brain absorb the information you've been studying.

COMING UP...

In this chapter and the two preceding chapters, you've seen a range of essay examples. In the next part of this book, you'll learn (or review) the important aspects of formal training in rhetoric and composition that will prepare you to craft essays that equal—or exceed—the ones that you've examined so far.

REFLECT

Think about what you've learned in Part IV, and respond to the following questions:

- How long will you spend on multiple-choice questions?
- How will you change your approach to multiple-choice questions?
- What is your multiple-choice guessing strategy?
- How much time will you spend on the first essay? The second? The third?
- What will you do before you begin writing an essay?
- How will you change your approach to the essays?
- Will you seek further help, outside of this book (such as a teacher, tutor, or AP Students website), on how to approach multiple-choice questions, the essays, or a pacing strategy?

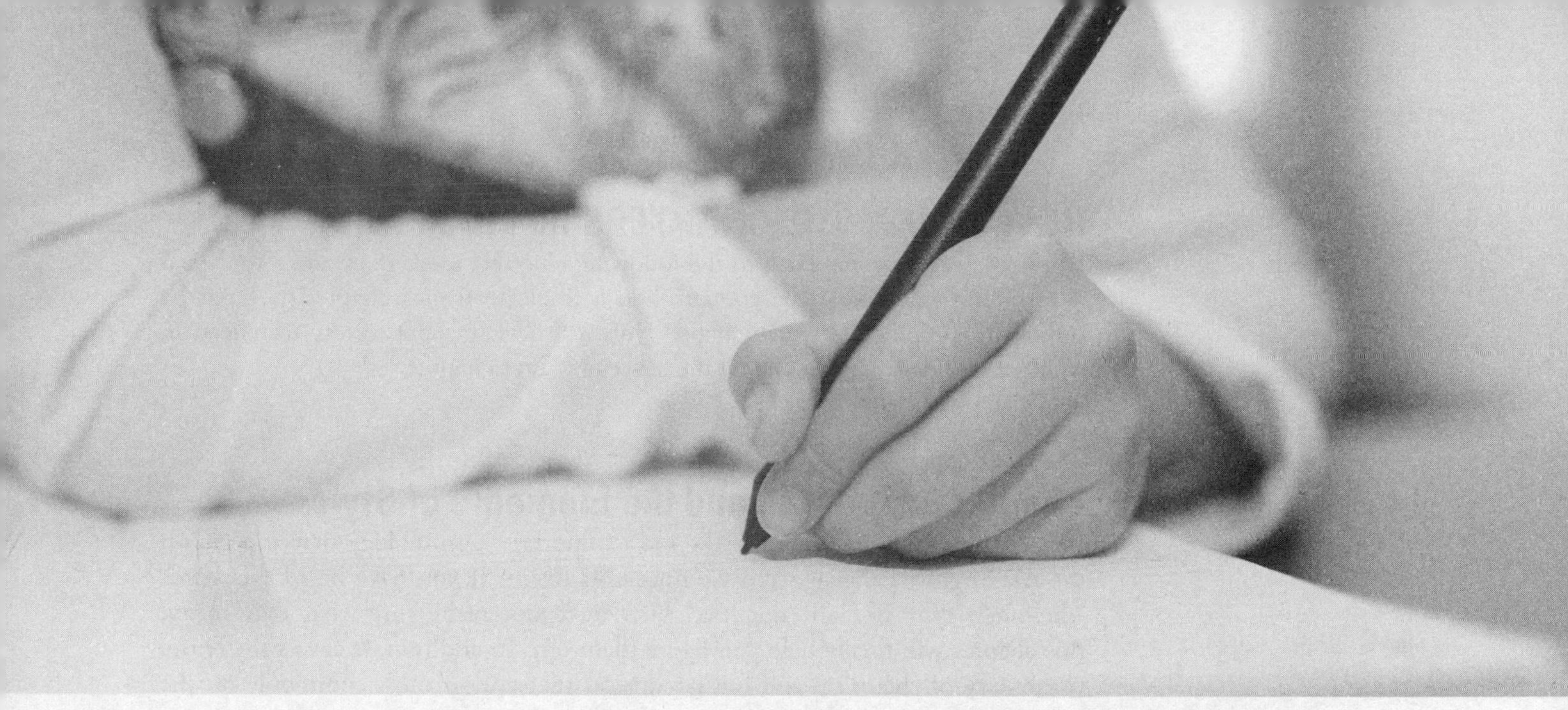

Part V
Terms and Modes Review for the AP English Language and Composition Exam

HOW TO USE THE CHAPTERS IN THIS PART

You may need to come back to the following chapters more than once. Your goal is to obtain mastery of the content, and a single read of a chapter may not be sufficient. At the end of each chapter, you will have an opportunity to reflect on whether you truly have mastered the content of that chapter.

Chapter 8: Rhetoric and the Elements of Style

This chapter introduces you to the most important terminology that appears on the AP English Language and Composition Exam. If you have heard the words "diction," "syntax," and "rhetoric," but you're not really sure what they mean, this chapter will finally help you figure them out. In addition, it covers the entire vocabulary of rhetorical and literary devices that appear most commonly on the exam.

Chapter 9: Basic Rhetorical Modes

"Rhetorical modes" refers to the ways that writers organize their arguments. What is the difference between an illustration and a classification? Why do some authors structure their essays around comparisons and contrasts? This brief chapter will help you identify these structures quickly on the multiple-choice passages.

Chapter 10: Complex Rhetorical Modes

This chapter expands on the content of the previous chapter and goes much deeper into analyzing how authors conceptualize their evidence and arguments. If you are running low on time, you can skim through this chapter and jump right to Practice Test 2.

Chapter 11: Rhetorical Fallacies

This brief chapter introduces you to the kinds of faulty reasoning that commonly appear in student writing. The errors may even be lurking in the background of the passages you have to analyze on the AP English Language and Composition Exam.

Chapter 8
Rhetoric and the Elements of Style

THE GOOD NEWS AND THE BAD NEWS ABOUT THE AP ENGLISH LANGUAGE AND COMPOSITION EXAM

The Good News

While the title of this exam allows people to differentiate between this test and the AP English *Literature* Exam, it's still somewhat misleading. The AP English *Language* Exam is not a language exam—at least not in the sense that you may think. For example, it is possible not to know the difference between a gerund and a present participle—or even a gerund and a giraffe—and still score a 5 on this exam.

In the multiple-choice section of the exam, test-writers will attempt to evaluate your ability to analyze how writers use language to explain or to argue; in the free-response, or essay, section they will expect *you* to use language to explain or to argue. Naturally, you should avoid making egregious errors in grammar or usage on the test, but don't get hung up on the rules of language as you study. If you're considering taking the AP Exam, your language skills are probably sufficient for the task. Now, you may be wondering what *is* tested on the exam. The answer is *composition,* and we'll spend Chapters 9 through 11 of this book reviewing all you need to know about composition to be fully prepared for the test.

The Bad News

Now for the bad news. Despite the test's lack of emphasis on the rules of language, there are some aspects of language that we must examine here to make sure you're ready for test day. We'll start by discussing diction, syntax, style, tone, and point of view. We'll move on to rhetoric and the many types of figurative language, and then discuss circumlocution and euphemism. Finally, we will review irony and satire.

RHETORIC AND LANGUAGE STYLE, TONE, AND THEME

Rhetoric and Language

Rhetoric is the art of speaking or writing persuasively. The terms covered later in this section are terms you should know cold before taking the exam. Multiple-choice questions may use them in answer choices, and you are certainly expected to use them in your essays.

First of all, what *is* rhetoric? It is often referred to as the stylistic devices an author uses to appeal successfully to a specific audience and is usually persuasive in nature. Before we get into the nitty gritty of figurative language and how it's used, let's review the three classical rhetorical appeals—methods of persuasion—you should know for the exam.

Classical Appeals

Aristotle identified three methods of appealing to an audience in order to persuade them to your point of view: *logos*, *pathos*, and *ethos*.

Logos is an appeal to reason and logic. An argument that uses logos to persuade needs to provide things like objective evidence, hard facts, statistics, or logical strategies such as cause and effect to back up its claim. (*Logos* is the root of our word "logic," which is a good way to remember which of the appeals this is!)

Also preparing for the SAT? Check out *Essential SAT Flashcards*, 2nd Edition to help you improve your vocabulary for both tests.

Ethos is an appeal to the speaker's credibility—whether he or she is to be believed on the basis of his or her character and expertise. For example, the prosecution in a murder trial might put a renowned psychiatrist on the stand to testify that the defendant is able to identify right and wrong and is thus capable of standing trial. Their argument would be using an appeal to *ethos* to persuade the jury (their audience) that the testimony of this expert is to be trusted. (*Ethos* is related to our word "ethics"—the principles of conduct that govern people and organizations and give them the authority to speak on certain topics.)

Advanced terms such as logos, ethos, and pathos are not likely to be used on the AP English Language and Composition Exam. However, the concepts behind these terms will be tested, and your teacher may use these terms, so it's good to be aware of them.

Pathos is an appeal to the emotions, values, or desires of the audience. Aristotle felt that, although ideally people would be persuaded by appeals to logic (*logos*, remember?), they would probably most often be persuaded by their emotions and beliefs instead. This is why, in that same murder trial, a defense attorney might tell the jury about the lonely childhood and difficult life of the defendant—he would be appealing to the *pathos* of the audience to convince them that his client should not be convicted. (*Pathos* is also the root of "pathetic," a word we use to describe something that is, shall we say, *suffering* from inferiority.)

As you review the following elements of style and consider how they are used in context, ask yourself the following question: How does an author's use of diction, syntax, and/or figurative language develop these appeals with the text?

Style, Tone, and Theme

You can count on seeing some combination of the terms *style, tone,* and *theme* in both multiple-choice and essay questions on this exam, so let's make sure you're familiar with their definitions.

Style is the manner of expression. It describes how the author uses language to get his or her point across (e.g., pedantic, scientific, and emotive).

Tone is the attitude, mood, or sentiments revealed by the style. Tone describes how the author seems to be feeling (e.g., optimistic, ironic, and playful).

Theme is the stance revealed by the style and the tone of the writing. The author's point of view expresses his or her position on the topic discussed.

Consider this excerpt.

> Our left fielder couldn't hit the floor if he fell out of bed! After striking out twice (once with the bases loaded!), he grounded into a double-play. My grandmother runs faster than he does! In the eighth inning, he misjudged a routine fly ball, which brought in the winning run. What a jerk! Why didn't the club trade him last week when it was still possible? What's wrong with you guys?

The *style* is simple, direct, unsophisticated, truculent, and even crass. The style helps evoke a simple sentiment: anger. The *tone* is angry, brash, emotional, and even virulent.

The *theme* is clear; the author appears to be a disgruntled spectator who doesn't like the player at all and wants the team to get rid of him.

Now let's try a sample question with an excerpt from Fyodor Dostoyevsky's *Notes from Underground.*

> The long and the short of it is, gentlemen, that it is better to do nothing! Better conscious inertia!

1. The tone of the speaker is best characterized as

    (A) ironic
    (B) nihilistic
    (C) reflective
    (D) optimistic
    (E) accusatory

You probably immediately eliminated (C) and (D) because the passage did not sound particularly reflective or optimistic. The author is not accusatory, so eliminate (E) as well. Choice (B) may have confused you a bit; nihilism refers to a belief in nothing. (Again notice the importance of vocabulary!) The speaker's tone can indeed be described as more "nihilistic" (referring to nothing) than "ironic," so the correct answer is (B).

The rest of this chapter reviews the basic elements of style: diction, syntax, and figurative language. Pay attention to how these work together to develop the style, tone, and theme within a text.

Diction

The basic definition of **diction** is "word choice." Generally, the diction questions you'll see on the test will ask you to evaluate why an author's choice of words is particularly effective, apt, or clear. Often, the test will ask you to consider what style and/or tone an author's use of diction develops. However, as we explained in the chapters on the multiple-choice section, more often than not it is the test-writers' diction that you have to crack. While knowledge of grammar and usage is almost irrelevant for this exam, a broad vocabulary is a necessity.

> Vocabulary is important for both the multiple-choice section AND the essays. Start creating flashcards: write down any unfamiliar words from this book and look up their definitions and write them down on index cards. There is a good chance you will see many of these words on your test!

Consider the following example question:

2. The style of the first paragraph on the previous page can best be described as

   (A) pedantic
   (B) lyrical
   (C) terse
   (D) ludic
   (E) edifying

While it's possible that none of the answers stands out to you as the correct choice, you could rule out "pedantic" if you know that it means narrowly, stodgily, and often ostentatiously learned. Likewise, an AP Exam and lyricism (intense, intimate display of emotion) make for an unlikely pair, so you can use POE to get rid of that choice too. The test-writers slipped "ludic" (pertaining to game, playful) in there in case you wanted to misremember some Latin (*ludus*). Finally, "terse" (concise, without superfluous detail) shows up regularly on this exam but probably doesn't describe the writing in this book very well. Given that the last choice can mean both enlightening and informative, (E) is the best answer.

But as you can see, if you knew none of these words, the question may as well have read as follows:

3. The style of the paragraph above can best be described as

   (A) pompom
   (B) banana
   (C) dog
   (D) tire iron
   (E) Susan

And then which would seem like the correct answer? Obviously, vocabulary is important, so start that vocabulary journal.

Denotation and Connotation

Denotation refers to a word's primary or literal significance, while **connotation** refers to the vast range of other meanings that a word suggests. Context (and at times, author's intent) determines which connotations may be appropriate for a word. An author will carefully pick a particular word for its connotations, knowing or hoping a reader will make an additional inference as a result. Some literary critics argue that it is impossible to distinguish between denotation and connotation. Who, they ask, is to determine which meaning to assign as a primary significance? Let's move on and look at an example.

> I am looking at the sky.

The denotation of the underlined word should be as clear as a cloudless sky (the space, often blue, above the Earth's surface). However, there can be connotations associated with the word. The sky is often associated with heaven; it can also evoke the idea of freedom or vast openness. Because of connotation, one can't help but believe that the sky evokes in the writer a sense of longing for freedom from work, the computer, or the AP English Language and Composition Exam.

Syntax

Tactics for Syntax

Syntax is simply another way of talking about grammar and sentence structure.

Syntax is another language term that you should be familiar with for the AP English Language and Composition Exam. Syntax is the ordering of words in a sentence; it describes sentence structure. Syntax is not a topic that excites many high school students—or teachers—and therefore is not discussed very much. However, *syntax* is a word that finds its way onto AP English Language and Composition Exams on a regular basis. Don't worry: you don't need to be an expert on this subject, but you should know how manipulating syntax can enhance an author's meaning, tone, or point of view. Let's look at an example from *Candide,* taken from the famous opening of Chapter 3.

> Never was anything so gallant, so well outfitted, so brilliant, and so finely disposed as the two armies. The trumpets, fifes, reeds, drums, and cannon made such harmony as never was heard in Hell.

The first sentence poses as a fairly simple sketch of a glorious battle scene. The second begins in the same fashion, but its words are arranged in a way that maximizes the effect of surprise that comes at the end of the sentence. The cannons are slipped in as the final member of a list of military musical instruments; the formation of the list creates an expectation that the final element will fit nicely into the set. It doesn't, but we don't have time to register our surprise because we're immediately distracted by a new setup with the phrase "such harmony as never was heard...." We expect harmony to be something beautiful, and we already begin to supply the final word (Earth? Heaven?) when—surprise—we are jolted by the word that Voltaire chose instead: Hell. The syntax in this sentence is brilliant.

Here's another slightly different example. In the following example, Candide asks about the proper etiquette for greeting the King of Eldorado through his servant and sidekick, Cacambo.

> When they drew near to the royal chamber, Cacambo asked one of the officers in what manner they were to pay their respects to His Majesty; whether it was the custom to fall upon their knees, or to prostrate themselves upon the ground; whether they were to put their hands upon their heads, or behind their backs; whether they were to lick the dust off the floor; in short, what was the usual ceremony for such occasions.

The syntax of this long sentence is very carefully constructed; Voltaire uses all of the parallel clauses that begin with "whether" to achieve great comic effect. At first, the text is fairly straightforward—after all, going down on one's knees before a king would have been fairly standard for a European reader of the 18th century; however, with each clause, the groveling etiquette becomes more extreme, and the final image—of licking the dust off the floor—pushes the concept beyond the believable. The syntax of this sentence is structured in a way that allows us to see the absurdity of *all* forms of ceremonial deference. In fact, in this story, the enlightened King of Eldorado simply embraces both Cacambo and Candide.

Note that punctuation is a critical aspect of syntax. In both of these examples, Voltaire's syntax revolves around punctuation: serial commas to create an extended list, and semicolons to unite the clauses that begin with "whether." Further, writers often use exclamation points to create an excited or emphatic tone.

FIGURATIVE LANGUAGE

As we stated at the beginning of this chapter, you don't need to be an expert in rhetoric to ace the AP English Language and Composition Exam; however, you do need to have some understanding of how language works. With the exception of technical manuals (like the one that helped you assemble your entertainment center), few texts are written such that all of their language is meant to be taken literally. **Figurative language** is strictly defined as speech or writing that departs from literal meaning to achieve a special effect or meaning. Take, for example, the end of one of Abraham Lincoln's inaugural speeches.

> With malice toward none, with charity for all, with firmness in the right as God gives us to see the right, let us strive on to finish the work we are in, to bind up the nation's wounds, to care for him who shall have borne the battle and for his widow and his orphan, to do all which may achieve and cherish a just and lasting peace among ourselves and with all nations.

Are we supposed to take "to bind up the nation's wounds" literally? Of course not. Lincoln has personified our country to make the suffering of particular individuals relatable to all the people of the nation. And what about "him who shall have borne the battle"? Clearly, Lincoln is using the singular (a man) to represent the collective mass of soldiers, and when he adds "his widow and his orphan," we understand that "shall have borne the battle" really means "shall have died in battle." Lincoln personalizes the suffering of this group of people by instead speaking of individual sacrifice, which he knows is far more likely to strike a profound emotional chord in his listeners.

Despite the effectiveness of Lincoln's speech, you should keep in mind that many other perfectly convincing arguments and explanations are conveyed primarily through literal language. On this exam, there's no need for you to strain yourself attempting to use figurative language in the free-response section. But it will be very helpful for you to review the common terms associated with figurative language that we've listed below because you will be obliged to analyze texts that contain figurative language on this test.

With all this in mind, here is a list of some common terms related to figurative language; we've put them in order of their decreasing relevance to the test.

Why use sensory imagery?

By activating one of the five senses, authors can often evoke particular emotions from their audience. For example, an author might mention the smell of salty sea air in order to garner a sense of relaxation or adventure from their audience. In other words, sensory imagery can develop pathos within an argument.

Imagery

For the purposes of this exam, you may consider **imagery** to be synonymous with figurative language. However, in a more restricted sense, imagery is figurative language that is used to convey a sensory perception (visual, auditory, olfactory, tactile, or gustatory).

Hyperbole

Hyperbole is overstatement or exaggeration; it is the use of figurative language that significantly exaggerates the facts for effect. In many instances, but certainly not all, hyperbole is employed for comic effect. Consider the following example.

> If you use too much figurative language in your essays, the AP readers will crucify you!

Clearly, this statement is a gross exaggeration; while the readers may give you a poor grade if you use figurative language that doesn't suit the purposes of your essay, they will not kill you.

Understatement

Understatement is figurative language that presents the facts in a way that makes them appear much less significant than they really are. Understatement is almost always used for comic effect.

> After dinner, they came and took into custody Doctor Pangloss and his pupil Candide, the one for speaking his mind and the other for appearing to approve what he heard. They were conducted to separate apartments, which were extremely cool and where they were never bothered by the sun.

Taking the last sentence literally would lead you astray. The understatement in this case ("They were conducted to separate apartments, which were extremely cool and where they were never bothered by the sun") should be taken to mean that the poor men were thrown into horribly dark, dank, and cold prison cells.

Simile

A **simile** is a comparison between two unlike objects, in which the two parts are connected with a term such as *like* or *as.* Here's an example of a simile:

> The birds are like black arrows flying across the sky.

You can easily identify a simile—and distinguish it from a metaphor—because of the use of *like* or *as.*

Authors often use similes and metaphors to compare new information to ideas the audience is already familiar with. Depending on what is being compared, this can develop both logos and/or pathos within a text. However, this consistently develops ethos: if the author uses an effective comparison, it reveals that the author understands the perspective of his/her audience, which can build trust and sympathy between the two.

Metaphor

A **metaphor** is a simile without a connecting term such as *like* or *as.* Here's an example of a metaphor.

> The birds are black arrows flying across the sky.

Birds are not arrows, but the commonalities (both are long and sleek, and they travel swiftly through the air—and both have feathers) allow us to easily grasp the image.

Extended Metaphor

An **extended metaphor** is precisely what it sounds like—it is a metaphor that lasts for longer than just one phrase or sentence. A word of caution for the exam, however; do not use extended metaphors in your own AP essays, for many scholars (and many AP graders) believe that the extended metaphor is a poor expository or argumentative technique. Consider this example:

> During the time I have voyaged on this ship, I have avoided the cabin; rather, I have remained on deck, battered by wind and rain, but able to see moonlight on the water. I do not wish to go below decks now.

As surprising as this may seem, this passage is not about nautical navigation. The ship's voyage is the central metaphor (representing the course of life); the writer extends the metaphor by relating elements of figurative language: cabin, deck, wind and rain, moonlight, water, and decks. The cabin is a safe place, but it's a place where you can't experience much; on deck, you're exposed to the elements, but you can experience beauteous sights. Having made the difficult, dangerous, but rewarding choice of staying on deck, it would be a personal defeat, a kind of surrender to wish for the safety, comfort, and limited horizons of the cabin later in life.

Metaphors vs. Symbols

Sometimes, it is difficult to distinguish between metaphor and symbol. Remember that a metaphor always contains an implied comparison between two elements. Recall the metaphorical image of the birds and the arrows: the birds remain birds, and the arrows remain arrows—and the metaphor serves to give us an image of the flight of the birds by suggesting a visualization of arrows. However, in the case of a symbol, the named object really doesn't count. There is no lamb; *lamb* is merely an object that's meant to conjure up another object or element.

Symbolism

A **symbol** is a concrete object that represents an abstract idea. Here's an example:

> The Christian soldiers paused to remember the lamb.

In this case, the lamb is a symbol. The lamb is a concrete object that represents an abstract idea. In this case, the lamb symbolizes the legacy of Jesus Christ.

Use your knowledge of denotations and connotations to analyze symbols. When you identify a symbolic object, here's how to start your analysis:

Step 1: Denotation: Define the concrete object acting as a symbol in the text.

Step 2: Brainstorm five connotations for the object. What does it remind you of? Are there any other well-known examples of this object?

Step 3: Ask yourself, how do these connotations develop main ideas in the text?

Here's how you can remember the difference between personification and anthropomorphism:

Personification comes from the Latin root *persona* meaning [person]. So if a non human object behaves like a person, you're dealing with personification.

Anthropomorphism comes from the Greek roots *anthrop* meaning [human] and *morph* meaning [shape]. So if an object or idea has the shape of human, you have anthropomorphism on your hands.

Personification

Personification is the figurative device in which inanimate objects or concepts are given the thoughts, feelings, or actions of a human. It can enhance our emotional response because we usually attribute more emotional significance to other humans than to things or concepts. Consider this example of personification:

> He had been wrestling with lethargy for days, and every time that he thought that he was close to victory, his adversary escaped his hold.

This figurative wrestling match, in which lethargy is personified as the opponent to the author of this sentence, brings the struggle to life—human life. If you don't believe this, think about the literal alternative: he tried to stop being lethargic, but he was not successful. This doesn't sound very lively.

Anthropomorphism occurs when non-human objects are given the physical shape of a human, e.g., the legs of a table, the face of a clock, the arms of a tree.

Metonymy and Synecdoche

Both *metonymy* and *synecdoche* are terms that mean the use of figurative language in which characteristics are substituted for the things with which they are associated.

In **metonymy,** one term is substituted for another term with which it is closely associated. Consider this example:

The sailors drank a glass of hearty red.

Red is a color; sailors cannot drink it. However, metonymically, the color represents wine (red wine), which sailors over the age of twenty-one may drink.

Synecdoche is a form of metonymy that's restricted to cases in which a part is used to signify the whole. Here's an example of synecdoche:

All hands on deck!

The hands (part of each sailor) represent the sailors (the whole).

If you have an aversion to learning rhetorical terms, then for the purposes of this exam, you can feel free to forget the definition of synecdoche; you can get away with using the term *metonymy* for any situation in which a characteristic of a certain thing is used to represent the thing.

Meto-WHAT?

Don't worry! Metonymy and synecdoche are tested very rarely on the AP English Language and Composition Exam, but you should be familiar with these definitions anyway.

Malapropism

Malapropism is the intentional use of a word that resembles the word intended but that has a very different meaning.

He was a man of great statue.

Malapropism can be used to develop an author's ethos. It characterizes the speaker as witty and comedic. Malapropism can also be used to characterize or satirize others within a text.

Though you may spot malapropism in an excerpt on the exam, it isn't a technique you should try within your written responses. The AP English Language and Composition readers often collect unintentional malapropisms to share with friends and colleagues as they read through the free-response essays; it isn't in your best interest to provide them with any good laughs, so try to avoid them.

Circumlocution and Euphemism

Circumlocution has two meanings, and you should be familiar with both of them. For the purposes of this exam, we'll say that one meaning of circumlocution is "talking around a subject" and that the other is "talking around a word."

AP is unlikely to test you on these terms.

It is entirely possible that you have used circumlocution when addressing your parents. For instance, instead of simply asking them straight out if you may borrow the car, have you ever said something such as, "I understand that you guys are going to stay in tonight and watch a DVD, right? If so, since I've already seen that movie, I was thinking about maybe going downtown. It's a nice summer evening and all that, but it's still too far to walk, and I'll be with Nina, anyway, and she'd never agree to walk downtown. We were thinking that she could drive, but, unfortunately, Nina's parents are going out, so she can't take their car. I know that I forgot to put gas in your car the last time that I drove to the mountains, but I learned my lesson. That won't happen again." You may even have gone on speaking for longer. You might never have gotten to the point where you actually asked to borrow the car, but your parents understood what you wanted and put you out of your misery by saying something such as, "We already told your sister that she could use the car tonight."

On the AP English Language and Composition Exam, you're more likely to encounter the second type of circumlocution—"talking around a word"—that is, using several words or a phrase in place of a specific word (or specific words). You may have noticed that sometimes it is more effective to be wordy than to be precise. For example, some people consider their automobiles cars, and, not surprisingly, they refer to these objects just as cars. Other people, however, use evocative circumlocutions when referring to their heap of metal—one of which is "cruisin' machine" (and the other of which is "heap of metal"). The point is that circumlocution is often an effective means for communicating points of view. Take a look at the following sentence.

> Candide was court-martialed, and he was asked which he liked better, to run the gauntlet six and thirty times through the whole regiment, or to have his brains blown out with a dozen musket-balls.

In this sentence, we read that in a spirit of compassion and justice, the military court is giving Candide a choice: he may choose to be either beaten to death or executed by firing squad. The wording of the second choice, in particular, provides a wonderful example of the evocative power of well-used circumlocution. While using the phrase "execution by firing squad" would have allowed both the author and the reader to remain distant from the event and dispassionate, the circumlocution that the author employed with "to have his brains blown out with a dozen musket-balls" vividly describes the horror and brutality of the event. In this sentence, Voltaire succeeds in relating his feelings about the court-martial without commenting on it.

A **euphemism** is a word or words that are used to avoid employing an unpleasant or offensive term. Again, you probably (hopefully) use euphemisms all the time. In both fiction and nonfiction, the most common euphemisms have to do with sex. In these cases, the author knows what he or she means, you know what he or she means, and the author knows that you know what he or she means. Let's look at another example from Voltaire's *Candide*. In this passage, Voltaire uses euphemism for comic effect.

> One day when Mademoiselle Cunégonde went to take a walk in a little neighboring wood that was called a park, she saw—through the bushes—the sage Doctor Pangloss giving a lecture in experimental philosophy to her mother's chambermaid, a little brown wench, very pretty and very accommodating.

Voltaire knows that his readers know what is really going on here. This particular example of euphemism is used for comic effect rather than direct avoidance of the word *sex*. One may expect Pangloss to limit his sagacity to philosophical matters, but clearly his "lecture in experimental philosophy" is most prosaic.

OTHER LINGUISTIC DEVICES

Oxymoron

In an **oxymoron,** two seemingly contradictory words (or sometimes brief phrases) are paired together. However, the two elements only appear to contradict each other. Look deeper, and the contradiction can be resolved.

One common example is "jumbo shrimp." Since "shrimp" is an edible creature as well as a term meaning "small," there is really no contradiction. The oxymoron describes a large version of an edible creature.

What does an oxymoron add to a written work? Look at some other common examples: open secret, civil war, freezer burn, old news, deafening silence. How about the title of George Romero's zombie film, *Night of the Living Dead?* Or Juliet's "Parting is such sweet sorrow" in the first balcony scene from Shakespeare's *Romeo and Juliet*?

As these examples show, oxymorons give authors a couple of tools: a way to describe a new or unusual thing, and economy of expression. For instance, the oxymoron "cold comfort" describes an unusual case in which something (perhaps a friend's comment) that one would expect to be warm and helpful has the opposite effect instead. Notice how many words it just took to describe that concept, compared with the vivid image economically conveyed by the oxymoron "cold comfort."

By using an oxymoron, an author can also jolt readers into paying attention if they've been skimming through the work on autopilot. Something doesn't sound quite right; they go back to reread the seemingly contradictory words and try to figure out what those words mean. Perhaps the readers then pay more attention to the next few paragraphs or pages.

Don't Be a "Moron"!

Oxymorons and paradoxes both involve contradictions, but there are two main differences.

1. The contradiction in an oxymoron is only apparent; it can be resolved. In a paradox, it cannot.
2. Oxymorons almost always involve only words or brief phrases, whereas paradoxes (in written work) involve statements.

Paradox

A **paradox** contains two elements which cannot both be true at the same time (although usually each one could be true on its own).

The classic example is the Cretan Liar Paradox, attributed to the sixth-century BCE philosopher and poet Epimenides. He was from Crete, and his famous paradox says, "All Cretans are liars."

Think about it. He's a Cretan; therefore (if his statement is true), he must also be a liar. But if he's a liar, he can't be making a true statement, so the statement must be false. As you can imagine, many philosophers and logicians have puzzled over how to resolve Epimenides's paradox.

Here's another ancient Greek example, this time from Socrates, the 5th-century BCE philosopher: "One thing only I know, and that is that I know nothing." Well if it's true that he knows nothing, then it can't also be true that he knows even that one thing. And if he knows that one thing, it can't be true that he knows nothing.

A great real-life example comes from the 17th-century witch trials. If a woman passed the test, thereby proving she was not a witch, she could live and go free. Failing the test proved she was indeed a witch and she was burned at the stake. So far, so good. But here's the test—and the paradox. The suspect was bound, attached to a large rock and thrown into a nearby deep body of water. If she sank to the bottom, that meant the water (symbolizing baptism) accepted her and that she was not a witch. However, since she would have drowned in the process of passing the test and proving her innocence, she could hardly live and go free. If you're innocent, you live, but you're dead.

What's the point of putting a paradox in a piece of writing? It depends on the author's purpose and point of view—both of which you should have identified as you were reading the passage.

Perhaps the writer is describing a world—or advancing an argument—where things are not always what they seem. A paradox is a good way to encourage readers to look at familiar things in new ways, or to question their assumptions. The writer might also be asking readers to suspend logical reasoning and use intuition or a more spiritual type of perception instead. Or, quite simply, the author might just be trying to jolt readers out of a habitual, absorption-type mode of reading—to make them think and return to reread and analyze the paradoxical statement.

Whatever the specific reason, the writer is trying to get your attention by using a paradox. You need to figure out why.

Anytime you identify a simile, metaphor, or personification, you have identified a comparison between two different things that add meaning to the text. Here's how to start your analysis:

Step 1: Identify the two things being compared. Be as specific as possible.

Step 2: Brainstorm the similarities and differences between these two things.

Step 3: Ask your self, how do these similarities and differences develop main ideas in the text?

Rhetorical Question

A **rhetorical question** is a question whose answer is obvious; these types of questions do not need to be answered—and usually aren't. Rhetorical questions attempt to prove something without actually presenting an argument; sometimes they're used as a form of irony, in which something is stated, but its opposite is meant.

> With all the fast food restaurants in the United States, is it any wonder obesity is on the rise? (no irony)

Since it has already been determined that you agree (even if you don't), the writer need not substantiate this remark.

> Aren't AP Exams great fun? (with irony)

Here, there is an assumption that you would answer in the negative, although there is no way for you to respond—unless you write a letter. Rhetorical questions allow a writer to make a point without further support, whether it's a straightforward remark or one with a touch of irony.

Bombast

Bombast (adjective = bombastic) is language that is overly rhetorical (pompous), especially when considered in context. Generally speaking, graduation speeches contain bombast; pedantic people (those who use their learning ostentatiously) tend to use bombast. Occasionally, a passage on the AP English Language and Composition Exam will contain bombast.

> We are here in these hallowed halls, accompanied by genial kin and erudite mentors, surrounded by Corinthian columns and the three wisdoms of the ages, to celebrate the conjunction of fare thee well and many happy returns and to proffer advice worthy of Athena to these prodigal sons and daughters as they depart our august institution. You happy survivors are not graduates, but champions who have been assailed on all sides by demons of mathematics, dragons of science, and inhuman beasts of humanities, but who have emerged victorious from each and every battle. In this respect, one is reminded of Thucydides, who writes: "So long as a vessel was coming up to charge another boat, the men on the decks rained darts, arrows, and stones upon her, but once alongside, the heavy infantry tried to board each other's vessel, fighting hand to hand. In many quarters it happened, because of the restricted space, that a vessel was charging an enemy on one side and being charged herself on another, and that two or even more ships were entangled all around one, obliging the helmsmen to attend to defense here, offense there, not to one thing at a time, but to many things on all sides, while the huge commotion caused by the number of ships crashing together not only spread terror, but also made the orders of the boatswains inaudible." I urge you to remember Attica, and to remember the Spartan way.

The passage on the previous page is marked by pretentious and inflated speech; it is a perfect example of bombast.

Getting Punny

Why do authors use puns? In titles, puns capture the attention and interest of the audience. Puns can also lighten the tone and add humor or optimism to heavy subjects.

But be careful—puns can also be used to trivialize important matters or distract the audience from unpopular implications of an author's argument.

Pun

A **pun** is a play on words. In general, a pun either plays on the multiple meanings of a word or replaces one word with another that is similar in sound but very different in meaning. Puns are almost always used for comic effect.

In *Star Wars,* why did the Empire leave the Catholic nuns alone? Force of habit.

If you know anything about the significance of "the Force" in *Star Wars* and about the double meaning of "habit," you'll get the play on words here. In the response "Force of habit," both "force" and "habit" carry multiple meanings. First, it is a common phrase used to describe an impulse or routine action. "Habit" refers to the action, and "force" refers to the impulse to do it.

However, "Force" also refers to the mystical energy harnessed by the Jedi in the *Star Wars* universe. "Habit" refers to the clothing traditionally worn by Catholic nuns. The humor stems from the ridiculous juxtaposition of images: a routine action alongside a Jedi nun.

There are several literary terms that have similar meanings. The AP will not test the terms but rather your familiarity with the concepts behind them.

Aphorism: "Power tends to corrupt, and absolute power corrupts absolutely." (Lord Acton)

Adage/Proverb: "Nothing ventured, nothing gained."

Maxim: "Where there's life, there's hope."

Motto: "All the news that's fit to print." (*The New York Times*)

Aphorism

An **aphorism** is a concise, pithy statement of an opinion or a general truth.

Life is short, the art [of medicine] is long, opportunity fleeting, experimentation dangerous, reasoning difficult.

That aphorism is attributed to Hippocrates, the "Father of Medicine." Note that his statement is more sophisticated than the "commonplace wisdom" of a saying like "Haste makes waste."

IRONY AND SATIRE

When reading the passages on the AP English Language and Composition Exam, you cannot always take what you see at face value; in fact, when reading, you must always be on the lookout for slightly or very veiled meanings behind the words.

Isn't It Ironic?

Irony: Most people use the term without really knowing its definition. Alanis Morissette's 1996 song about irony didn't help the situation. If you don't believe this, ask one of your friends to define irony and see what kind of answer you receive. Generally speaking, irony refers to the relationship between the text and the audience's expectations. If the audience anticipates certain events or dialogue, and alternate events or dialogue occur, you're likely dealing with irony. Let's look at the two basic types of irony that you'll need to be familiar with for this test: verbal irony and situational irony.

Rain on Your Wedding Day

Irony is not mere misfortune. It is a set of circumstances that wind up the opposite of how the reader would expect them to turn out or how the characters had planned.

Verbal Irony

Verbal irony refers to the process of stating something but *meaning* the opposite of what is stated. In cases of verbal irony, the audience can anticipate the dialogue or specific language used in a text. The author may use a common saying, situation, or emotional experience to build up the audience's expectation. For example, an author may describe an experience while shopping. When the author enters the store, the salesperson says, "Hello, how can you help me?" This would be ironic because the expectation is that the salesperson would say the opposite, "How can I help you?"

Take a minute to review the rhetorical diamond on page 121. To develop irony, the author uses the context of the text to guide the audience's expectation. The author then subverts those expectations with surprising events or dialogue.

Verbal irony can refer to irony that's used in spoken language as well as in print. In spoken language, intonation is often a clue to ironic intent; however, in writing, it is not possible to imply things through intonation, so there's always a danger that the irony may be missed; in essence, the writer who employs irony risks communicating the exact opposite of what is intended. For example, let's say that you write, "This Princeton Review book is really interesting." Unless your listener or reader hears your remark in context, he or she won't know if this is high praise for this book, or if you're bored silly and have chosen to express your sentiment more forcefully by using verbal irony.

Consider the following excerpt, again from *Candide*. The philosopher Pangloss has just given a rather personalized history of venereal disease, a veritable uncontrollable—and uncontrolled—plague in 18th-century Europe.

> "O sage Pangloss," cried Candide, "what a strange genealogy is this! Is not the devil at the root of it all?"
>
> "Not at all," replied the great man, "it was unavoidable, a necessary ingredient in the best of worlds."

The student Candide shows sincere respect for Pangloss when he addresses him as "sage Pangloss"; Candide has no ironic intent. However, the same cannot be said of the narrator. In *Candide,* one of Voltaire's principal aims is to excoriate (to censure scathingly) the "philosophers of optimism," of whom Pangloss is a caricature. He does this through the frequent use of verbal irony; in the passage above, his use of "great man" is ironic—even though Candide's tone is not. After all, neither the narrator nor the careful reader views Pangloss as a great man—he is just the opposite.

In essence, to fully appreciate the passage, we must read in stereo, simultaneously picking up on Candide's serious tone and the narrator's ironic tone. This is a pretty complicated case of verbal irony.

Sarcasm is simply verbal irony used with the intent to injure. It's often impossible to discern between irony and sarcasm, and, more often than not, sarcasm is in the mind of the beholder. Let's say that your close friend and soccer teammate missed a wide-open goal from ten feet away, and you smiled and shouted, "Nice shot!" Presumably your friend, used to your jests, would interpret your quip as playful irony. If the opposing team's goalie said the same words, however, it is far more likely that your friend would take the remark as sarcasm—and reply with a not-so-kind word or two. In written form, irony and sarcasm can be considered to be fairly synonymous—but just think of sarcasm as malicious. Here is an example from Henrik Ibsen's *Hedda Gabbler.*

> Brack: There's a possibility that the appointment may be decided by competition—
>
> Tesman: Competition! By Jove, Hedda, fancy that!
>
> Hedda: [*motionless in her chair*] How exciting, Tesman.

Of course, it is easier to see the sarcasm when you are familiar with the play, but it is sufficient for you to know that Tesman is the rather boring, plodding husband and that Hedda is an unfulfilled wife. The stage direction ("motionless in her chair") helps us see that her words are at least full of irony; if you add the bitter, malignant intent, which the husband misses but we do not, then you have sarcasm.

Situational Irony

Situational irony refers to a circumstance that runs contrary to what was expected.

Suppose you live in Seattle during the rainy season and plan a vacation to sunny Phoenix. While you are in Phoenix, it rains every day there, but is sunny the entire week in Seattle. This is situational irony.

Situational Irony

A simple example of situational irony can be found in the classic tale "The Gift of the Magi." Jim and Delia are a poor couple who have no money to buy each other gifts for Christmas. Jim sells his watch to buy Delia a comb for her hair. Delia sells her hair to buy Jim a watch-chain. Both gifts wind up useless to their respective recipients—the ultimate in irony.

Satire

In **satire,** something is portrayed in a way that's deliberately distorted to achieve comic effect. Implicit in most satire is the author's desire to critique what is being mocked. Voltaire's *Candide* is principally a satire of optimism, the philosophy that, given that the first "cause" was perfect (God's creation of the world), all causes and effects must naturally be part of this original perfect plan. The French satirist takes on many other causes, however, and one of his favorite targets is the part of religion that he considers no more than fanatical superstition. Here is what happens after Candide and Pangloss are caught in the infamous earthquake of Lisbon, Portugal.

After the earthquake, which had destroyed three-fourths of the city of Lisbon, the sages of that country could think of no better manner to preserve the kingdom from complete ruin than to entertain the people with an *auto-da-fe,* it having been decided by the University of Coimbra that burning a few people alive over low heat and with great ceremony is an infallible way to prevent earthquakes.

In consequence, they had seized a Biscayan for marrying his godmother and two Portuguese for taking out the bacon of a larded chicken they were eating; after dinner, they came and took into custody Doctor Pangloss and his pupil Candide, the one for speaking his mind and the other for appearing to approve what he heard. They were conducted to separate apartments, which were extremely cool and where they were never bothered by the sun. Eight days later, they were each dressed in a *sanbenito* and their heads were adorned with paper *mitres*. The *mitre* and *sanbenito* worn by Candide were painted with upside down flames and with devils that had neither tails nor claws, but Doctor Pangloss's devils had both tails and claws, and his flames were right side up. In these clothes they marched in the procession and heard a very pathetic sermon, which was followed by an anthem accompanied by bagpipes. Candide was flogged to the beat of the music while the anthem was being sung; the Biscayan and the two men who would not eat bacon were burned, and Pangloss was hanged, which is not a common custom at these solemnities. The same day there was another earthquake, which created the most dreadful havoc.

After the real earthquake of 1755, there were real *auto-da-fes* ("acts of faith"), during which "evil" inhabitants of Lisbon were sacrificed to appease God, who, ostensibly (to all outward appearances), had provoked the earthquake to punish the city. The "evils" that are being punished say more about the ridiculous prejudices of the persecutors than they do about the so-called evil victims. The two Portuguese who refrained from eating the bacon are guilty of nothing—but they are taken for Jews; the man who married his godmother, who, presumably, is not tied to him by blood, is guilty of no more than infringing on a technicality of the religious code (Catholicism, in this case).

Note that the satire is heightened by Voltaire's use of verbal irony ("the sages"), situational irony (right after the ceremony there is a second earthquake), and a comical circumlocution ("burning a few people alive over low heat and with great ceremony" is a circumlocution for *auto-da-fe*). Satire can be effective in both fiction and nonfiction, and *Candide,* a philosophical story that combines both, is thought to be one of the most brilliant satires of all.

The following terms are similar, but not identical. Know the differences.

Satire: A social or political criticism that relies heavily on irony, sarcasm, and often humor

Parody: Imitation for comic effect

Lampoon: Sharp ridicule of the behavior or character of a person or institution

Caricature: A ludicrous exaggeration of the defects of persons or things

Most critics, however, relegate satire—and satirists—to a secondary sphere in the universe of writing; satire makes for good entertainment, but mocking others does not measure up to the conviction of cogent writing. Had Voltaire been nothing more than a satirist, he would not have been remembered as a brilliant *philosophe,* but as a clever joker—if he were remembered at all. Although Voltaire's satire in *Candide* is quite brilliant, some other examples of satire are a little easier to figure out. Let's look at a sample question based on a passage from Jonathan Swift's *Gulliver's Travels.*

For about seventy moons past there have been two struggling parties in this empire, under the names of *Tramecksan* and *Slamecksan,* from the high and low heels of their shoes, by which they distinguish themselves. It is alleged, indeed, that the high heels are most agreeable to our ancient constitution; but, however this be, his majesty has determined to make use only of low heels in the administration of the government, and all offices in the gift of the crown, as you cannot but observe; and particularly that his majesty's imperial heels are lower at least by a *drurr* than any of his court (*drurr* is a measure about the fourteenth part of an inch). The animosities between these two parties run so high, that they will neither eat, nor drink, nor talk with each other. We compute the *Tramecksan*, or high heels, to exceed us in number; but the power is wholly on our side. We apprehend his imperial highness, the heir to the crown, to have some tendency towards the high heels; at least we can plainly discover that one of his heels is higher than the other, which gives him a hobble in his gait.

4. The above passage is an example of

(A) an analysis of court customs
(B) a satire of British footwear
(C) a study of British eccentricities
(D) a satire of the British court
(E) a nonsensical account of life at court

Well, the correct answer must be either (B) or (D) because this section is all about satire. The correct answer is (D). The passage serves to satirize the Whig-Tory discord (the Whigs dominated politics during much of the 18th century) and the relationship of the "parties" (the Whigs and Tories were not really political parties as we know them today) and the king. Unless you recognize that the passage is satirical, you will not have a good grasp of what is going on—which will lead to major problems with all of the multiple-choice questions on that passage.

THEME

Once you've considered the rhetorical diamond, as well as the use of diction, syntax, and figurative language, you're ready to consider a text's theme. As stated, a **theme** is an argument contained in the text; the theme may be stated explicitly or only suggested. A theme is not just an idea; it is *an idea that is developed,* often over the course of a chapter or an entire book. Usually, one can identify a central theme and several minor ones. Sometimes both are overtly stated, as in the example that follows:

> Many scholars agree that the central theme in *The Adventures of Huckleberry Finn* is the conflict between nature and civilization. But clearly, the book contains other themes, such as the worth of honor and the voyage of self-discovery.

Read the following passage, and see if you can identify a central theme.

We now touch on civilization's most sensitive spot; it is an unpleasant task to raise one's voice against the folly of the day, against chimeras that have caused a downright epidemic.

To speak against the absurdities of trade today means to expose oneself to anathemas, just as much as if one had spoken against the tyranny of the popes and the barons in the twelfth century. If it were a matter of choosing between two dangerous roles, I think it would be less dangerous to offend a sovereign with bitter truths than to offend the mercantile spirit that now rules like a despot over civilization—and even over sovereigns!

And yet a superficial analysis will prove that our commercial systems defile and disorganize civilization and that in trade, as in all other things, we are being led further and further astray.

The controversy on trade is barely half a century old and has already produced thousands of books, and yet the participants in the controversy have not seen that the trade mechanism is organized in such a way that it is a slap in the face to all common sense. It has subordinated the whole of society to one class of parasitic and unproductive persons: the merchants. All the essential classes of society—the proprietor, the farmer, the manufacturer, and even the government—find themselves dominated by a non-essential, contingent class, the merchant, who should be their subordinate, their employed agent, removable and accountable, and who, nevertheless, directs and obstructs at will all the avenues of circulation.

It should not surprise you that the title of the essay that this passage is excerpted from is "On Trade." In his essay, the French socialist Charles Fourier develops a central theme: merchants, through trade, have both corrupted society and become its tyrant.

Identifying themes in a text is critical to both the multiple-choice and free-response sections of the text. In the analysis essay, your primary aim is to identify the speaker's theme and analyze how that theme was developed within the text.

REFLECT

Respond to the following questions:

- For which topics discussed in this chapter do you feel you have achieved sufficient mastery to answer multiple-choice questions correctly?
- For which topics discussed in this chapter do you feel you have achieved sufficient mastery to discuss effectively in an essay?
- For which topics discussed in this chapter do you feel you need more work before you can answer multiple-choice questions correctly?
- For which topics discussed in this chapter do you feel you need more work before you discuss them effectively in an essay?
- What parts of this chapter are you going to re-review?
- Will you seek further help, outside of this book (such as a teacher, tutor, or AP Students website), on any of the topics in this chapter—and, if so, on which ones?

Chapter 9
Basic Rhetorical Modes

Don't confuse rhetorical modes with the elements of style discussed in the previous chapter. Rhetorical modes refer to the overall organization of an argument; the elements of style refer to the specific decisions an author makes when constructing the words and sentences that comprise the argument.

WHAT ARE RHETORICAL MODES?

The rhetorical modes (or patterns) contained in this chapter are worth studying for two reasons. First, they will provide you with ready-made approaches for writing your essays on the exam, and second, the multiple-choice questions on the test also often include some of the rhetorical mode terminology.

As you prepare for the exam by taking practice tests, you'll see that 40 minutes is not much time in which to write a sophisticated essay, and the shortcuts you'll learn in this chapter will be invaluable in helping you write a great essay in the allotted time. However, you do not need to cram and memorize all the material in this section. If you read and understand the explanations and just make sure you retain the basics, you'll be comfortable enough with the process to do well on the exam.

Another important point to remember is that, more often than not, rhetorical modes are used in combination. Breaking them up into individual components is a somewhat arbitrary process—but for our purposes, it makes the material easier to understand. Let's begin.

CLASSIFICATION

How do you classify things? Well, you probably start by dividing up whatever you have into groups according to certain characteristics. For example, if you wanted to explain "new music" to someone, you might divide the artists into groups by type (female vocalists, male vocalists, and bands) and classify the groups by genre (heavy metal, punk rock, alternative, and so on). This would make the material easier for someone to understand because it would be organized. In other words, *We classify to more easily analyze and explain.*

When you place things into categories on the AP English Language and Composition Exam, avoid creating classifications that overlap. For example, it would not make sense to classify your favorite foods in the following way: sweets, barbecued meats, vegetables, and chocolates; logically, the last group is a smaller subset of the first group.

All of this boils down to the following: classification is nearly the same thing as organization. And organization is important. As you know by now, the directions in the free-response section of the AP English Language and Composition Exam request that you write "a well-organized essay." It may seem obvious that the test-writers would request this of you—but then you'd be surprised how poorly organized many of the AP essays that students write are. Classify before you write.

There is almost always more than one way to classify things. Right now, you may group your teachers as being either cool or uncool. Later, it's more likely that you'll classify them according to what they helped you learn: the new categories may be teachers who inspired you, teachers who taught you the most, teachers who taught you about life, and teachers who should not have been teachers.

Aristotle liked to classify, and he did so quite often. Some of his classifications have stood the test of time, including the one below, which is the beginning of Part 6 of an essay entitled "Categories."

> Quantity is either discrete or continuous (…). Instances of discrete quantities are number and speech; instances of continuous quantities are lines, surfaces, solids, and, besides these, time and place.
>
> In the case of the parts of a number, there is no common boundary at which they join. For example: two fives make ten, but the two fives have no common boundary, but are separate; the parts three and seven also do not join at any boundary. Nor, to generalize, would it ever be possible in the case of number that there should be a common boundary among the parts; they are always separate. Number, therefore, is a discrete quantity.
>
> The same is true of speech. That speech is a quantity is evident: for it is measured in long and short syllables. I mean here that speech which is vocal. Moreover, it is a discrete quantity for its parts have no common boundary. There is no common boundary at which the syllables join, but each is separate and distinct from the rest.
>
> A line, on the other hand, is a continuous quantity, for it is possible to find a common boundary at which its parts join. In the case of the line, this common boundary is the point; in the case of the plane, it is the line, for the parts of the plane have also a common boundary. Similarly you can find a common boundary in the case of the parts of a solid, namely either a line or a plane.
>
> Space and time also belong to this class of quantities. Time, past, present, and future, forms a continuous whole. Space, likewise, is a continuous quantity; for the parts of a solid occupy a certain space, and these have a common boundary; it follows that the parts of space also, which are occupied by the parts of the solid, have the same common boundary as the parts of the solid. Thus, not only time, but space also, is a continuous quantity, for its parts have a common boundary.

Here, Aristotle's division of quantity into two categories (discrete and continuous) makes sense. The examples that he uses to illustrate the nature of his categories reveal a great deal about his interests: time, space, language, and mathematics. This is a well-organized passage; the categories are well-defined and Aristotle clearly explains how the members of each category have been classified.

Laundry List for Classification

- When you're asked to analyze and explain something, classification will be very useful.
- Make sure you have a central idea (thesis).
- Sort your information into meaningful groups. Are there enough elements in each group to allow you to write a convincing, useful paragraph? Sometimes you'll find that you need to combine categories.
- Make sure you have a manageable number of categories—three or four. Remember that you have only about 40 minutes to plan and execute each essay.
- Make sure the categories (or the elements in the categories) do not overlap.
- Before writing, make sure the categories and central idea (thesis) are a good fit. Sometimes you'll want to modify your thesis statement based on the categories that you've found.
- As you write, do not justify your classification unless this is somehow necessary to address a very bizarre free-response question. Justify your thesis, not your categories.

Sample Classification Question

Write a short essay in which you analyze the different methods a teacher uses to convey information to his or her class. In your essay, be sure to use classification to organize your ideas. Once you've written your essay, show it to your AP teacher or tutor. You might want to show it to a fellow AP student for peer review.

Drill: Reflect on How You Could Use Classification to Address the Following Topics

As you read each of the topics, think about how you would organize your essay in terms of classification. Come up with a possible thesis (central idea), and plan how you could categorize the information you have on these topics into three or four meaningful divisions.

TOPIC 1: Television commercials

TOPIC 2: Movies

TOPIC 3: Students

TOPIC 4: Cars

EXAMPLE OR ILLUSTRATION

Our first rhetorical mode consists of using specific examples to illustrate an idea. Now, this may seem like a pretty simple idea, but one of the most common mistakes students make when writing their AP English Language and Composition essays is to use poor examples. Remember that all examples are not created equal. If you use poor illustrative examples, your ideas will be communicated much less clearly and effectively than if you'd used solid, appropriate ones. In writing these essays, your principal goal is clarity.

Read the following student essay based on *Candide*, and as you do so, evaluate the effectiveness of the examples that it uses.

> Pangloss is correct when he claims that everything is for the best in the best of all possible worlds. First of all, we are seeing more and more technological innovation every year. Computer technology, in particular, has helped us in many ways, and breakthroughs in medicine have helped raise the life expectancy significantly. Furthermore, in most cities, there are bustling restaurants and great nightlife. Finally, travel has become affordable for most people, and paradises like Aruba and Hawaii await us all!

Surely you agree that the examples are not convincing, but you should also understand that they are not even relevant. Implicit in the examples chosen is the reduction of the best of all possible worlds to the writer's own tiny corner. A better approach would be something as follows:

> Pangloss is correct when he claims that everything is for the best in the best of all possible worlds. First of all, the challenges that we have faced or are facing have inspired some of our most important scientific advances. Great famines have led scientists to exciting new agricultural discoveries, such as drought-resistant crops; great droughts have inspired engineers to develop cost-effective desalination plants. In essence, the evils in the world have been necessary stimulants for changes for the better. Furthermore, advances in medicine are no longer restricted to the wealthy nations of the world, and there is reason to hope that coordinated efforts to help developing countries will become more effective; take, for example, the international relief efforts to help the people whose homes were destroyed by the recent tsunami. Not only will the victims have better and safer homes now, but also the cooperation among the developed nations will translate into a better, safer world. Indeed, everything is for the best.

While the second essay may be naive, at least it does its best to substantiate an untenable position. Without any doubt, the examples in the second passage are much more appropriate for the argument than those that were used in the first passage.

Just as it is important to choose relevant, convincing examples to substantiate your own ideas, it is essential to constantly evaluate the examples that others use in their attempts to explain or to convince.

Tricksters, dogmatists, and charlatans usually illustrate their positions with scanty, inappropriate details. Be critical.

Laundry List for Example (Illustration)

- Use examples that your reader (the person who reads your essays) will identify with and understand. Do not assume that the AP reader has seen the latest teen cult film or knows any pop culture icons younger than Britney Spears.
- Draw your examples from "real life," "real" culture (literature, art, classical music, and so on), and well-known folklore.
- Make sure the example really does illustrate your point. Don't use a fancy example just to show off your knowledge; find ones that really work!
- Introduce your examples using transitions, such as *for example, for instance, case in point,* and *consider the case of.*
- A single example that is perfectly representative can serve to illustrate your point.
- A series of short, less-perfect (but still relevant) examples can, by their accumulation, serve to illustrate your point.
- The ideal approach is to construct a well-developed, representative example supported by several shorter examples.
- Remember that you are in control of what you write. As you brainstorm, discard examples that may disprove your point. Your AP essays will have little or nothing to do with your beliefs or with a balanced examination of an issue. You will be defending a point of view (argumentative essay) or explaining something (expository essay)—don't feel as if you have to be fair to all sides of an argument; your aim is to get your point across.
- Quality is more important than quantity; poorly chosen examples detract significantly from your presentation. Make sure examples are detailed, specific, and concrete.

When you're drafting free-response essays, use the basic rhetorical modes to guide you. Start by classifying your ideas and organizing them into paragraphs. Then, brainstorm examples and/or analogies to support and illustrate your ideas.

Sample Question for Using Examples

Write a thoughtful and carefully constructed essay in which you use specific examples to defend, challenge, or qualify the assertion that Hollywood movies are a reflection of a decaying society.

Drill: Reflect on How You Could Use Examples to Address the Following Topics

As you read each of the topics listed below, make a list of five examples you could use to support them. Are your examples all relevant? Do they support just this side of the argument? Treat each as the basis for your thesis statement in a practice free-response question.

TOPIC 1: High schools unwittingly encourage students to cheat.

TOPIC 2: Studying the humanities is important.

TOPIC 3: A person's attitude toward diversity reveals much about that person.

ANALOGY

Although analogies are not that useful in argumentative writing, they *are* useful in expository writing—this means that analogies will be useful when you write your expository essay for this test.

Analogies are sometimes used to explain things that are difficult to understand by comparing them with things that are easier to understand. Let's say that you want to explain how a well-run corporation works. You might explain that it functions like a football team. In both cases there are owners or stockholders. In the corporation, there's a CEO, who is similar to the coach of a football team. The CEO directs the managers (or vice presidents), just as the coach directs the assistant coaches; these work directly with the employees—the players. When an employee doesn't heed directions, the success of the enterprise is put at risk, just like when a player fails to execute a block or a tackle. The most important thing about using analogies is that you choose one that will be readily understood by your audience.

Think of an **analogy** as a comparison used to explain something.

In this case, if the reader knows nothing about football, this analogy may do more harm than good.

You can also use an analogy to explain something that's abstract by comparing it with something that's concrete. Throughout history, people have used analogies to explain their god or gods. Christians explain God, for example, through analogy. They say that God is like a father who loves his children and, thus, both punishes and rewards them. The only difference is that they consider God's judgment to be perfect. They believe that God is like a father in that both are good, but that the difference is that God is *perfectly* good.

The most famous philosophical analogy serves as the basis for Plato's "allegory of the cave." The analogy purportedly evolved from a conversation between Socrates and Glaucon.

> Imagine human beings living in an underground cave; here they have been from their childhood, and they have their legs and necks chained so that they cannot move and can only see before them, being prevented by the chains from turning round their heads. Above and behind them, a fire is blazing at a distance, and between the fire and the prisoners there is a raised way; and there is a low wall built along the way, like the screen which marionette players have to hide them and over which they show the puppets.
>
> Men are passing along the wall (and screened by the wall) and are carrying all sorts of things and animals made of wood and stone and various materials that appear over the wall. Some of them are talking, others are silent.
>
> Like ourselves, they see only their own shadows, or the shadows of one another, or the shadows of the things and animals, which the fire throws on the opposite wall of the cave.
>
> And if the human beings were able to converse with one another, would they not suppose that they were naming what was actually before them (even though they were seeing only shadows of those things)?
>
> And suppose further that the prison had an echo which came from the other side, would they not be sure to fancy when one of the passers-by spoke that the voice which they heard came from the passing shadow?
>
> To them, I said, the truth would be literally nothing but the shadows of the images.

This is only part of the analogy, but you probably get the idea. Socrates uses this analogy to explain that we think that we see things just as they really are in our world, but that we are seeing only reflections of a greater truth, an abstraction that we fail to grasp. The cave is our world; the shadows are the objects and people that we "see." We are like the prisoners, for we are not free to see what creates the shadows; the truth, made up of ideal forms, is out in the light.

Laundry List for Analogy

- Use analogy for expository writing (explanation).
- Do not use analogy for argumentative writing (argumentation).
- Use analogy to explain something that is abstract or difficult to understand.
- Make sure your audience will readily understand your "simple" or concrete subject.

Sample Analogy Question

Write an essay in which you explain the process of applying to college. Use analogy when appropriate. Once you've written your essay, show it to your AP teacher or tutor. You might want to show it to a fellow AP student for peer review.

Drill: Reflect on How You Could Use Analogy to Address the Following Topics

As you read each topic, think of it as the basis for the thesis of an expository essay. Come up with a simpler subject that you can use as an analogy for this more complex topic. Write down a basic plan for an essay.

TOPIC 1: The way your school functions

TOPIC 2: The benefits of honesty

MOVING ON...

In this chapter we discussed three rhetorical modes: example, classification, and analogy. Make sure you are familiar with the laundry lists in this chapter. If you get into good habits now when using these rhetorical modes, you'll be much better off on test day!

Further proving how useful these modes will be, we guarantee that both your expository and argumentative essay questions will fit into some combination of these modes.

Of course, remember to plan your essay before you begin writing. It often helps to write your thesis statement along with this plan so that you can keep in mind whether the parts of your plan are relevant to your central idea. This will ensure that you write the best organized, most coherent essay you can.

Now that we've covered the three basic rhetorical modes, let's move on to review a few complex modes in the next chapter.

REFLECT

Respond to the following questions:

- For which topics discussed in this chapter do you feel you have achieved sufficient mastery to answer multiple-choice questions correctly?
- For which topics discussed in this chapter do you feel you have achieved sufficient mastery to discuss effectively in an essay?
- For which topics discussed in this chapter do you feel you need more work before you can answer multiple-choice questions correctly?
- For which topics discussed in this chapter do you feel you need more work before you can discuss them effectively in an essay?
- What parts of this chapter are you going to re-review?
- Will you seek further help, outside of this book (such as a teacher, tutor, or AP Students website), on any of the topics in this chapter—and, if so, on which ones?

Chapter 10
Complex Rhetorical Modes

In this chapter, we'll discuss a few more—and more complex—rhetorical modes, including process analysis, cause and effect, definition, description, narration, and induction and deduction. As was the case with the rhetorical modes you learned about in the last chapter, it will be extremely beneficial to you to know all you can about these modes on test day. It will not only help you recognize when these modes are used in the sample passages, but also enable you to use them in your essays.

So let's jump right in.

PROCESS ANALYSIS

Mnemonics

If you're having trouble remembering rhetorical modes, make some flashcards and memorize them like vocabulary words.

Process analysis is a rhetorical mode that's used by writers when they want to explain either how to do something or how something was done. When your science teacher hands you instructions for a lab, she is giving you a rather dry sheet of process analysis that says, "first do this; then do that; then examine the data; then explain such-and-such." When you write your lab report, you're also indulging in process analysis, saying, "first we did this; then we did that; then we examined the data; then we determined such-and-such." If you like to follow recipes when you cook, then you've already been exposed to process analysis. However, process analyses used in writing generally aren't as dry as recipes or how-to manuals; they usually have a few examples to spice them up a little.

Process analysis can be an effective way of relating an experience. Take, for example, this excerpt from "On Dumpster Diving" from *Travels with Lizbeth* by Lars Eighner.

> I learned to scavenge gradually, on my own. Since then I have initiated several companions into the trade. I have learned that there is a predictable series of stages a person goes through in learning to scavenge.
>
> At first the new scavenger is filled with disgust and self-loathing. He is ashamed of being seen and may lurk around, trying to duck behind things, or he may try to dive at night. (In fact, most people instinctively look away from a scavenger. By skulking around, the novice calls attention to himself and arouses suspicion. Diving at night is ineffective and needlessly messy.)
>
> Every grain of rice seems to be a maggot. Everything seems to stink. He can wipe the egg yolk off the found can, but he cannot erase the stigma of eating garbage out of his mind.
>
> That stage passes with experience. The scavenger finds a pair of running shoes that fit and look and smell brand-new. He finds a pocket calculator in perfect working order. He finds pristine ice cream, still frozen, more than he can eat or keep. He begins to understand: people do throw away perfectly good stuff, a lot of perfectly good stuff.
>
> At this stage, Dumpster shyness begins to dissipate. The diver, after all, has the last laugh. He is finding all manner

of good things which are his for the taking. Those who disparage his profession are the fools, not he.

He may begin to hang onto some perfectly good things for which he has neither a use nor a market. Then he begins to take note of the things which are not perfectly good but are nearly so. He mates a Walkman with broken earphones and one that is missing a battery cover. He picks up things which he can repair.

At this stage he may become lost and never recover. Dumpsters are full of things of some potential value to someone and also of things which never have much intrinsic value but are interesting. All the Dumpster divers I have known come to the point of trying to acquire everything they touch. Why not take it, they reason, since it is all free.

Here's a good example of process analysis in writing. Although the material is organized in chronological stages, the author inserts explanatory examples and personal commentary that make the passage more lively. In this passage, the author is not instructing the reader on how to scavenge for food in Dumpsters; rather, he is explaining the psychological evolution of a homeless scavenger—based on his own experience—and illustrating the excesses of a consumerist society.

Remember that process analysis is a rhetorical mode that serves to organize something in a step-by-step manner, and it can serve both scientific and persuasive ends.

Laundry List for Process Analysis

- Sequence is chronological and usually fixed—think of recipes.
- When you use this device, make sure the stages of the process are clear, by using transitions (e.g., *first, next, after two days, finally*).
- Make sure your terminology is appropriate for the reader. For example, the person who will read your essays probably does not know much about the embryonic development of frogs, so you should avoid using too-specialized terms like *Spemann organizer* or *Nieuwkoop center.*
- Verify that every step is clear; an error or omission in an intermediate step may make the rest of the process analysis very confusing. Let's say you were describing how to braid hair, and wrote the following instructions: "First, comb or brush your hair so that it is untangled and manageable to work with. Next, take the far-right section of hair and put it over the middle section and under the far-left section." This could be confusing to your reader because you never said to divide the hair into three sections before starting the actual braiding process.

Sample Process Analysis Question

Write a short essay in which you describe the process of how you selected the colleges to which you applied (or are going to apply to). Once you've written your essay, show it to your AP teacher or tutor. You might want to show it to a fellow AP student for peer review.

Drill: Reflect on How You Could Use Process Analysis to Address the Following Topics

Try making a numbered list with a few examples. Make sure you have included all the necessary steps and have used appropriate language and terminology for your reader. Remember to use transition words when you write the essay.

TOPIC 1: How decisions are made at your school

TOPIC 2: How to get through high school successfully

TOPIC 3: How to choose and keep close friends

CAUSE AND EFFECT

You just saw how process analysis is a useful rhetorical mode for explaining how to do things or how things were done; the rhetorical mode known as **cause and effect** explains *why things should be done* or *should have been done.* In a sense, cause and effect explains the processes responsible for the process.

Some cause-and-effect relationships are easy to describe. For instance, read the example below from *Candide*'s Dr. Pangloss.

> "It is demonstrable," said Pangloss, "that things cannot be otherwise than as they are; for as all things have been created for some end, they must necessarily be created for the best end. Observe, for instance, the nose is formed for spectacles; therefore we wear spectacles. The legs are visibly designed for stockings; accordingly we wear stockings. Stones were made to be hewn and to construct castles; therefore My Lord has a magnificent castle, for the greatest baron in the province ought to be the best lodged. Swine were intended to be eaten; therefore we eat pork all the year round."

In this passage, Pangloss is using a series of cause-and-effect relationships to prove his point, that "things cannot be otherwise than as they are." This rhetorical mode is everywhere, however. You see examples of this rhetorical mode all around you.

On this exam, the causes and effects that you choose to explore will depend on what you're asked to explain. You may have to use cause and effect in your essays, possibly in combination with one or more other rhetorical modes; you may also see a few questions in the multiple-choice section that deal with how the author uses cause and effect to make a point. When making critical decisions, writers will often consider both the immediate and the long-term effects; when analyzing an important event, writers will often examine both the immediate and the underlying causes.

If you were writing about the poor average of AP English Language and Composition test scores at your school, you could go about it in two ways. First, you could examine some *immediate* causes: Ms. What's-Her Name retired and was replaced by a teacher who had no experience teaching and no background in English, we didn't have a good review book for the exam, or the exam is administered in Room Z during school band practice. Alternatively, you could examine some *underlying* causes for the poor exam scores: The superintendent of schools changed hiring policies (so a terrible teacher was hired); last year, funds for buying books were diverted to buying new lockers for the football team (so we had no good review book); and the room that the school band normally practices in was flooded when a pipe broke.

Laundry List for Cause and Effect

- Do not confuse the relating of mere circumstances with a cause-and-effect relationship. For example, it is not logical to assume that socialism in Chile necessarily caused socialism in Argentina.
- Turn your causal relationships into causes and effects by using carefully chosen examples. Remember that not all causal relationships are causes and effects. However, careful use of evidence and examples can turn causal relationships into causes and effects.
- Make sure to carefully address each step in a series of causal relationships; if you don't, you risk losing your reader. Imagine the attendance secretary when she hears, "I'm sorry I'm late. We had a fire, so I had to find my cat." A better (clearer) explanation would have been as follows: "I'm sorry I'm late. This morning at 4:00 A.M. there was an electrical fire in the garage; fortunately, there was an alarm that woke my dad, who put out the fire, but when he opened the garage door, my cat ran outside. I think it was frightened so it ran up a tree. I decided to climb up the tree and get the cat but I fell, and my mother had to take me to the emergency room." Although this explanation is longer, it is far more detailed and answers any questions your reader may have.

Sample Cause-and-Effect Question

Write an essay in which you examine the possible causes and effects of violence in the United States today. Once you've written your essay, show it to your AP teacher or tutor. You might want to show it to a fellow AP student for peer review.

Drill: Reflect on How You Could Use Cause and Effect to Address the Following Topics

In a T-chart, compare the possible causes and effects of the topics below. Then for at least one topic, make sure to give examples to back up your claims.

TOPIC 1: Academic dishonesty in high schools

TOPIC 2: The fear of domestic terrorism in the United States

TOPIC 3: The changing face of ethnic America

DEFINITION

You are probably familiar with definitions; you see them every time you look up a word in the dictionary. Hopefully when you write, you try to make sure your reader understands the words that you use.

For the AP Exam, we have to consider *definition* in its meaning as a rhetorical mode.

When writing your essays for the AP English Language and Composition Exam, if you happen to leave a key term unexplained or explained vaguely, even a carefully crafted essay will fall apart. This is especially true of very specialized terminology and obscure words. For example, if you are explaining a wonderful new tradition at your school and define it by synonym, you may write, "Basically, it's a Mexican *feis*." If your readers are Irish, this would be all right; if your readers were from just about anywhere else, you would need to define *feis* by putting it into a **category** (defining it in terms everyone will understand): "a *feis* is a competition for Irish dance, song, and instrumental music." Then, you could explain your project: "We want to do the same thing with traditional Mexican dance, song, and music."

In this case, a paragraph—or an entire essay—is devoted to the definition of a term. Here, for example, is a paragraph that defines *feis* (pronounced "fesh").

> A *feis* is a day of competition in Irish dancing, music, and song. Perhaps you were wondering where all the Irish dancers from *Lord of the Dance* came from. All first performed at a *feis* and honed their skills through competitions

at various levels. A *feis* is a living legacy of Irish culture; it is where beginners, trying to remember their left from right, unknowingly dance the ancient steps of Ireland and pass this legacy on to the next generation. On the more practical side, a *feis* is to Irish performers what a soccer game is to athletes the world over. Competitions are organized by ability (Beginner, Advanced Beginner, Novice, Open, Preliminary Championships, and Championships) and by age (Under 6, Under 7, etc.). At a typical *feis*, there might be as many as 2,500 dancers.

The passage begins with a straightforward definition, but the definition is extended and rhetorical modes are mixed. You noted, I'm sure, the *analogy* to a soccer game; then, there is an inchoate (imperfectly formed) stab at *classification* (the divisions in the competition). You could even argue that the mention of *Lord of the Dance* serves as a kind of *example*. The rhetorical mode of *definition* can be used simply to explain a word or concept, but typically the author using it also wants to interest the reader in what's being explained.

Let's take a look at another good example of definition.

The *Palio* is a horse race that's held twice each year in Siena, Italy: on July 2nd in honor of the Madonna of Provenzano, and on August 16th in honor of the Assumption of the Virgin. But saying that the Palio is just another horse race would be like calling the Superbowl just another football game. The Palio is not just a race. It is blood, sweat, and tears; it is part competition and part festival. According to some, it is the world's craziest horse race; according to others, it is Italy's most honored tradition. One thing is clear to everyone, however: the Palio represents the tradition, culture, and soul of Siena. The actual race lasts only about a minute, but those moments represent an entire year's worth of anticipation and preparation.

Again, the passage begins with a simple definition; but here, too, we have an example of another rhetorical mode—analogy (to the Super Bowl).

However, the author of this passage uses an important additional tactic, known as *definition by negation.* You should be aware of this rhetorical device and use it where appropriate. In the passage above, the negation is partial—the Palio is, indeed, a race, but it is not "just a race." Most negations work in that manner; definition by negation is usually used to impress upon the reader the importance of the item under discussion or create a distinction between the item under discussion and the item with which it is being "negatively" compared. For instance, you may write, "Madonna is not a pop singer; she's a phenomenon, a true diva, a multitalented musical ambassador, and savvy businesswoman." Perhaps this statement is true, but she's still a pop singer.

You may be able to use definition as a mode in your free-response essays, but most likely, you will see definition used in the passages in the multiple-choice sections.

For example, you may be asked to answer a question that deals with how an author uses definition to analyze a topic.

Laundry List for Definition

- Keep your reason for defining something in mind as you're writing.
- Define key terms according to what you know of your audience, in other words, the readers of the essays; you don't want to bore your reader by defining terms unnecessarily, nor do you want to perplex your reader by failing to define terms that may be obscure to your audience. Keep in mind that for you, your readers are the AP English Language and Composition Exam graders.
- Explain the background (history) when it is relevant to your definition.
- Define by negation when appropriate.
- Combine definition with any number of other rhetorical modes when applicable.

Sample Definition Question

Write an essay in which you use definition to analyze the role of integrity in your life. Once you've written your essay, show it to your AP teacher or tutor. You might want to show it to a fellow AP student for peer review.

Drill: Reflect on How You Could Use Definition to Address the Following Topics

First define each word by category; then, define each word by negation.

WORD 1: Hip-hop

WORD 2: Success

WORD 3: Love

WORD 4: Cool

DESCRIPTION

Description can help make expository or argumentative writing lively and interesting and hold the reader's interest, which is vital, of course. Think of how many essays those test graders have to read every day; as we mentioned in the techniques chapters, a large part of scoring well on the free-response section is keeping your audience interested.

Oftentimes description serves as the primary rhetorical mode for an entire essay—or even an entire book. It's typically used to communicate a scene, a specific place, or a person to the reader. Although writers tend to concentrate most on the visual aspects of descriptions, they can be used to appeal to any of the reader's senses.

Objective:
Based on facts

Subjective:
Based on feelings or opinions

It is important to keep in mind that sometimes description can be objective; in these cases, the author is not describing something in a sentimental or otherwise subjective way—he or she is merely stating the facts. As an example of this, take a look at Charles Darwin's depiction of Valparaíso, the chief seaport in Chile, in *Voyage of the Beagle*.

> The town is built at the very foot of a range of hills, about 1,600 feet high, and rather steep. From its position, it consists of one long, straggling street, which runs parallel to the beach, and wherever a ravine comes down, the houses are piled up on each side of it. The rounded hills, being only partially protected by very scanty vegetation, are worn into numberless little gullies, which expose a singularly bright red soil. From this cause, and from the low whitewashed houses with tile roofs, the view reminded me of St. Cruz in Tenerife. In a northwesterly direction there are some fine glimpses of the Andes, but these mountains appear much grander when viewed from the neighboring hills: the great distance at which they are situated can then more readily be perceived.

This type of objective description tends to be drier than more subjective description. The degree of objectivity exhibited above probably doesn't thrill you—nor will it thrill the AP readers.

Fortunately, unlike most other rhetorical modes, description allows for a significant degree of subjectivity. In most descriptions, the writer attempts to communicate personal impressions of something or someone. To do so, it is necessary to draw on the powers of figurative writing; simile, metaphor, and personification are the most common.

Here is another description of a city: Nathaniel Hawthorne's impressions of Florence. The description comes not from one of Hawthorne's novels, but from one of the notebooks that he kept during his travels in Europe.

> By and by, we had a distant glimpse of Florence, showing its great dome and some of its towers out of a sidelong valley, as if we were between two great waves of the tumultuous sea of hills, while, far beyond, rose in the distance the blue peaks of three or four of the Apennines, just on the remote horizon. There being a haziness in the atmosphere, however, Florence was little more distinct to us than the Celestial City was to Christian and Hopeful, when they spied at it from the Delectable Mountains.
>
> Florence at first struck me as having the aspect of a very new city in comparison with Rome; but, on closer acquaintance, I find that many of the buildings are antique and massive, though still the clear atmosphere, the bright sunshine, the light, cheerful hues of the stucco, and—as much as anything else, perhaps—the vivacious character

of the human life in the streets, take away the sense of its being an ancient city.

As we returned home over the Arno River, crossing the Ponte di Santa Trinitá, we were struck by the beautiful scene of the broad, calm river, with the palaces along its shores repeated in it, on either side, and the neighboring bridges, too, just as perfect in the tide beneath as in the air above—a city of dream and shadow so close to the actual one. God has a meaning, no doubt, in putting this spiritual symbol continually beside us.

Along the river, on both sides, as far as we could see, there was a row of brilliant lamps, which, in the far distance, looked like a cornice of golden light; and this also shone as brightly in the river's depths. The lilies of the evening, in the quarter where the sun had gone down, were very soft and beautiful, though not so gorgeous as thousands that I have seen in America. But I believe I must fairly confess that the Italian sky, in the daytime, is bluer and brighter than our own, and that the atmosphere has a quality of showing objects to better advantage. It is more than mere daylight; the magic of moonlight is somehow mixed up with it, although it is so transparent a medium of light.

This is a much more personal vision of a city. Hawthorne uses one simile to give us a better visual image of the countryside around Florence ("as if we were between two great waves of the tumultuous sea of hills") and another to communicate the effect of the gas lamps ("like a cornice of golden light"); and he employs a metaphor ("a city of dream and shadow") to evoke his impression of the reflections in the river. In fact, virtually all of the description serves to communicate or explain *Hawthorne's* impressions of the city; here, the writer wishes to evoke and is not interested in scientific exactitude.

Keep in mind that this rhetorical device allows you a certain amount of freedom of language, but it also allows you certain liberties in organization. In Hawthorne's passage, for example, the author put down in writing his impressions in whatever order they came to him. In more objectively written descriptions, however, it often makes sense to think spatially when writing a visual description. You might describe a scene from left to right or front to back, for example; you might start a description of a person with the head (and end with the feet).

In the following passage, Fyodor Dostoyevsky gives us both a spatial description and a barrage of sensory impressions.

In the first place, on entering this house, one passes into a very bare hall, and thence along a passage to a mean staircase. The reception room, however, is bright, clean, and spacious, and is lined with redwood and metalwork. But the scullery you would not care to see; it is greasy, dirty, and odoriferous, while the stairs are in rags, and the walls so covered with filth that the hand sticks fast wherever it touches them. Also, on each landing there is a medley of boxes, chairs, and dilapidated wardrobes; while the windows have had most of their panes shattered, and everywhere stand washtubs filled with dirt, litter, eggshells, and fish bladders. The smell is abominable. In short, the house is not a nice one.

As to the disposition of the rooms, I have described it to you already. True, they are convenient enough, yet every one of them has an atmosphere. I do not mean that they smell badly so much as that each of them seems to contain something which gives forth a rank, sickly sweet odor. At first the impression is an unpleasant one, but a couple of minutes will suffice to dissipate it, for the reason that everything here smells—people's clothes, hands, and everything else—and one grows accustomed to the rankness. Canaries, however, soon die in this house. A naval officer here has just bought his fifth. Birds cannot live long in such an air. Every morning, when fish or beef is being cooked, and washing and scrubbing are in progress, the house is filled with steam. Always, too, the kitchen is full of linen hanging out to dry; and since my room adjoins that apartment, the smell from the clothes causes me not a little annoyance. However, one can grow used to anything.

Note that Dostoyevsky's description first takes us through the ground floor and leads us up the staircase. Unlike the previous passages, this one appeals to our tactile ("so covered with filth that the hand sticks") and, even more prominently, olfactory senses. Choice of detail is important, and the choice of fish bladders, for example, conveys wonderfully the disgusting sights and smell. This is great writing—not only is the description effective, it's also humorous, thanks to the short comment at the end of each paragraph.

Laundry List for Description

- When possible, call on all five senses: visual, auditory, olfactory (smell), gustatory (taste), and tactile.
- Place the most striking examples at the beginnings and ends of your paragraphs (or essay) for maximum effect.
- Show, don't tell, using anecdotes and examples.
- Use concrete nouns and adjectives; nouns, not adjectives, should dominate.
- Concentrate on details that will convey the sense you're trying to get across most effectively. (Remember the fish bladders!)
- Employ figures of speech, especially similes, metaphors, and personification, when appropriate.
- When describing people, try to focus on distinctive mannerisms; if possible, you should go beyond physical appearance.
- Direct discourse (using dialogue or quotations) can be revealing and useful.
- A brief illustrative anecdote is worth a thousand words. Instead of simply using a general statement ("My friend Kai is a very generous person"), use an example ("My friend Kai is known for his generosity; the whole school knows about the time that he spent an entire weekend volunteering at a homeless shelter").

- To the extent possible, use action verbs. You could write, "The delightful aroma of chocolate chip cookies baking in the oven *crept around the corner and filled the den* with its sweetness" instead of just "The baking chocolate chip cookies *smelled* sweet."

Sample Description Question

Write an essay in which you describe your local shopping mall. Remember that you are not limited to physical descriptions. Once you've written your essay, show it to your AP teacher or tutor. You might want to show it to a fellow AP student for peer review.

Drill: Reflect on How You Could Use Description to Address the Following Topics

First decide the general feeling you'd like to convey, and second begin to list some specifics; don't forget examples or anecdotes. When describing people, go beyond just the physical.

TOPIC 1: A party

TOPIC 2: Your parents

TOPIC 3: A natural disaster (seen from personal experience or on television)

TOPIC 4: Your favorite place to relax

TOPIC 5: The campus of your school

NARRATION

A narrative is a story in which pieces of information are arranged in chronological order. Narration can be an effective expository technique. Decades after her experience in a Japanese internment camp, Jeanne Wakatsuki Houston decided to narrate her experiences before, during, and immediately after imprisonment. She did not want to tell the story just for the story's sake; she wanted to relay her experience to the public to exorcize personal demons and to raise public awareness about this period in history. Here is a passage from this personal narrative. The passage describes the period after the Wakatsuki family had lost their house in Ocean Park, California, when they were forced into detention.

> My own family, after three years of mess hall living, collapsed as an integrated unit. Whatever dignity or feeling of filial strength we may have known before December 1941 was lost, and we did not recover it until many years after the war, not until after Papa died and we began to come together, trying to fill the vacuum his passing left in all our lives.

The closing of the camps, in the fall of 1945, only aggravated what had begun inside. Papa had no money then and could not get work. Half of our family had already moved to the East Coast, where jobs had opened up for them. The rest of us were relocated into a former defense workers' housing project in Long Beach. In that small apartment there never was enough room for all of us to sit down for a meal. We ate in shifts, and I yearned all the more for our huge round table in Ocean Park.

Soon after we were released I wrote a paper for a seventh-grade journalism class, describing how we used to hunt grunion before the war. The whole family would go down to Ocean Park Beach after dark, when the grunion were running, and build a big fire on the sand. I would watch Papa and my older brothers splash through the moonlit surf to scoop out the fish, then we'd rush back to the house where Mama would fry them up and set the sizzling pan on the table, with soy sauce and horseradish, for a midnight meal. I ended the paper with this sentence: "The reason I want to remember this is because I know we'll never be able to do it again."

You may be asked to use personal narrative when writing your essays on the AP English Language and Composition Exam; and you will certainly be asked to *analyze* narratives that employ this rhetorical mode.

In the following passage, Booker T. Washington uses narrative to explain how his view on education developed. Watch for changes between the first- and third-person style of narration.

When a mere boy, I saw a young colored man, who had spent several years in school, sitting in a common cabin in the South, studying a French grammar. I noted the poverty, the untidiness, the want of system, and thrift that existed about the cabin, notwithstanding his knowledge of French and other academic subjects. Another time, when riding on the outer edges of a town in the South, I heard the sound of a piano coming from a cabin of the same kind. Contriving some excuse, I entered and began a conversation with the young colored woman who was playing, and who had recently returned from a boarding-school, where she had been studying instrumental music among other things. Despite the fact that her parents were living in a rented cabin, eating poorly cooked food, surrounded with poverty, and having almost none of the conveniences of life, she had persuaded them to rent a piano for four or five dollars per month. Many such instances as these, in connection with my own struggles, impressed upon me the importance of making a study of our needs as a race, and applying the remedy accordingly.

Some one may be tempted to ask, Has not the negro boy or girl as good a right to study a French grammar and instrumental music as the white youth? I answer, Yes, but in the present condition of the negro race in this country there is need of something more. Perhaps I may be forgiven for the seeming egotism if I mention the expansion of my own life partly as an example of what I mean. My earliest recollection is of a small one-room log hut on a large slave plantation in Virginia. After the close of the war, while working in the coal-mines of West Virginia for the support of my mother, I heard in some accidental way of the Hampton Institute.

When I learned that it was an institution where a black boy could study, could have a chance to work for his board, and at the same time be taught how to work and to realize the dignity of labor, I resolved to go there. Bidding my mother good-by, I started out one morning to find my way to Hampton, though I was almost penniless and had no definite idea where Hampton was. By walking, begging rides, and paying for a portion of the journey on the steam-cars, I finally succeeded in reaching the city of Richmond, Virginia. I was without money or friends. I slept under a sidewalk, and by working on a vessel next day I earned money to continue my way to the institute, where I arrived with a surplus of fifty cents. At Hampton I found the opportunity—in the way of buildings, teachers, and industries provided by the generous—to get training in the class-room and by practical touch with industrial life, to learn thrift, economy, and push. I was surrounded by an atmosphere of business, Christian influence, and a spirit of self-help that seemed to have awakened every faculty in me, and caused me for the first time to realize what it meant to be a man instead of a piece of property.

While there I resolved that when I had finished the course of training I would go into the far South, into the Black Belt of the South, and give my life to providing the same kind of opportunity for self-reliance and self-awakening that I had found provided for me at Hampton.

Notice that in the first paragraph, the narration slips briefly into the third person—Washington is telling the story of the girl, not his own. Likewise, Washington presents the story of the boy studying French from his point of view. In these two instances, Washington switches from first to third person with ease, so that the transition is optimally effective and unnoticeable. The second paragraph effortlessly transitions to a personal anecdote, which is continued in the third paragraph. The final paragraph justifies the narrative: Washington's life story leads to his commitment to establish his own institute—called the Tuskegee Normal and Industrial Institute—deep in the South.

Laundry List for Narration

- When possible, structure the events in chronological order.
- Make your story complete: make sure you have a beginning, middle, and end.
- Provide a realistic setting (typically at the beginning). Notice how Booker T. Washington provides a setting in this passage with just a few details: "a young colored man," "a common cabin in the South," "the poverty, the untidiness, the want of system, and thrift that existed about the cabin."
- Whenever possible, use action verbs; for example, write "the fighters *tumbled* to the ground," rather than "there *were* fallen soldiers on the ground."
- Provide concrete and specific details.
- Show, don't tell. This is another way of saying that you should use anecdotes and examples whenever possible.
- Establish a clear point of view—if it's clear who is narrating and why, then it will be easier to choose relevant details.
- Include appropriate amounts of direct discourse (dialogue or quotations).

Sample Narration Question

"A college education is not necessary for success." Relate an experience of someone you know (directly or indirectly) that defends, challenges, or qualifies this statement. Once you've written your essay, show it to your AP teacher or tutor. You might want to show it to a fellow AP student for peer review.

Drill: Reflect on How You Could Use Narration to Address the Following Topics

Think of a personal experience (or an experience of someone you know) that pertains to the topic. Determine how you would best describe this experience. Come up with a few anecdotes or examples.

TOPIC 1: Danger when eating becomes an obsession

TOPIC 2: Hardship is a necessary part of our education

INDUCTION AND DEDUCTION

Induction:
PART to WHOLE

Deduction:
WHOLE to PART

You will probably find that the rhetorical modes of induction and deduction are most useful when you're writing the argument essay, although they will be helpful on the rhetorical analysis essay too.

Induction is a process in which specific examples are used to reach a general conclusion. If you took the AP European History Exam and did not like the experience, and then took the AP Calculus BC Exam and did not like the experience, you might arrive at the following general conclusion: AP Exams are always an unpleasant experience. If, when you were young, you found that you didn't like broccoli, asparagus, or cabbage, your parents might have concluded that you didn't like vegetables. In both cases, the conclusion would be of questionable value because there is not enough evidence to justify the generalization.

Assume that you want to argue that your English teacher is in a bad mood every time the Boston Red Sox lose a game to the New York Yankees. You could substantiate that generalization by recalling certain tantrums that he or she threw and comparing those days with the dates of Red Sox losses. This would substantiate your claim but not prove it, especially if you didn't even know whether your teacher saw the games. After all, what if something else happened to coincide with the games and was the real cause of his or her bad temper, such as traffic jams on the way home from school?

We tend to believe in generalizations arrived at through induction, whether or not they can actually be proved. The Food and Drug Administration, for example, has to follow the inductive reasoning of scientists; just because a certain drug produced the desired results—and didn't produce an undesirable result, such as death—20,000 experimental cases does not prove that the same results will occur when 20,000,000 people take the drug.

Deduction involves the use of a generalization to draw a conclusion about a specific case. For example, if you read in the morning paper that all schools in your county would be closed that day because of inclement weather, you could conclude that you won't have to go to school. You just used deductive reasoning.

Laundry List for Induction and Deduction

- Induction proceeds from the specific to a generalization. For example, your classmate Ricky plays on the school's football and basketball teams, and he has ice hockey posters all over his bedroom at home. You could conclude that Ricky likes all sports in general.
- Make sure you have sufficient evidence to support your claim.
- Deduction is the process of applying a generalization to a specific case. For example, your cousin Jennifer told you that she hates dancing and loud music. From this, you could safely say that she probably wouldn't want to come with you to the hot new nightclub opening this weekend.

- Make sure your generalization has sufficient credibility before applying it to specific cases. For example, it would be an unfair generalization to assume that all baseball players use or have used anabolic steroids.

Sample Induction and Deduction Question

Write a short essay in which you analyze the following statement using induction or deduction: *Contemporary films are a reflection of today's values.* Once you've written your essay, show it to your AP teacher or tutor. You might want to show it to a fellow AP student for peer review.

Drill: Reflect on How You Could Use Induction to Substantiate the Following Theses

THESIS 1: Academic honesty is alive and well.

THESIS 2: High schools don't really care about their mission to educate.

THESIS 3: Computer games have beneficial effects.

THESIS 4: Children generally demonstrate more wisdom than their parents.

In this chapter, we looked at a few more rhetorical modes that will be extremely useful to you on test day. Remember that these can be used in combination with each other *and,* further complicating matters, in combination with the modes in the previous chapter. Hopefully, these modes have given you some ideas about how you can structure your essays into coherent works that the test readers will understand and maybe even enjoy.

Here we are at the end of the review section of the book. You are now ready to take the second practice test; depending on how you did on the first one, you may have been dreading this moment, but we know that once you begin, you'll see that you know a lot more than you think you do! If you've worked through the book up to this point and complete these practice exams, you'll certainly be ready for test day.

Good luck!

REFLECT

Respond to the following questions:

- For which topics discussed in this chapter do you feel you have achieved sufficient mastery to answer multiple-choice questions correctly?
- For which topics discussed in this chapter do you feel you have achieved sufficient mastery to discuss effectively in an essay?
- For which topics discussed in this chapter do you feel you need more work before you can answer multiple-choice questions correctly?
- For which topics discussed in this chapter do you feel you need more work before you can discuss them effectively in an essay?
- What parts of this chapter are you going to re-review?
- Will you seek further help, outside of this book (such as a teacher, tutor, or AP Students website), on any of the topics in this chapter—and, if so, on which ones?

Chapter 11
Rhetorical Fallacies

The AP will test whether you understand logical fallacies. However, you are unlikely to be tested on the exact terms for the different fallacies.

THE RHETORICAL FALLACY TRAP

Have you ever seen commercials or billboard ads showing a happy, carefree crowd walking on a blissful beach at a 5-star resort? Don't they always seem to be enjoying a wonderful vacation, enticing you to want to also take a vacation at that same resort?

Ads like this rely on rhetorical fallacy: a way to persuade you to buy into what they are selling. They don't explain the advantages of the resort. Instead, they promote the resort by showcasing a fun-loving couple on the beach. The people in the ad might not be anything like you; their lives might be completely different from yours. Who's to say your experience would be the same if you were to visit the same resort? This is a prime example of how rhetorical fallacy is used in everyday life.

A rhetorical fallacy is basically faulty reasoning leading to a conclusion the advertiser, author, or speaker wants you to make. They pop up often—in ads, in statements by politicians, in appeals from charities, in arguments from your own friends and family. Skilled communicators such as political speech writers use them deliberately. Others use them unconsciously—the conclusion seems so obvious to them that "everybody else has one" sounds like irrefutable evidence. You might have used rhetorical fallacies subconsciously too.

Rhetorical fallacies also pop up on the AP English Language and Composition Exam, since this test covers how language works and how it is used. A rhetorical fallacy uses (or rather, *mis*-uses) language in order to trick you into accepting the author's conclusion. This conclusion appears to be truth at first, but the evidence supporting it crumbles when your active reading or listening skills kick in. You then ask yourself, "*why* should I do or believe this?".

> On the test, you might find rhetorical fallacies lurking in the passages for the multiple-choice questions or in the sources provided for the synthesis and analysis essays. You need to be able to recognize them so you won't be led astray in your answers. You also need to avoid them in your own essays.

Spotting and Avoiding Rhetorical Fallacies

Think of a rhetorical fallacy as "fake evidence." It seems to support a conclusion that the author wants the reader to accept, but—on close examination—it doesn't really lead to that conclusion.

You can identify rhetorical fallacies (and avoid them in your own work) by following this process:

1. Identify the conclusion. What position does the author want you to accept? What action does the author want you to take? What inference does he or she want you to draw?
2. Identify the evidence. How does the author lead you to that conclusion? What does the author present as evidence that the conclusion is correct?
3. Examine the evidence. Is it
   a. relevant to the conclusion?
   b. accurate?
   c. credible?
   d. logical?
   e. complete?

If it's not, then you've likely encountered a rhetorical fallacy.

Common Rhetorical Fallacies

Let's look at some common types of rhetorical fallacies so you can understand how they try to mislead you. The name of each specific fallacy is given, but what's most important for the exam is being able to recognize faulty reasoning when you see it, and avoiding it in the essays you write.

Emphasizing the Person

In this class of rhetorical fallacies, the evidence focuses on the person who supports a conclusion, not on the merits of the conclusion itself.

***Ad Populum* or "bandwagon":** A certain political candidate is ahead in the polls. Since most people are going to vote for him, you should too. Otherwise you'll just be wasting your vote.

The happy crowd on the beach described at the beginning of this chapter is another instance of the "bandwagon" fallacy. All of these people are having a great vacation at this resort; you should go there, and you'll have fun too.

The conclusion is an action the author (or the advertiser) wants you to take—vote for this candidate, book a vacation at this resort. No support is provided to explain *why* the candidate is the best choice, or *why* the resort is better than others. The very thin evidence is only that others are doing it.

Argument from Authority: Dr. X recommends this medication to his patients, or well-known musician Y always drives this brand of car. Are they being paid by the manufacturers to endorse those products, or do the products have attributes that really make them superior? You'll never know. This rhetorical fallacy focuses solely on the credentials or fame of the person recommending the product, without saying anything about the product itself.

And watch those credentials—is Dr. X really a recognized specialist in the illness the medication is intended to treat? What does musician Y know about cars?

You're My Hero—or Not

"Argument from Authority" is really *"Ad Hominum"* turned upside down.

***Ad Hominem*:** This rhetorical fallacy turns to the other side of the coin and points out negative characteristics of the person who promotes an idea or action. By implication, the action is as negative as the person who endorses it. The mayor was caught plagiarizing an essay in college and was accused of embezzlement by a former employer. Therefore, his claim that municipal taxes must increase to cover necessary road repairs has to be a lie and an attempt to steal taxpayers' money. Nothing is said about the actual condition of the roads.

Dogmatism: The conclusion must be correct because the author or speaker says it is and she can't possibly be wrong. After all, she is an internationally recognized authority on the subject, or she is the CEO of the most profitable company on the planet. She wouldn't have risen to that position if she were ever wrong. No other reasons are presented to support the conclusion, and no opposing viewpoints are even considered.

Presenting Only Part of the Truth

Equivocation: This type of fallacy leaves out facts that a reader or listener would need in order to make a thorough assessment of the conclusion. Equivocation often relies on ambiguous definitions of words.

For example, your home insurer might say that for an extra $50 premium, you'll be covered for $100,000 in water damage. Look at the "definitions" section of your policy, though, and you might see that the insurer considers "water damage" to be damage caused by a sewer backup. "Overland flooding" or "ice dams on roof" are separate categories that are not covered. You probably assumed those events would all result in "water damage," and the insurer is counting on that to lead you to the conclusion that it's worth spending the extra $50.

> In the movie *Pink Panther*, Inspector Clouseau enters a quaint European hotel and, upon spying a cute little dog, asks the owner, "Does your dog bite?" The manager responds, "No," and Clouseau attempts to pet the dog, which growls and bites him. "You told me that your dog does not bite!" exclaims Clouseau. "That's not my dog," responds the owner.

Sentimental Appeals: Charities often use this tactic when they ask for donations. Poor, starving children living in deplorable surroundings, or clear-cut hillsides that were once covered by beautiful forests—these scenes appeal to your emotions rather than your intellect. This rhetorical fallacy omits rational explanations about why the charity deserves your donation. What has it achieved recently to right the wrong it presents? How much of your donation is used for its programs, and how much goes into executive salaries or "team-building" events? How much is it spending in order to raise the donations it's seeking?

Arousing Fear

Slippery Slope: It may seem minor now, but the end result will inevitably be a catastrophe. According to this rhetorical fallacy, if you eat at a fast-food takeout once, pretty soon you'll never want to eat healthy, nourishing home-cooked meals again. Therefore, you can never allow yourself to eat at a fast-food takeout, not even once. The author uses the fear of the disaster waiting at the bottom of the slippery slope to trick the reader into agreeing that the first action must not be allowed to occur.

Scare Tactics: Here the speaker or author is trying to frighten you into agreeing with him. If you don't commit to a two-year contract, your monthly rate won't be protected and prices are going to go through the roof in the next couple of years. Who says? On what evidence does he make that prediction?

Weakening an Opposing Argument

These rhetorical fallacies present an opposing view in such a weak light that almost nobody would agree with it. Readers would, instead, accept the author's apparently stronger conclusion.

Red Herring: Instead of addressing the key issues of an opposing argument, a red herring fallacy focuses attention on an insignificant or irrelevant factor. For instance, you should avoid eating green vegetables (the conclusion) because of the risk of salmonella contamination (the red herring). This fallacy avoids the main points of the opposing argument in favor of green vegetables (such as nutritional content and health benefits).

Straw Man: The writer creates a straw man—something that's easy to knock down and tear apart—as the opposing viewpoint. The straw man could be either an over-simplification of an opponent's position, or a completely fictitious argument. In contrast, the writer's conclusion seems strong and reasonable.

For instance, suppose the mayor wants taxpayers to fund a new bridge that will lead directly to a large new subdivision. People who oppose this expense, she says, don't believe the new bridge is necessary because subdivision residents can simply spend an extra half hour driving downtown, across the existing bridge and back up the other side of the river to the new subdivision. That opposing viewpoint is pretty easy to knock down if you live, work, or shop in the new subdivision, so of course you favor a new bridge.

Making Inaccurate Connections

Faulty analogy: One thing is compared with a second thing, but the comparison is exaggerated or misleading or unreasonable. Nevertheless, that comparison colors the reader's impression of the first thing. "Hiking on that trail is like descending into a dungeon of horrors from which you might never return." Perhaps it's just a challenging trail that leads through thick woods and would give you a good workout. But not many people would try it after hearing the speaker's comparison.

Reverse Causation

Causal arguments are often faulty because the reverse causation is equally plausible. For example, "Eating too much chocolate can make you depressed." Well, it's just as likely that depressed people might feel the urge to eat too much chocolate. If the author says "A caused B," ask yourself, "Is it also possible that B caused A?"

Faulty causality (also called ***Post hoc ergo propter hoc***)**:** This type of fallacy assumes that because one event happened shortly before another, the first event must have caused the second. (That's what the long Latin name refers to, by the way). "She wore her old Brand X runners instead of her new Brand Y runners, therefore she lost the race." Well, maybe. But perhaps she lost the race because she hadn't trained sufficiently, or because her knee was sore that day, or because others were simply faster. No evidence is presented to prove that the first event caused the second.

Twisting the Language

Begging the Question: In this rhetorical fallacy, an assumption which is not proven is used as evidence that the conclusion is correct. For instance, "high-altitude skiing is such a dangerous sport (the evidence) that no one under the age of 18 should be allowed to do it (the conclusion)." That might be a logical argument if the writer had proven—with statistics or with specific examples—that high-altitude skiing is dangerous for young people in particular. But he doesn't. He states that assumption as if it were a proven fact and then uses the assumption to prove his conclusion.

Circular Argument: This fallacy says essentially the same thing in both the conclusion and in the evidence that allegedly supports it. For example, someone might say that Sally cares about other people (the conclusion) because she is always willing to help them (the evidence). Someone who is always willing to help others obviously cares about them. Both the conclusion and the evidence describe the same idea. If the speaker had given specific examples of times when Sally helped someone else, and other actions that show she cares about others, he would have provided more credible proof for his conclusion.

Rhetorical fallacies in this category can be tough to spot, particularly when you're reading quickly under pressure. You need keen active reading skills to be able to say, "wait a minute, how do you know that piece of evidence is true?" or "didn't your evidence and your conclusion just say the same thing in different words?".

Mismatch Between Evidence and Conclusion

Missing the point: The author offers evidence that supports a conclusion—it's just not the same conclusion that the author reaches. Imagine a presenter with gorgeous slides of meadows and grasslands in the northern plains, dense forests and subarctic tundra—the preferred habitats of grizzly bears. She cites research that reveals the grizzly population is declining and being pushed into smaller and smaller territories as humans take over the bears' habitats for their own uses. As a result, she continues, we should experiment with relocating small groups of grizzlies to see if they can adapt to habitats where they won't get so much competition from humans for use of the land. She suggests wetlands and high up on western mountains.

Her evidence does support the conclusions that we should take steps to protect the remaining grizzly population and should be more conscious of the impact our land use has on other creatures. However, it doesn't lead to a radical relocation scheme that ignores factors such as food sources, climate, and the bears' likely reaction.

Non Sequitur: This Latin term means, "it doesn't follow." In this rhetorical fallacy, the conclusion is not logically related to the evidence that preceded it. "Violent crime in this city has increased by 10 percent year over year for the past five years. Adding to the police force hasn't improved the situation. Therefore, we should build more private schools."

What do private schools have to do with the violent crime rate? Perhaps more than half of violent crimes occur around schools, private schools have the money for much better security measures, and the existing private schools all have long waiting lists. The author doesn't explain that, though; he has left serious gaps in the connection between his evidence and his conclusion.

It's easy to fall into this fallacy in your own work when the conclusion seems obvious to you. Think about your readers, though—would they need a few more steps before they could follow you to your conclusion?

Unstated Assumptions

Conclusions in this class of rhetorical fallacies rest on assumptions that the author doesn't even state, let alone prove. These, too, can be tough to spot in a pressure-cooker exam setting.

False Dichotomy: This rhetorical fallacy assumes a black-and-white world in which there is no middle ground, no other alternative. "If we don't launch a preemptive attack and destroy the enemy first, they will destroy us." No consideration is given to other possibilities, such as a diplomatic solution or a small-scale limited strike.

Hasty Generalization: Here the author or speaker assumes that a limited experience foreshadows the entire experience. The result is insufficient evidence to support the conclusion. "I could tell from the first few minutes that the movie was going to be unbearably boring, so I left rather than waste any more of my time." Maybe the director deliberately starts off slowly in order to intensify viewers' reactions to the terrifying monster that is about to appear.

Non-testable hypothesis: In this rhetorical fallacy, anything that has not been proven false is assumed to be true; the author doesn't need to prove it's true. For example, suppose an environmental group claims that average temperatures across the entire North American continent would fall by 1° Celsius if we switched completely to renewable energy. Since we have never abandoned fossil fuels entirely, it's impossible to prove that the group's claim is false. Therefore, the argument assumes it must be true.

You Can't Prove I'm Not Right

The absence of evidence to the contrary does not, in fact, prove anything.

Drill—Catch the Rhetorical Fallacies

The following examples are similar to parts of passages you might encounter in the multiple-choice section of the AP English Language and Composition Exam, or to parts of the sources given in the essay questions. Before you read the explanation that follows each selection, try to identify how the author is misleading you into reaching the conclusion he or she wants you to accept. Remember to look for the claim or action or belief that the author is endorsing. Then find and assess the evidence the author presents. And think about how your answer on the exam might be different depending on whether you noticed the rhetorical fallacy or not.

(Hint: One example does not contain a rhetorical fallacy. See if you can identify that one too.)

In this selection, a detective is questioning a woman in order to gather evidence about a crime he is investigating.

> … it is on me that all this weight lies. If the police begin investigations they come close upon the fact that I went there to meet a man whom my husband has forbidden me to meet. Any little turn of evidence that involves me, any little accident that obliges me to admit it, and I am lost,"—her voice thrilled and pleaded.
>
> "It is you who are lost," he echoed dully. "I can understand how you feel. If I can ease your burden or lessen the anxiety you suffer from, you may depend upon me, Mrs. Wilder. This matter is a dark road where I, too, walk blind, not knowing the path I follow, but, at least, I can give you my word that under no circumstances shall I be led to mention your name. You can be sure of that, Mrs. Wilder. If I can add your trouble to my own burden I shall not feel its weight, …
>
> Excerpt from *The Pointing Man: A Burmese Mystery*
> by Marjorie Douie, 1920

Now suppose a multiple-choice question asks:

> What technique does the detective use to try to gain Mrs. Wilder's confidence?
>
> (A) Deceit
> (B) Sympathy
> (C) Threats
> (D) Empathy
> (E) Begging

What conclusion is Mrs. Wilder supposed to reach?—that it's safe to answer the detective's questions. He won't tell anyone who gave him the information, so Mr. Wilder won't find out that his wife met the forbidden man. What evidence does the detective offer to support that conclusion? None. Mrs. Wilder can count on him keeping her name out of the investigation because she can depend on him (circular argument). She should believe him because he understands how she feels (non-testable hypothesis) and because he says she can (dogmatism).

Choices (C) and (E) are clearly not supported in the passage. If you didn't notice the rhetorical fallacies, though, you might be tempted to choose (D) or perhaps (B), both of which are incorrect. If you spotted the faulty evidence, you'd know the correct choice is (A). The detective's only objective is to get answers to his questions, and he'll tell this frightened woman whatever she needs to hear before she'll answer them.

This paragraph appears in "Maintenance and Safety of Hybrid and Plug-In Electric Vehicles," a resource from the U.S. Department of Energy's Vehicle Technologies Office. It is the type of source you might find in the synthesis essay question.

> **Safety Requirements**
>
> HEVs [hybrid electric vehicles], PHEVs [plug-in hybrid electric vehicles], and EVs [all-electric vehicles] have high-voltage electrical systems that typically range from 100 to 600 volts. Their battery packs are encased in sealed shells and meet testing standards that subject batteries to conditions such as overcharge, vibration, extreme temperatures, short circuit, humidity, fire, collision, and water immersion. Manufacturers design these vehicles with insulated high-voltage lines and safety features that deactivate the electrical system when they detect a collision or short circuit. EVs tend to have a lower center of gravity than conventional vehicles, making them more stable and less likely to roll over.

Suppose the synthesis prompt asked you to defend, challenge, or qualify the claim that electric vehicles are unsafe. How would you evaluate this excerpt when you're choosing sources for your essay? Is it a strong, reliable source, or does it contain faulty reasoning that misleads you into accepting a conclusion?

Start by identifying the conclusion: electric vehicles are safer than you might think because of the safety features designers have built into them. Now what evidence does the author give to support that conclusion? The selection lists specific examples of safety features (such as sealed cases and automatic shutoff) intended to shield people from the dangers of high voltage. It also describes a design feature (low center of gravity) that helps prevent instability and rollovers. And it acknowledges the high voltage instead of trying to hide the danger.

This author gives relevant, specific, logical evidence supporting the conclusion, and does not resort to rhetorical fallacies. This would be a good choice as one of your sources.

The following excerpt from a mobile app's End User License Agreement (EULA) illustrates the type of source you might see in the analysis essay question, for which you're asked to identify the strategies an author uses to achieve his or her purpose.

> Bazaar Bonanza is a free, powerful, user-friendly tool to get you to the best deals on things that will make your life easier, more fulfilling and just plain more fun. Millions of users are saving money and time on products they want and need with Bazaar Bonanza. We take your privacy very seriously, and are committed to providing you with choice and transparency. We'd like you to know about the benefits you'll gain when you create an account and download our app.
>
> In order to make sure you never miss a great deal, we track your location and maintain a database of your favorite places and the times and days you usually visit them. We also access your contacts, your messages and your emails because we know you'll want to share amazing bargains with your friends and family members. Since you'll want to return to the same shops that offered outstanding deals in the past, we track and store data about all of the purchases you make via a mobile payment service. Over time, we build a complete profile of your travel and shopping habits. So we can provide you with an ever-expanding universe of wonderful products and services at unbelievable prices, we share your profile with other companies that may be of interest to you. We also give those companies access to your reviews and endorsements so they can share them with other users who may be looking for similar deals.

What rhetorical strategies is this author using to achieve her purpose of gaining new users? Are rhetorical fallacies among those strategies?

This excerpt is full of rhetorical fallacies. First is the bandwagon ("millions of users") and then dogmatism—there's no evidence that the company values the privacy of its users or that it is offering them any choice. It's true because the company says it's true. The commitment to transparency is actually well supported, though, in the extensive list of data the company collects and descriptions of what it does with that data. Next comes a scare tactic (missing a great deal). Then there are a few *non sequiturs*—for instance, if you want to share information about bargains with your friends, why does it follow that the app needs access to your contacts and messages? Throughout the entire excerpt is the unstated assumption that your desire to find a deal outweighs your desire to protect your personal information.

This is the type of prompt you might see in the argument essay question:

> In order to save time, reduce costs, and avoid security risks, many companies are encouraging their employees to substitute technology (such as video conferencing) for business trips that can involve long absences, expensive travel, and potentially dangerous locations. In contrast, some executives and sales professionals claim there's no substitute for the personal relationships they can develop through meeting someone face to face or attending an industry event in person. Political leaders often seem to agree, traveling halfway around the world for a meeting that might last only an hour or two.

> Think about the trade-off between savings and security on the one hand, and the gains that can result from an in-person meeting on the other. Then write an essay explaining your position on whether travel is worth the costs and risks. Use appropriate evidence from your reading, experience, or observations to support your argument.

Before you read the suggestions below, consider what position you would take on this question. Then think about the conclusions you'll need to persuade readers so they can follow your argument and eventually agree with it.

You could argue for using technology, for in-person travel or—most likely in this case—for a combination of the two. You might say, for example, that travel is justified for an initial meeting or two in order to establish a personal relationship, but after that, little more would be gained from the expense and potential risks of traveling to meet in person. Electronic communication or phone calls would serve the purpose.

To lead readers to agree with this argument, you'll need to get them to concede that travel is expensive, time-consuming, and depending on the destination, can be dangerous. They'll have to acknowledge the importance of saving money, saving time, and avoiding risks. They also need to accept that an in-person relationship can form a foundation that leads to a better outcome in later long-distance dealings.

Now what evidence can you use to support each of those conclusions? And how can you avoid rhetorical fallacies in presenting that evidence? This prompt is particularly vulnerable to fallacies that emphasize the person or group instead of the merits of an idea, to fallacies that arouse fear, and to mismatches between the evidence and the conclusion.

Under the time pressure of the exam, you won't have time to do a thorough assessment of your evidence for each conclusion. But as you're writing, you can ask yourself if you're really addressing the conclusion itself, or only the people who would advocate that course of action. Are you trying to frighten readers by describing the consequences that might result from not following your recommendation? Have you left any gaps in the evidence that leads to your conclusion? Are you covering the key issues and most relevant aspects of the topic?

Don't let clever rhetorical fallacies lead you down the wrong path!

Rhetorical fallacies can be very convincing. They're also easy errors to make in your own writing, particularly when you have a strong opinion about a subject, when you're making broad claims or when you're experiencing stress during an exam. By training yourself to think in terms of relevant, complete, logically presented evidence, you can avoid falling into the trap of believing—or creating—rhetorical fallacies.

Another Course? Of Course!

If you can't get enough AP English Language and Composition and want to review this material with an expert, we also offer an online Cram Course that you can sign up for here: www.princetonreview.com/college/ap-test-prep.

REFLECT

Respond to the following questions:

- Do you understand how rhetorical fallacies work? How they can trick people?
- Are there any types of rhetorical fallacies that you are particularly susceptible to believing?
- Are there any types of rhetorical fallacies that you tend to use automatically when you're trying to convince a listener or reader to agree with your argument?
- What are the characteristics of valid evidence?
- What techniques could you use to avoid rhetorical fallacies in your own work?
- How can you avoid rhetorical fallacies when you're writing essays under the time pressure of the AP English Language and Composition Exam?
- For which topics in this chapter do you feel you need more practice or more examples?

Part VI
Practice Test 2

Practice Test 2

AP® English Language and Composition Exam

SECTION I: Multiple-Choice Questions

DO NOT OPEN THIS BOOKLET UNTIL YOU ARE TOLD TO DO SO.

At a Glance

Total Time
1 hour

Number of Questions
45

Percent of Total Grade
45%

Writing Instrument
Pencil required

Instructions

Section I of this examination contains 45 multiple-choice questions. Fill in only the ovals for numbers 1 through 45 on your answer sheet.

Indicate all of your answers to the multiple-choice questions on the answer sheet. No credit will be given for anything written in this exam booklet, but you may use the booklet for notes or scratch work. After you have decided which of the suggested answers is best, completely fill in the corresponding oval on the answer sheet. Give only one answer to each question. If you change an answer, be sure that the previous mark is erased completely. Here is a sample question and answer.

Sample Question

Chicago is a
(A) state
(B) city
(C) country
(D) continent
(E) village

Sample Answer

(A) 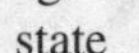 (C) (D) (E)

Use your time effectively, working as quickly as you can without losing accuracy. Do not spend too much time on any one question. Go on to other questions and come back to the ones you have not answered if you have time. It is not expected that everyone will know the answers to all the multiple-choice questions.

Many candidates wonder whether or not to guess the answers to questions about which they are not certain. Multiple-choice scores are based on the number of questions answered correctly. Points are not deducted for incorrect answers, and no points are awarded for unanswered questions. Because points are not deducted for incorrect answers, you are encouraged to answer all multiple-choice questions. On any questions you do not know the answer to, you should eliminate as many choices as you can, and then select the best answer among the remaining choices.

GO ON TO THE NEXT PAGE.

This page intentionally left blank.

ENGLISH LANGUAGE AND COMPOSITION
SECTION I
Time—1 hour

Directions: This part consists of selections from prose works and questions on their content, form, and style. After reading each passage, choose the best answer to each question and completely fill in the corresponding oval on the answer sheet.

Note: Pay particular attention to the requirement of questions that contain the words NOT, LEAST, or EXCEPT.

Questions 1–11. Read the following passage carefully before you choose your answers.

This is from the Lincoln-Douglas Debates of 1858.

Now, I hold that Illinois had a right to abolish and prohibit slavery as she did, and I hold that Kentucky has the same right to continue and protect slavery that Illinois had to abolish it. I hold that New York had as much right to abolish slavery as Virginia has to continue it, and that each and every State of this Union is a sovereign power, with the right to do as it pleases upon this question of slavery, and upon all its domestic institutions. Slavery is not the only question which comes up in this controversy. There is a far more important one to you, and that is, what shall be done with the free negro? We have settled the slavery question as far as we are concerned; we have prohibited it in Illinois forever, and in doing so, I think we have done wisely, and there is no man in the State who would be more strenuous in his opposition to the introduction of slavery than I would; but when we settled it for ourselves, we exhausted all our power over that subject. We have done our whole duty, and can do no more. We must leave each and every other State to decide for itself the same question. In relation to the policy to be pursued toward the free negroes, we have said that they shall not vote; whilst Maine, on the other hand, has said that they shall vote. Maine is a sovereign State, and has the power to regulate the qualifications of voters within her limits. I would never consent to confer the right of voting and of citizenship upon a negro, but still I am not going to quarrel with Maine for differing from me in opinion. Let Maine take care of her own negroes, and fix the qualifications of her own voters to suit herself, without interfering with Illinois, and Illinois will not interfere with Maine. So with the State of New York. She allows the negro to vote provided he owns two hundred and fifty dollars' worth of property, but not otherwise. While I would not make any distinction whatever between a negro who held property and one who did not, yet if the sovereign State of New York chooses to make that distinction it is her business and not mine, and I will not quarrel with her for it. She can do as she pleases on this question if she minds her own business, and we will do the same thing. Now, my friends, if we will only act conscientiously and rigidly upon this great principle of popular sovereignty, which guarantees to each State and Territory the right to do as it pleases on all things, local and domestic, instead of Congress interfering, we will continue at peace one with another. Why should Illinois be at war with Missouri, or Kentucky with Ohio, or Virginia, with New York, merely because their institutions differ? Our fathers intended that our institutions should differ. They knew that the North and the South, having different climates, productions, and interests, required different institutions. This doctrine of Mr. Lincoln, of uniformity among the institutions of the different States, is a new doctrine, never dreamed of by Washington, Madison, or the framers of this government. Mr. Lincoln and the Republican party set themselves up as wiser than these men who made this government, which has flourished for seventy years under the principle of popular sovereignty, recognizing the right of each State to do as it pleased. Under that principle, we have grown from a nation of three or four millions to a nation of about thirty millions of people; we have crossed the Allegheny mountains and filled up the whole Northwest, turning the prairie into a garden, and building up churches and schools, thus spreading civilization and Christianity where before there was nothing but savage barbarism. Under that principle we have become, from a feeble nation, the most powerful on the face of the earth, and if we only adhere to that principle, we can go forward increasing in territory, in power, in strength, and in glory until the Republic of America shall be the north star that shall guide the friend of freedom throughout the civilized world. And why can we not adhere to the great principle of self-government upon which our institutions were originally based? I believe that this new doctrine preached by Mr. Lincoln and his party will dissolve the Union if it succeeds. They are trying to array all the Northern States in one body against the South, to excite a sectional war between the free States and the slave States, in order that the one or the other may be driven to the wall.

GO ON TO THE NEXT PAGE.

1. In this passage the speaker's purpose is to
   (A) analyze the causes of slavery
   (B) argue in favor of states' rights
   (C) criticize individual states
   (D) describe the advantages of a federal government
   (E) argue in favor of slavery

2. Which of the following best describes the tone of the passage?
   (A) Mock enthusiasm
   (B) Righteous indignation
   (C) Well-reasoned polemic
   (D) Objective rationalization
   (E) Ironic detachment

3. In the first two sentences (lines 1–8), the speaker grounds his central idea on which of the following rhetorical strategies?
   (A) Inductive reasoning
   (B) Deductive reasoning
   (C) Description
   (D) Classification
   (E) Appeal to ignorance

4. In line 36, the word "it" most closely refers to
   (A) "property" (line 33)
   (B) "State" (line 34)
   (C) "the State of New York" (line 34)
   (D) "distinction" (line 34)
   (E) "quarrel" (line 35)

5. The sentence that begins "Now, my friends, if we will..." (lines 37–42) contains all of the following EXCEPT
   (A) a classification
   (B) an appeal to a principle
   (C) a call to action
   (D) a definition
   (E) an accusation

6. The author suggests that which of the following is true of Maine, Illinois, and New York?
   (A) They have relatively liberal policies toward "negroes."
   (B) They prove that popular sovereignty has been generally successful.
   (C) They exemplify the principle of popular sovereignty.
   (D) They create inconsistent laws for both "negroes" and citizens.
   (E) They create laws concerned more with wealth than justice.

7. The speaker substantiates his central idea with
   (A) clever anecdotes
   (B) innovative symbols
   (C) unusual paradoxes
   (D) extended metaphors
   (E) appeal to authority

8. From the passage, it appears that the speaker's personal view is that African Americans
   (A) should be slaves and should not be allowed to hold property
   (B) should not be slaves and should be allowed to vote
   (C) should not be free but should be allowed to hold some property
   (D) should be free but not allowed to vote
   (E) should be allowed to hold property and to vote

9. The author implies that Abraham Lincoln's policies would have all of the following potential negative effects EXCEPT
   (A) consolidating power
   (B) hindering westward expansion
   (C) dissolving the Union
   (D) initiating war
   (E) hindering population growth

10. In the final lines of the passage, the speaker attempts to win over his audience by
    (A) inspiring confidence
    (B) shifting blame
    (C) instilling fear
    (D) reconciling differences
    (E) overstating a problem

11. The development of the passage can best be described as the
    (A) argument for a particular solution to a political problem
    (B) rebuttal of those who challenge the authority of Congress
    (C) explanation of the failings of a political opponent
    (D) exploration of the various meanings of a universal principle
    (E) comparison between two political entities

GO ON TO THE NEXT PAGE.

Questions 12–23. Read the following passage carefully before you choose your answers.

This passage is excerpted from a recent work that examines popular conceptions of the history of medieval Spain.

If you have read anything about medieval Spain, then you probably know about *convivencia*—the peaceful "coexistence" of Muslims, Christians, and Jews for nearly eight hundred years on the Iberian peninsula. The story is invariably told in the same way: "once upon a time,"[1] after the Muslim invasion of the Iberian peninsula in 711, a "culture of tolerance"[2] was created among Muslims, Christians, and Jews. Tolerant adherents of these three Abrahamic faiths shared philosophical and scientific learning, translating previously unknown sources (especially the works of Aristotle) for the rest of Europe. "But," the author or narrator intones in his gravest voice, "this world too quickly vanished. Greed, fear, and intolerance swept it away. Puritanical judgments and absolutism snuffed out the light of learning." Then the author or narrator laments the loss of this vanished world: "it was truly a bright light in what was largely a dark and ignorant medieval landscape. Its loss is one of the great tragedies in history."[3] This is almost always followed by a didactic—and dramatic—moral about the relevance of medieval Spain for contemporary problems: "Humanity has never completely found the way back. Medieval Spain might help point the way."[4] This is a fairy tale for adults who, like children, know nothing about the actual (medieval) world it attempts to describe. The story of *convivencia* fulfills the requirements of the genre, replete as it is with exotic journeys in faraway lands and epic battles between noble heroes and depraved villains. And like all fairy tales, this story of *convivencia* tells us much more about the world of storytelling in which it was created than about the historical past or objective reality, on which it is only loosely based.

While some of the recent books on *convivencia* have gestured in the direction of scholarly discourse, more often than not, they cannot resist the temptation to indulge our basest tendencies to Orientalism and exoticism. In nearly every popular recounting of *convivencia,* images of an Islamic *locus amoenus* abound: we hear of gardens, bath-houses, exotic fruits, and enchanting mosques. Chris Lowney, in *A Vanished World,* emphasized that "daily life was transformed as exotic new species like cotton, figs, spinach, and watermelon burgeoned in fields nourished by new irrigation techniques." The "luxury and sophistication" of the Islamic city of Cordoba "undoubtedly surpassed anything found elsewhere in Europe." Maria Rosa Menocal's syrupy confection, *The Ornament of the World,* simmers under a thick layer of Orientalized cheese. Some of her chapter titles themselves suffice to prove the point, "The Palaces of Memory," "The Mosque and the Palm Tree," "A Grand Vizier, A Grand City," "The Gardens of Memory," and "Sailing Away, Riding Away." And when these authors describe Islam, it is with the wonderment and delight of a tourist. We, their audience, are supposed to share in their surprise—and in the delicious irony—that Islam was a peaceful, tolerant religion, while Christianity was persecutory, cruel, and violent.

1 Maria Rosa Menocal, *Ornament of the World: How Muslims, Christians, and Jews Created a Culture of Tolerance in Medieval Spain* (New York: Little, Brown, 2002), 5.

2 The subtitle of Menocal's *Ornament of the World.*

3 Chris Lowney, *A Vanished World: Muslims, Christians, and Jews in Medieval Spain* (Oxford: Oxford University Press, 2005).

4 Lowney, *A Vanished World,* 14.

12. One purpose of the first paragraph is to

(A) discount the importance of medieval history
(B) reinforce a popular perception of medieval Spain
(C) suggest that historical research will need to explore new sources
(D) define *convivencia* for non-specialists
(E) distinguish among the various historical accounts of medieval Spain

13. The primary purpose of the quotes in the first paragraph is to

(A) emphasize the author's bewilderment with the narrative of medieval history offered by most historians of medieval Spain
(B) reinforce the author's position that proponents of *convivencia* misinterpret their evidence by quoting directly from their works
(C) suggest an alternate interpretation of the historical record
(D) recount the conventional narrative of *convivencia* in the words of its historians
(E) provide a comprehensive survey of the history of medieval Spain

14. The footnotes serve to

(A) demonstrate the range of sources he cites
(B) reveal that all the quotes are from the same source
(C) provide documentation for the sources of his quotes
(D) impress the reader with the technical expertise of the author
(E) explain the complexity of the argument at hand

15. The content of the second footnote

(A) undermines the claims made by Maria Rosa Menocal
(B) provides a citation for more information about the subject
(C) introduces information that will turn out to be essential to the main argument
(D) informs the reader of the whereabouts of a certain text
(E) clarifies the source of the expression used in the text

GO ON TO THE NEXT PAGE.

16. In line 25, the word "genre" refers to

(A) "fairy tale" (line 23)
(B) "*convivencia*" (line 25)
(C) "children" (line 23)
(D) "it" (line 26)
(E) "exotic journeys" (line 26)

17. Which one of the following characteristics of the scholarship on *convivencia* is most troublesome to the author?

(A) Its inherent lack of documentary evidence
(B) Its misleading emphasis on the importance of religion
(C) Its lack of methodological rigor or complexity
(D) Its preoccupation with Islamic historical trends
(E) Its tendency to exaggerate historical reality

18. All of the following accurately describe the tone of the second paragraph EXCEPT

(A) emphatic
(B) acerbic
(C) relieved
(D) comic
(E) vituperative

19. Which of the following sentences best represents the author's main point in the passage?

(A) "If you have read anything about medieval Spain, then you probably know about *convivencia*—the peaceful "coexistence" of Muslims, Christians, and Jews for nearly eight hundred years on the Iberian peninsula." (lines 1–4)
(B) "And like all fairy tales, this story of *convivencia* tells us much more about the world of storytelling in which it was created than about the historical past or objective reality, on which it is only loosely based." (lines 27–31)
(C) "While some of the recent books on *convivencia* have gestured in the direction of scholarly discourse, more often than not, they cannot resist the temptation to indulge our basest tendencies to Orientalism and exoticism." (lines 32–35)
(D) "And when these authors describe Islam, it is with the wonderment and delight of a tourist." (lines 50–52)
(E) "We, their audience, are supposed to share in their surprise—and in the delicious irony—that Islam was a peaceful, tolerant religion, while Christianity was persecutory, cruel, and violent." (lines 52–55)

20. The author's observation about Maria Rosa Menocal's *The Ornament of the World* (lines 44–46) is best described as an example of which of the following?

(A) Alliteration
(B) Metaphor
(C) Allegory
(D) Linguistic paradox
(E) Personification

21. The speaker mentions the chapter titles in lines 47–50 as examples of which of the following?

(A) Islamic history
(B) Poetic imagery
(C) Hyperbolic language
(D) Orientalist excess
(E) Failed metaphors

22. Which of the following best describes the rhetorical function of the phrase "and in the delicious irony" (line 53)?

(A) It raises a question the author answered at the beginning of the second paragraph.
(B) It alludes to a contention made in the first paragraph.
(C) It reiterates the thesis of the passage as stated in the first paragraph.
(D) It critiques the scholarly discourse of *convivencia*.
(E) It extends the metaphorical language of the second paragraph.

23. The passage as a whole is best characterized as

(A) a treatise on history
(B) an ironic attack
(C) a qualified dismissal
(D) an analysis of historical evidence
(E) a vituperative comparison

GO ON TO THE NEXT PAGE.

Questions 24–32 are based on the following passage.

This passage below is a draft.

(1) Cities around the United States have been put into a tenuous situation due to the practice of offering stadium subsidies. (2) Stadium subsidies refer to funds given by city municipalities to fund professional sports stadiums and have real budgetary consequences.

(3) The impact that stadiums have had on cities such as Detroit, which subsidized a hockey arena for its hockey team in 2014 by decreasing pensions, and Oakland, which chopped its police department by 18% to continue funding the Oakland Coliseum, make it clear that the practice of building new stadiums must come to an end. (4) Four-fifths of all stadiums constructed since the turn of the century have benefited from tax-free bonds, leaving taxpayers to foot a total bill exceeding three billion dollars.

(5) Why, then, does this practice persist? (6) Some feel that stadiums bring economic benefits that outweigh the costs of the stadiums, though this claim has been categorically denied by economists. (7) The few studies that support the use of stadium subsidies are funded by sports franchises and cannot be used as serious evidence.

(8) While stadium subsidies make little economic sense, they do occur under some significant pressure: cities pass new budgets annually and must meet the needs of a multitude of interests. (9) The monopoly held by the major sports leagues lead municipalities to feel that they must cower to the demands of their local teams, lest they lose their beloved franchise to a city that will pay the subsidy. (10) Therefore, cities with professional sports teams will likely face this quandary for the foreseeable future.

24. Which of the following sentences, if placed before sentence 1, would both capture the audience's interest and provide the most effective introduction to the topic of the paragraph?

(A) Professional sports teams have long brought a sense of civic pride to American cities.
(B) Even though professional sports teams are large revenue generators, they can be a financial drain on local resources.
(C) The Las Vegas football franchise, Arlington baseball team, and Detroit's hockey organization are all sports franchises that have been rewarded with expensive stadiums in recent years.
(D) In 2018, Las Vegas celebrated its acquisition of a professional football team, but the joy may have been overshadowed by a steep budgetary hit to the tune of $750 million in tax-free municipal bonds.
(E) Stadium subsidies for professional sports teams are among the most wasteful items on a municipal budget.

25. In sentence 2 (reproduced below), the writer wants an effective transition from the introductory paragraph to the main idea of the passage.

Stadium subsidies refer to funds given by city municipalities to fund professional sports stadiums and have real budgetary consequences.

Which of the following versions of the underlined text best achieves this purpose?

(A) (as it is now)
(B) are important to attracting professional sports teams to a city.
(C) can exceed hundreds of millions of dollars.
(D) are heavily supported by local politicians as well as several powerful interest groups.
(E) are more prevalent in football than in other sports.

26. In sentence 3 (reproduced below), which of the following versions of the underlined text best establishes the writer's position on the main argument of the passage?

The impact that stadiums have had on cities such as Detroit, which subsidized a hockey arena for its hockey team in 2014 by decreasing pensions, and Oakland, which chopped its police department by 18% to continue funding the Oakland Coliseum, make it clear that the practice of building new stadiums must come to an end.

(A) (as it is now)
(B) using public land to build stadiums
(C) offering tax-payer funded subsidies for new stadiums
(D) allowing the public to privately donate to developing sports venues
(E) developing single use sports arenas

27. The writer wants to add a phrase at the beginning of sentence 7 (reproduced below), adjusting the capitalization as needed, to set up a relationship with the idea discussed in sentence 6.

The few studies that support the use of stadium subsidies are funded by sports franchises and cannot be used as serious evidence.

Which of the following choices best accomplishes this goal?

(A) However,
(B) By contrast,
(C) Nevertheless,
(D) On the other hand,
(E) Furthermore,

GO ON TO THE NEXT PAGE.

28. In sentence 8 (reproduced below), the writer wants to provide a convincing explanation for why cities feel they must give in to the demands of sports franchises.

While stadium subsidies make little economic sense, they do occur under some significant pressure: cities pass new budgets annually and must meet the needs of a multitude of interests.

Which version of the underlined text best accomplishes this goal?

(A) (as it is now)
(B) a limited number of sports teams in each league make cities feel that they could ill-afford to lose their teams.
(C) cities have large surpluses and are more than willing to move the extra money to vanity projects. allowing the public to privately donate to developing sports venues.
(D) sports is only part of the interests of city residents, and politicians do not want to alienate potential voters by supporting stadium subsidies.
(E) finding land close to public transportation could drive up the price of developing a stadium.

29. The writer wants to add the following sentence to the third paragraph (sentences 5–7) to provide additional explanation.

Whatever the case, the process for generating and approving stadium subsidies is generally quite byzantine and hidden from public view.

Where would the sentence best be placed?

(A) Before sentence 5
(B) After sentence 5
(C) After sentence 6
(D) After sentence 7
(E) This sentence is irrelevant and therefore should not be included.

30. The writer wants to add more information to the third paragraph (sentences 5–7) to support the main argument of the paragraph. All of the following pieces of evidence help achieve this purpose EXCEPT which one?

(A) A quote from an economist who has studied the detrimental impacts of stadium subsidies
(B) An explanation of the methodological flaws of the studies funded by sports franchises
(C) A short overview of why the economic benefits of stadium subsidies do not outweigh the costs
(D) Statistics that support the amount of jobs created by the development of a new stadium
(E) The percentage of economists who deny that the economic benefits of stadium subsidies outweigh the costs

31. In the fourth paragraph (sentences 8–10), the writer wants to expand on the claim that a sports franchise can be offered a stadium subsidy simply by threatening to leave its current city. Which of the following claims would best achieve this purpose?

(A) San Diego lost its football team to Los Angeles when residents of San Diego refused to fund a new stadium for the team.
(B) The city of St. Louis was left paying for its stadium even after its football team moved away.
(C) Teams have been leaving their cities for newer locations ever since Major League Baseball began try to expand its market westward.
(D) Sports franchises have lots of money and can therefore be very influential with local politicians.
(E) Finding public funds for a stadium does not always prevent a team from moving to another city.

32. In the fourth paragraph (sentences 8–10), the writer wants to conclude with a statement that best calls for an action supportive of the essay's central claim. Which of the following sentences would best achieve this purpose?

(A) (as it is now)
(B) However, for the sake of local budgets, lawmakers must find a way to prevent teams from demanding free state-of-the-art facilities at the expense of taxpayers.
(C) Accordingly, stadium subsidies should be avoided at all costs.
(D) Consequently, the stranglehold that professional sports teams maintain over their home cities will remain a budget killer for years to come.
(E) Nonetheless, the civic pride stemming from a successful sports franchise winning a championship will ultimately justify whatever costs the stadium brings the city.

GO ON TO THE NEXT PAGE.

Questions 33–40 are based on the following passage.

This passage below is a draft.

(1) As America's healthcare system becomes more complex and doctors more specialized, consumers of healthcare may wonder how to evaluate the quality of their physicians. (2) Surely one may consult the subjective "gut feeling" that a patient may feel about a physician: that they have a good "report" with their doctor. (3) In recent years, insurance companies, hospitals, and professional medical societies have posited a variety of "objective" metrics to inform patients of doctor quality.

(4) One such metric is patient evaluations, which can only be conducted in large healthcare systems. (5) In the pursuit of maximizing the patient experience, interested parties consult patients with a post-visit survey. (6) The physician and the facilities are therefore rated from the patient's perspective. (7) Another approach to quantifying doctor quality is examining outcomes. (8) For instance, when a patient visits a hospital for a surgery, they may be contacted for follow-up information on how the patient has recovered in the short, medium, and long terms.

(9) But these types of standardized approaches that aim to measure physician quality are flawed and unfair. (10) The patient experience may not accurately reflect the quality of healthcare the patient received. (11) Physicians could boost these ratings by simply decreasing waiting room time or offering more comfortable exam tables, regardless of the quality of medical attention offered. (12) Further, attributing patient outcomes solely to the performance of a doctor, with no regard to patient lifestyle (diet and tobacco use, for instance) will certainly push physicians away from treating the most vulnerable patients, such as those who suffer from obesity, poverty, and congenital diseases.

(13) Nobody wants to choose a doctor primarily based on the accoutrements of the waiting room. (14) Further, it would not be desirable to potentially leave the most vulnerable patients to fend for themselves. (15) Perhaps the best approach would be a system that allows doctors to be evaluated by experts in their field—their peers. (16) Medical professionals can look at data and outcomes within their proper context in order to best communicate essential information about a physician's quality to America's health care consumers.

33. After sentence 1, the writer wants to provide a convincing explanation for why it is important for healthcare consumers to learn more about physicians. Which sentence below best accomplishes this goal?

(A) Specialists are largely similar due to the nature of their work, so the most important factor in finding a doctor is a convenient schedule.
(B) No two doctors are alike, and quality healthcare stems from factors as diverse as a physician's experience to the physician's relationship with patients.
(C) The complexity of the healthcare system has made it nearly impossible to learn anything about a doctor before going in for a visit.
(D) Recent trends in medicine towards team-oriented healthcare have made doctors interchangeable with one another.
(E) Learning about the personal lives and interests of physicians is key to finding a doctor with whom a patient may develop a good relationship.

34. The writer wants to add a phrase at the beginning of sentence 3 (reproduced below), adjusting the capitalization as needed, to set up a relationship with the idea discussed in sentence 2.

In recent years, insurance companies, hospitals, and professional medical societies have posited a variety of metrics to inform patients of doctor quality.

Which of the following choices best accomplishes this goal?

(A) In other words,
(B) Similarly,
(C) For example,
(D) Furthermore,
(E) However,

35. The writer wants to add more information to the second paragraph (sentences 4–8) to further develop the examples in the paragraph. All of the following pieces of evidence help achieve this purpose EXCEPT which one?

(A) Information about the types of questions posed on patient surveys
(B) How patient feedback is translated into a doctor rating
(C) The types of illnesses that bring patients into a doctor's office
(D) Factors that are measured in the follow up patient visits
(E) How long patients are tracked following a medical procedure

GO ON TO THE NEXT PAGE.

36. In sentence 4 (reproduced below), the writer wants an effective transition from the topic sentence to the main idea of the paragraph.

One such metric is patient evaluations, which can only be conducted in large healthcare systems.

Which of the following versions of the underlined text best achieves this purpose?

(A) (as it is now)
(B) create a consumer-based assessment of the healthcare experience.
(C) look toward the medical community's perspective for feedback on a physician.
(D) are typically flawed approaches to understanding a doctor's effectiveness.
(E) are too time consuming to be done on a large scale.

37. In the third paragraph (sentences 9–12), the writer wants to provide further evidence that the current systems of evaluation are unfair. Which of the following pieces of evidence would best achieve this purpose?

(A) Patient feedback that typically aligns directly with other types of doctor evaluations
(B) Patients who do not always have the knowledge about what kind of medical care is optimal for a particular ailment
(C) Data that suggests that measuring long-term patient outcomes is a more effective method than patient surveys for evaluating physician quality
(D) A quote from a health-consumer advocacy organization
(E) A brief history of physician evaluations to provide context

38. In the third paragraph (sentences 9–12), the writer wants to expand upon the idea that attributing patient outcomes solely to the performance of the doctor could be harmful to certain patients. Which of the following claims would best achieve this purpose?

(A) The most effective physicians will continue to gravitate toward treating patients who suffer from congenital diseases.
(B) The systems of doctor evaluation currently proposed will take consideration of patient lifestyle when evaluating physician performance.
(C) Studies suggest that smokers evaluate their physicians most harshly.
(D) Obesity can be a treatable condition when addressed by a highly qualified doctor.
(E) People who live in poverty are more susceptible to adverse long-term health conditions regardless of the quality of their physicians.

39. The writer wants to add the following sentence to the fourth paragraph (sentences 13–16) to provide additional explanation.

The aforementioned approaches put both healthcare providers and consumers in an undesirable situation.

Where would the sentence best be placed?

(A) Before sentence 13
(B) After sentence 13
(C) After sentence 14
(D) After sentence 15
(E) After sentence 16

40. In sentence 16 (reproduced below), which of the following versions of the underlined text best establishes the writer's position on the main argument of the passage?

Medical professionals can look at data and outcomes within their proper context in order to best communicate essential information about a physician's quality to America's health care consumers.

(A) (as it is now)
(B) remove patients from the process of evaluating physicians.
(C) ensure that patients afflicted by poverty, obesity, and congenital diseases continue to receive quality healthcare.
(D) best enhance the patient experience during visits to doctors' offices and hospitals.
(E) treat both short- and long-term ailments faced by patients.

GO ON TO THE NEXT PAGE.

Questions 41–45 are based on the following passage.

This passage below is a draft.

(1) Zoos are the subject of controversy due to a fundamental misunderstanding of their role in the survival of various species. (2) The moral imperative of keeping some animals in captivity has unfortunately been clouded by less humane practices from a century ago. (3) In reality, most modern zoos provide necessary joy and entertainment to their thousands of annual visitors.

(4) Climate change has resulted in threats to nearly half of all small mammals and a quarter of the world's bird population. (5) However, repopulation programs hosted by zoos have shown only moderate effects in recent decades. (6) Even larger animals, such as wild horses, which were considered extinct a half century ago, have benefited from repopulation programs at zoos: the 12 horses in captivity at the time of extinction have now increased to over 2,000, with a significant number being reintroduced to the wild.

(7) While there have been questions about the effects of zoos on the health of animals due to small enclosures, there is a net benefit stemming from captivity due to the amount of scientific research that is possible. (8) One outcome of such research arises when zoo veterinarians use a comparison of disease surveillance in the wild with their own animals in captivity and can warn the public about possible outbreaks that are forthcoming.

(9) Zoos of the twenty-first century are a far cry from the circus sideshows that have informed our popular perception of zoos as inhumane animal prisons. (10) Nowadays, all it takes is a single visit to make it clear that park goers are primarily on an educational journey focused on the conservation of some of the planet's most threatened species. (11) The challenging living conditions are just an unfortunate side effect of a system that benefits humans as well as animals.

41. In sentence 3 (reproduced below), which of the following versions of the underlined text best establishes the writer's position on the main argument of the passage?

In reality, most modern zoos provide <u>necessary joy and entertainment to their thousands of annual visitors.</u>

(A) (as it is now)
(B) unjust and inhumane living quarter for its inhabitants.
(C) animals with an adequate habitat.
(D) animals with homes that are preferable to habitats in the wild.
(E) an indispensable service in promoting public education and the survival of threatened species.

42. In sentence 5 (reproduced below), the writer wants to provide a convincing explanation for why zoos provide a necessary service.

However, repopulation programs hosted by zoos have <u>shown only moderate outcomes in recent decades.</u>

Which version of the underlined text best accomplishes this goal?

(A) (as it is now)
(B) had dramatic effects in recent decades.
(C) failed to accomplish their goals.
(D) been met with unceasing successes.
(E) not been successful enough to justify caging animals.

43. The writer wants to add more information to the second paragraph (sentences 4–6) to support the main argument of the paragraph. All of the following pieces of evidence help achieve this purpose EXCEPT which one?

(A) American zoos have invested more than $25 million in research during a single year.
(B) Zoos have used their resources to help minority students access STEM training and careers.
(C) Conservation efforts in California zoos have helped increase the population of California condors from nine to over four hundred during a period of thirty years.
(D) Studies have confirmed that zoo visitors experience an increase in knowledge of both biodiversity and conservation efforts stemming from their visits.
(E) Polar bears in captivity were found to have an infant mortality rate of 65%.

GO ON TO THE NEXT PAGE.

44. The writer wants to add a phrase at the beginning of sentence 8 (reproduced below), adjusting the capitalization as needed, to set up a relationship with the idea discussed in sentence 7.

One outcome of such research arises when zoo veterinarians use a comparison of disease surveillance in the wild with their own animals in captivity and can warn the public about possible outbreaks that are forthcoming.

Which of the following choices best accomplishes this goal?

(A) Furthermore,
(B) However,
(C) In fact,
(D) By contrast,
(E) Consequently,

45. In the fourth paragraph (sentences 9–11), the writer wants to conclude with a statement that supports the essay's central claim. Which of the following sentences would best achieve this purpose?

(A) (as it is now)
(B) However, the controversy surrounding zoos will not disappear anytime soon.
(C) With any luck, animals caged in zoos will one day find the freedom they deserve.
(D) Any opposition to the mission of zoos is shrouded in misinformation and lacks compassion.
(E) We must therefore continue to support America's zoos on their path toward helping a wide array of species.

END OF SECTION I

AP® English Language and Composition Exam

SECTION II: Free-Response Questions

DO NOT OPEN THIS BOOKLET UNTIL YOU ARE TOLD TO DO SO.

At a Glance

Total Time
2 hours, plus a 15-minute reading period

Number of Questions
3

Percent of Total Grade
55%

Writing Instrument
Pen required

Instructions

Section II of this examination requires answers in essay form. To help you use your time well, the coordinator will announce the time at which each question should be completed. If you finish any question before time is announced, you may go on to the following question. If you finish the examination in less than the time allotted, you may go back and work on any essay question you want.

Each essay will be judged on its clarity and effectiveness in dealing with the requirements of the topic assigned and on the quality of the writing. After completing each question, you should check your essay for accuracy of punctuation, spelling, and diction; you are advised, however, not to attempt many longer corrections. Remember that quality is far more important than quantity.

Write your essays with a pen, preferably in black or dark blue ink. Be sure to write CLEARLY and LEGIBLY. Cross out any errors you make.

The questions for Section II are printed in the green insert. You are encouraged to use the green insert to make notes and to plan your essays, but be sure to write your answers in the pink booklet. Number each answer as the question is numbered in the examination. Do not skip lines. Begin each answer on a new page in the pink booklet.

GO ON TO THE NEXT PAGE.

ENGLISH LANGUAGE AND COMPOSITION
SECTION II
Total Time—2 hours, 15 minutes

Question 1

Suggested reading and writing time—55 minutes.
It is suggested that you spend 15 minutes reading the question, analyzing and evaluating the sources, and 40 minutes writing your response.
Note: You may begin writing your response before the reading period is over.

(This question counts for one-third of the total essay section score.)

Individuals have argued the concept of what it means to live a good life for thousands of years. Many have posited that happiness is an internal choice, a question of free will, and that it is something that can be reached every moment of every day. Others have pointed to external factors such as the slow accumulation of wealth and the construction of solid relationships—both of which require time and long-term strategy—as the primary drivers of a "life well-lived." More recently, some have even pointed to the role of genes in determining life satisfaction.

Carefully read the following seven sources, including the introductory information for each source. Then synthesize the information from at least three of the sources and incorporate it into a coherent, well-developed essay that argues a clear position on whether life satisfaction is better achieved by living in the moment or by working toward long-term goals.

Your argument should be the focus of your essay. Use the sources to develop your argument and explain the reasoning for it. Avoid merely summarizing the sources. Indicate clearly which sources you are drawing from, whether through direct quotation, paraphrase, or summary. You may cite the sources as Source A, Source B, and so forth, or by using the descriptions in parentheses.

Source A	(National Institute on Drug Abuse)
Source B	(Dixit)
Source C	(map)
Source D	(Helliwell, Layard, and Sachs)
Source E	(chart)
Source F	(Ferriss)
Source G	(Department of Labor)

GO ON TO THE NEXT PAGE.

Source A

"Drugs, Brains, and Behavior: The Science of Addiction." National Institute on Drug Abuse. 2014. Web. 2 Feb. 2017.

The following is excerpted from an article on the National Institute of Health's Web site.

How do drugs work in the brain to produce pleasure?

Most drugs of abuse directly or indirectly target the brain's reward system by flooding the circuit with dopamine. Dopamine is a neurotransmitter present in regions of the brain that regulate movement, emotion, motivation, and feelings of pleasure. When activated at normal levels, this system rewards our natural behaviors. Overstimulating the system with drugs, however, produces euphoric effects, which strongly reinforce the behavior of drug use—teaching the user to repeat it. Most drugs of abuse target the brain's reward system by flooding it with dopamine.

How does stimulation of the brain's pleasure circuit teach us to keep taking drugs?

Our brains are wired to ensure that we will repeat life-sustaining activities by associating those activities with pleasure or reward. Whenever this reward circuit is activated, the brain notes that something important is happening that needs to be remembered, and teaches us to do it again and again without thinking about it. Because drugs of abuse stimulate the same circuit, we learn to abuse drugs in the same way.

Why are drugs more addictive than natural rewards?

When some drugs of abuse are taken, they can release 2 to 10 times the amount of dopamine that natural rewards such as eating do. In some cases, this occurs almost immediately (as when drugs are smoked or injected), and the effects can last much longer than those produced by natural rewards. The resulting effects on the brain's pleasure circuit dwarf those produced by naturally rewarding behaviors. The effect of such a powerful reward strongly motivates people to take drugs again and again. This is why scientists sometimes say that drug abuse is something we learn to do very, very well.

What happens to your brain if you keep taking drugs?

For the brain, the difference between normal rewards and drug rewards can be described as the difference between someone whispering into your ear and someone shouting into a microphone. Just as we turn down the volume on a radio that is too loud, the brain adjusts to the overwhelming surges in dopamine (and other neurotransmitters) by producing less dopamine or by reducing the number of receptors that can receive signals. As a result, dopamine's impact on the reward circuit of the brain of someone who abuses drugs can become abnormally low, and that person's ability to experience *any* pleasure is reduced.

This is why a person who abuses drugs eventually feels flat, lifeless, and depressed, and is unable to enjoy things that were once pleasurable. Now, the person needs to keep taking drugs again and again just to try and bring his or her dopamine function back up to normal—which only makes the problem worse, like a vicious cycle. Also, the person will often need to take larger amounts of the drug to produce the familiar dopamine high—an effect known as tolerance.

GO ON TO THE NEXT PAGE.

Source B

Dixit, Jay. "The Art of Now: Six Steps to Living in the Moment." *Psychology Today*. 1 Nov. 2008. Web. 2 Feb. 2017.

The following is excerpted from an article published by a website dedicated to current psychology topics and research.

Life unfolds in the present. But so often, we let the present slip away, allowing time to rush past unobserved and unseized, and squandering the precious seconds of our lives as we worry about the future and ruminate about what's past.

When we're at work, we fantasize about being on vacation; on vacation, we worry about the work piling up on our desks. We dwell on intrusive memories of the past or fret about what may or may not happen in the future. We don't appreciate the living present because our "monkey minds," as Buddhists call them, vault from thought to thought like monkeys swinging from tree to tree.

Most of us don't undertake our thoughts in awareness. Rather, our thoughts control us. "Ordinary thoughts course through our mind like a deafening waterfall," writes Jon Kabat-Zinn, the biomedical scientist who introduced meditation into mainstream medicine. In order to feel more in control of our minds and our lives, to find the sense of balance that eludes us, we need to step out of this current, to pause, and, as Kabat-Zinn puts it, to "rest in stillness—to stop doing and focus on just being."

We need to live more in the moment. Living in the moment—also called mindfulness—is a state of active, open, intentional attention on the present. When you become mindful, you realize that you are not your thoughts; you become an observer of your thoughts from moment to moment without judging them. Mindfulness involves being with your thoughts as they are, neither grasping at them nor pushing them away. Instead of letting your life go by without living it, you awaken to experience.

Cultivating a nonjudgmental awareness of the present bestows a host of benefits. Mindfulness reduces stress, boosts immune functioning, reduces chronic pain, lowers blood pressure, and helps patients cope with cancer. By alleviating stress, spending a few minutes a day actively focusing on living in the moment reduces the risk of heart disease. Mindfulness may even slow the progression of HIV.

Mindful people are happier, more exuberant, more empathetic, and more secure. They have higher self-esteem and are more accepting of their own weaknesses. Anchoring awareness in the here and now reduces the kinds of impulsivity and reactivity that underlie depression, binge eating, and attention problems. Mindful people can hear negative feedback without feeling threatened. They fight less with their romantic partners and are more accommodating and less defensive. As a result, mindful couples have more satisfying relationships.

Mindfulness is at the root of Buddhism, Taoism, and many Native-American traditions, not to mention yoga. It's why Thoreau went to Walden Pond; it's what Emerson and Whitman wrote about in their essays and poems.

"Everyone agrees it's important to live in the moment, but the problem is how," says Ellen Langer, a psychologist at Harvard and author of *Mindfulness*. "When people are not in the moment, they're not there to know that they're not there." Overriding the distraction reflex and awakening to the present takes intentionality and practice.

Living in the moment involves a profound paradox: You can't pursue it for its benefits. That's because the expectation of reward launches a future-oriented mindset, which subverts the entire process. Instead, you just have to trust that the rewards will come.

GO ON TO THE NEXT PAGE.

Source C

Esteban Ortiz-Ospina and Max Roser. (2019). "Happiness and Life Satisfaction." *Published online at OurWorldInData.org*. Retrieved from: 'https://ourworldindata.org/happiness-and-life-satisfaction'

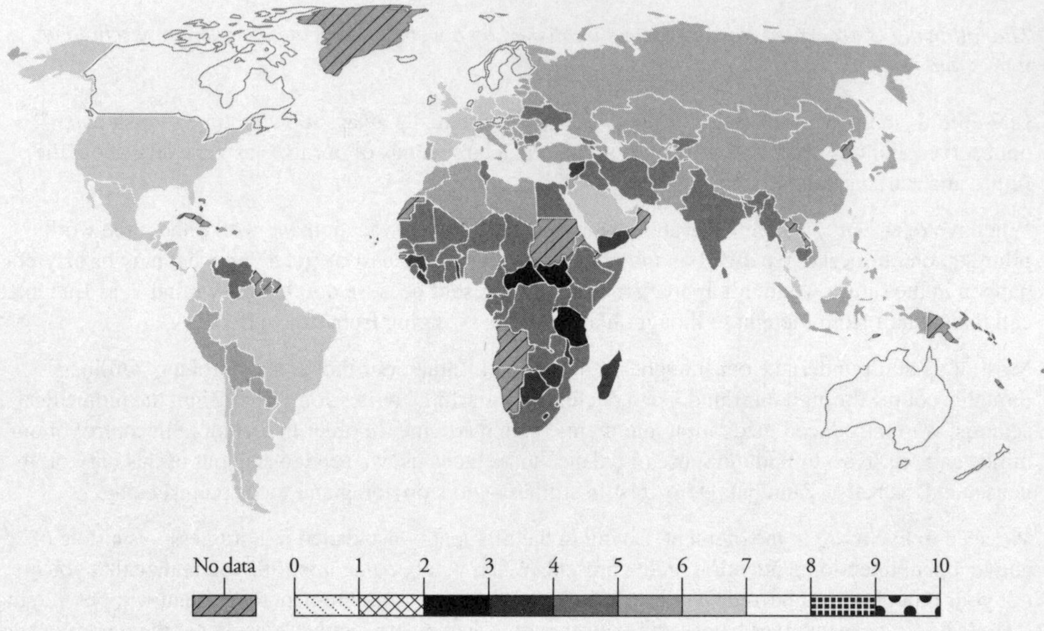

GO ON TO THE NEXT PAGE.

Source D

Helliwell, J., Layard, R., & Sachs, J. (2018). World Happiness Report 2018, New York: Sustainable Development Solutions Network.

The World Happiness Report is a landmark survey of the state of global happiness. The World Happiness Report 2018, ranks 156 countries by their happiness levels, and 117 countries by the happiness of their immigrants.[…]

The overall rankings of country happiness are based on the pooled results from Gallup World Poll surveys from 2015–2017, and show both change and stability. There is a new top ranking country, Finland, but the top ten positions are held by the same countries as in the last two years, although with some swapping of places. Four different countries have held top spot in the four most recent reports-Denmark, Switzerland, Norway and now Finland.

All the top countries tend to have high values for all six of the key variables that have been found to support well-being: income, healthy life expectancy, social support, freedom, trust and generosity. Among the top countries, differences are small enough that that year-to-year changes in the rankings are to be expected.

The analysis of happiness changes from 2008–2010 to 2015–2015 shows Togo as the biggest gainer, moving up 17 places in the overall rankings from the last place position it held as recently as in the 2015 rankings. The biggest loser is Venezuela, down 2.2 points on the 0 to 10 scale. […]

The importance of social factors in the happiness of all populations, whether migrant or not, is emphasized in Chapter 6, where the happiness bulge in Latin America is found to depend on the greater warmth of family and other social relationships there, and to the greater importance that people there attach to these relationships.

The Report ends on a different tack, with a focus on three emerging health problems that threaten happiness: obesity, the opioid crisis, and depression. Although set in a global context, most of the evidence and discussion are focused on the United States, where the prevalence of all three problems has been growing faster and further than in most other countries.

GO ON TO THE NEXT PAGE.

Source E

"8-channel model of flow," a concept in psychology based on the research of psychologist Mihály Csíkszentmihályi.

In positive psychology, flow, also known as the zone, is the mental state of operation in which a person performing an activity is fully immersed in a feeling of energized focus, full involvement, and enjoyment in the process of the activity. The chart below describes the balance that a person encounters, when doing an activity, between how much challenge the task presents and how much skill that person already possesses for the activity. Experts such as Mihály Csíkszentmihályi have suggested that happiness can be found by entering the upper right quadrant of this chart.

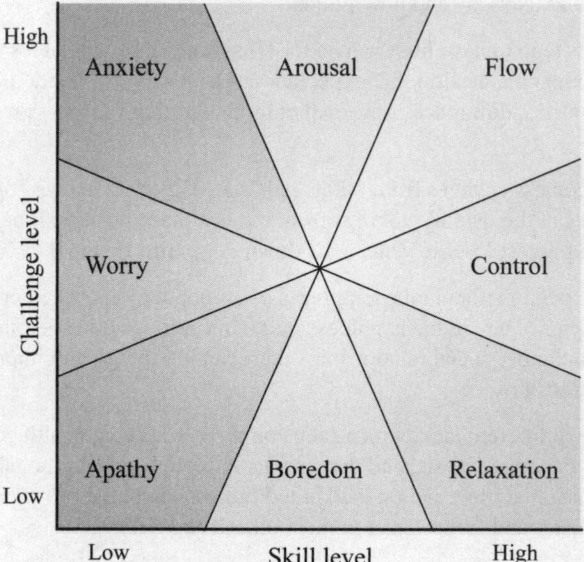

GO ON TO THE NEXT PAGE.

Source F

Ferriss, Timothy. *The 4-Hour Work Week.* 2007.

The following is excerpted from a book about redesigning your lifestyle in order to work less and increase your income.

To do or not to do? To try or not to try? Most people will vote no, whether they consider themselves brave or not. Uncertainty and the prospect of failure can be very scary noises in the shadows. Most people will choose unhappiness over uncertainty. For years, I set goals, made resolutions to change direction, and nothing came of either. I was just as insecure and scared as the rest of the world.

The simple solution came to me accidentally four years ago. At that time, I had more money than I knew what to do with—I was making $70K or so per month—and I was completely miserable, worse than ever. I had no time and was working myself to death. I had started my own company, only to realize it would be nearly impossible to sell.

Critical mistakes in its infancy would never let me sell it. I could hire magic elves and connect my brain to a supercomputer—it didn't matter. My little baby had some serious birth defects. The question then became, How do I free myself from this Frankenstein while making it self-sustaining? How do I pry myself from the tentacles of workaholism and the fear that it would fall to pieces without my 15-hour days? How do I escape this self-made prison? A trip, I decided. A sabbatical year around the world.

So I took the trip, right? First, I felt it prudent to dance around with my shame, embarrassment, and anger for six months, all the while playing an endless loop of reasons why my cop-out fantasy trip could never work. One of my more productive periods, for sure.

Then a funny thing happened. In my undying quest to make myself miserable, I accidentally began to backpedal. As soon as I cut through the vague unease and ambiguous anxiety by defining my nightmare, the worst-case scenario, I wasn't as worried about taking a trip. I could always take a temporary bartending job to pay the rent if I had to. I could sell some furniture and cut back on eating out. I could steal lunch money from the kindergarteners who passed by my apartment every morning. The options were many. I realized it wouldn't be that hard to get back to where I was, let alone survive. None of these things would be fatal—not even close.

I realized that on a scale of 1–10, 1 being nothing and 10 being permanently life-changing, my so-called worst-case scenario might have a temporary impact of 3 or 4. On the other hand, if I realized my best-case scenario, or even a probable-case scenario, it would easily have a permanent 9 or 10 positive life-changing effect.

In other words, I was risking an unlikely and temporary 3 or 4 for a probable and permanent 9 or 10, and I could easily recover my baseline workaholic prison with a bit of extra work if I wanted to. This all equated to a significant realization: There was practically no risk, only huge life-changing upside potential.

That is when I made the decision to take the trip and bought a one-way ticket to Europe. I started planning my adventures and eliminating my physical and psychological baggage. None of my disasters came to pass, and my life has been a near fairy tale since.

GO ON TO THE NEXT PAGE.

Source G

"Top 10 Ways to Prepare for Retirement." *Employee Benefits Security Administration/United States Department of Labor.* Web. 2 Feb. 2017.

The following is excerpted from a pamphlet on retirement savings.

Fewer than half of Americans have calculated how much they need to save for retirement.

In 2014, 30 percent of private industry workers with access to a defined contribution plan (such as a 401(k) plan) did not participate.

The average American spends roughly 20 years in retirement. Putting money away for retirement is a habit we can all live with. Remember…saving matters!

Start saving, keep saving, and stick to your goals. If you are already saving, whether for retirement or another goal, keep going! You know that saving is a rewarding habit. If you're not saving, it's time to get started. Start small if you have to and try to increase the amount you save each month. The sooner you start saving, the more time your money has to grow. Make saving for retirement a priority. Devise a plan, stick to it, and set goals. Remember, it's never too early or too late to start saving.

Know your retirement needs. Retirement is expensive. Experts estimate that you will need at least 70 percent of your preretirement income—lower earners, 90 percent or more—to maintain your standard of living when you stop working. Take charge of your financial future. The key to a secure retirement is to plan ahead.

Contribute to your employer's retirement savings plan. If your employer offers a retirement savings plan, such as a 401(k) plan, sign up and contribute all you can. Your taxes will be lower, your company may kick in more, and automatic deductions make it easy. Over time, compound interest and tax deferrals make a big difference in the amount you will accumulate. Find out about your plan. For example, how much would you need to contribute to get the full employer contribution and how long you would need to stay in the plan to get that money?

Learn about your employer's pension plan. If your employer has a traditional pension plan, check to see if you are covered by the plan and understand how it works. Ask for an individual benefit statement to see what your benefit is worth. Before you change jobs, find out what will happen to your pension benefit. Learn what benefits you may have from a previous employer. Find out if you will be entitled to benefits from your spouse's plan.

Consider basic investment principles. How you save can be as important as how much you save. Inflation and the type of investments you make play important roles in how much you'll have saved at retirement. Know how your savings or pension plan is invested. Learn about your plan's investment options and ask questions. Put your savings in different types of investments. By diversifying this way, you are more likely to reduce risks and improve return. Your investment mix may change over time depending on a number of factors such as your age, goals, and financial circumstances. Financial security and knowledge go hand in hand.

Don't touch your retirement savings. If you withdraw your retirement savings now, you'll lose principal and interest and you may lose tax benefits or have to pay withdrawal penalties. If you change jobs, leave your savings invested in your current retirement plan, or roll them over to an IRA or your new employer's plan.

GO ON TO THE NEXT PAGE.

Question 2

Suggested time—40 minutes.

(This question counts for one-third of the total essay section score.)

The passage below is excerpted from one of Mark Twain's most famous essays, "Fenimore Cooper's Literary Offenses." At the time Twain wrote his essay, Cooper's novels were generally well liked and respected. Read the passage carefully. Then, in a well-developed essay, analyze the rhetorical strategies Twain uses to convey his attitude.

If Cooper had been an observer his inventive faculty would have worked better; not more interestingly, but more rationally, more plausibly. Cooper's proudest creations in the way of "situations" suffer noticeably from the absence of the observer's protecting gift. Cooper's eye was splendidly inaccurate. Cooper seldom saw anything correctly. He saw nearly all things as through a glass eye, darkly. Of course a man who cannot see the commonest little every-day matters accurately is working at a disadvantage when he is constructing a "situation." In the *Deerslayer* tale Cooper has a stream which is fifty feet wide where it flows out of a lake; it presently narrows to twenty as it meanders along for no given reason, and yet when a stream acts like that it ought to be required to explain itself. Fourteen pages later the width of the brook's outlet from the lake has suddenly shrunk thirty feet, and become "the narrowest part of the stream." This shrinkage is not accounted for. The stream has bends in it, a sure indication that it has alluvial banks and cuts them; yet these bends are only thirty and fifty feet long. If Cooper had been a nice and punctilious observer he would have noticed that the bends were often nine hundred feet long than short of it.

Cooper made the exit of that stream fifty feet wide, in the first place, for no particular reason; in the second place, he narrowed it to less than twenty to accommodate some Indians. He bends a "sapling" to form an arch over this narrow passage, and conceals six Indians in its foliage. They are "laying" for a settler's scow or ark which is coming up the stream on its way to the lake; it is being hauled against the stiff current by rope whose stationary end is anchored in the lake; its rate of progress cannot be more than a mile an hour. Cooper describes the ark, but pretty obscurely. In the matter of dimensions "it was little more than a modern canal boat." Let us guess, then, that it was about one hundred and forty feet long. It was of "greater breadth than common." Let us guess then that it was about sixteen feet wide. This leviathan had been prowling down bends which were but a third as long as itself, and scraping between banks where it only had two feet of space to spare on each side. We cannot too much admire this miracle. A low-roofed dwelling occupies "two-thirds of the ark's length"—a dwelling ninety feet long and sixteen feet wide, let us say—a kind of vestibule train. The dwelling has two rooms—each forty-five feet long and sixteen feet wide, let us guess. One of them is the bedroom of the Hutter girls, Judith and Hetty; the other is the parlor in the daytime, at night it is papa's bedchamber. The ark is arriving at the stream's exit now, whose width has been reduced to less than twenty feet to accommodate the Indians—say to eighteen. There is a foot to spare on each side of the boat. Did the Indians notice that there was going to be a tight squeeze there? Did they notice that they could make money by climbing down out of that arched sapling and just stepping aboard when the ark scraped by? No, other Indians would have noticed these things, but Cooper's Indians never notice anything. Cooper thinks they are marvelous creatures for noticing, but he was almost always in error about his Indians. There was seldom a sane one among them.

The ark is one hundred and forty-feet long; the dwelling is ninety feet long. The idea of the Indians is to drop softly and secretly from the arched sapling to the dwelling as the ark creeps along under it at the rate of a mile an hour, and butcher the family. It will take the ark a minute and a half to pass under. It will take the ninety-foot dwelling a minute to pass under. Now, then, what did the six Indians do? It would take you thirty years to guess, and even then you would have to give it up, I believe. Therefore, I will tell you what the Indians did. Their chief, a person of quite extraordinary intellect for a Cooper Indian, warily watched the canal-boat as it squeezed along under him and when he had got his calculations fined down to exactly the right shade, as he judged, he let go and dropped. And missed the boat! That is actually what he did. He missed the house, and landed in the stern of the scow. It was not much of a fall, yet it knocked him silly. He lay there unconscious. If the house had been ninety-seven feet long he would have made the trip. The error lay in the construction of the house. Cooper was no architect.

There still remained in the roost five Indians. The boat has passed under and is now out of their reach. Let me explain what the five did—you would not be able to reason it out for yourself. No. 1 jumped for the boat, but fell in the water astern of it. Then No. 2 jumped for the boat, but fell in the water still further astern of it. Then No. 3 jumped for

GO ON TO THE NEXT PAGE.

the boat, and fell a good way astern of it. Then No. 4 jumped for the boat, and fell in the water away astern. Then even No. 5 made a jump for the boat—for he was a Cooper Indian. In that matter of intellect, the difference between a Cooper Indian and the Indian that stands in front of the cigar-shop is not spacious. The scow episode is really a sublime burst of invention; but it does not thrill, because the inaccuracy of details throw a sort of air of fictitiousness and general improbability over it. This comes of Cooper's inadequacy as observer.

GO ON TO THE NEXT PAGE.

Question 3

Suggested time—40 minutes.

(This question counts for one-third of the total essay section score.)

The French Enlightenment writer Voltaire wrote, “It is dangerous to be right in matters about which the established authorities are wrong.”

In a well-written essay, develop your position on Voltaire’s claim. Use appropriate evidence from your reading, experience, or observations to support your argument.

STOP

END OF EXAM

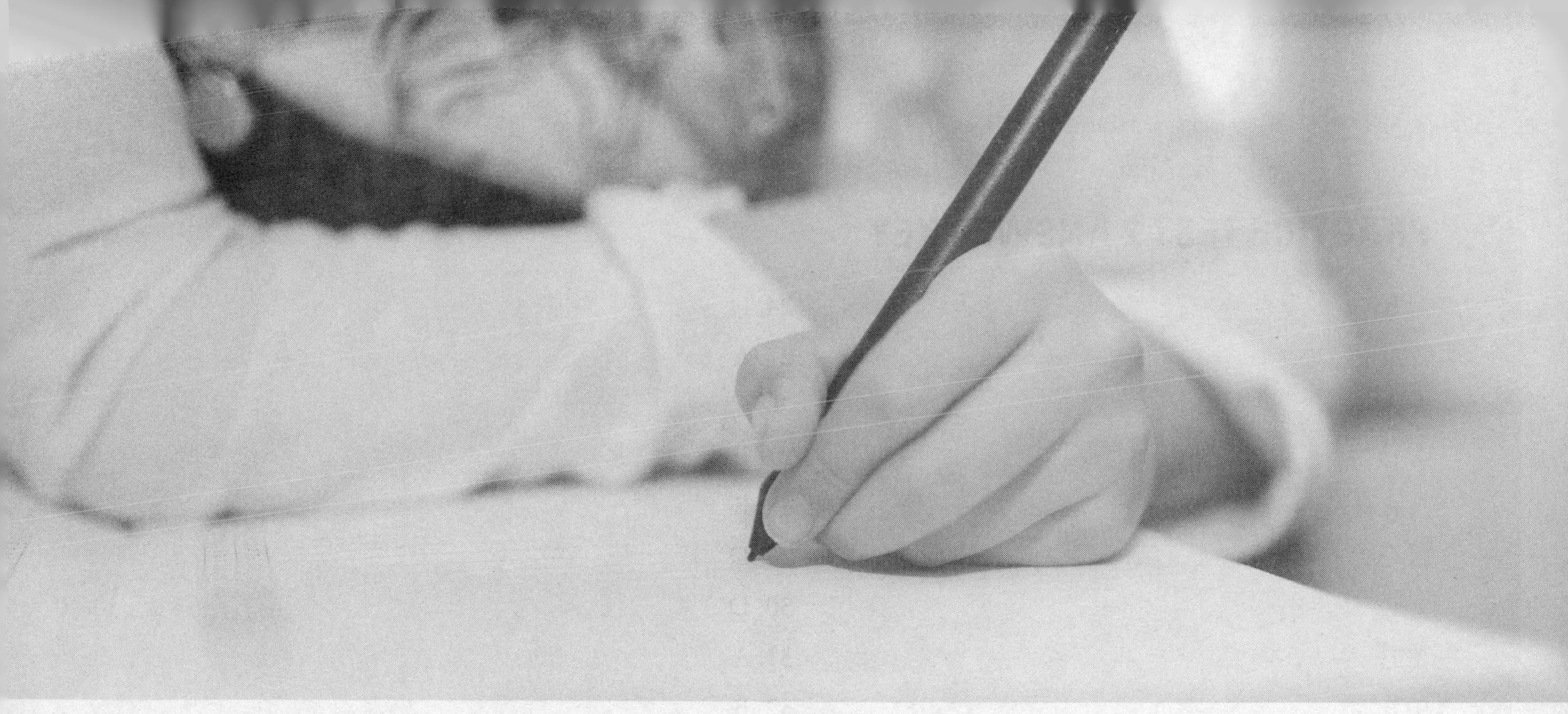

Practice Test 2: Answers and Explanations

PRACTICE TEST 2 ANSWER KEY

1. B
2. C
3. A
4. D
5. A
6. C
7. E
8. D
9. E
10. C
11. A
12. D
13. D
14. C
15. E
16. A
17. E
18. C
19. B
20. B
21. D
22. E
23. B
24. D
25. A
26. C
27. E
28. B
29. D
30. D
31. A
32. B
33. B
34. E
35. C
36. B
37. B
38. E
39. A
40. A
41. E
42. B
43. E
44. C
45. E

PRACTICE TEST 2 EXPLANATIONS

Multiple-Choice Questions

1. **B** This passage is from one of the famous Lincoln-Douglas debates; here, Douglas argues in favor of states' rights. You should note that it is possible to eliminate several of the choices based on the verb used. The speaker presents an argument; he does not *analyze*, (A), *criticize*, (C), or *describe*, (D). Douglas says directly that he is vehemently opposed to the idea of slavery in his home state of Illinois; he argues in favor of letting each state decide the issue for itself and goes on to claim that the greatness of the country rests on the sovereignty of the states to do so.

2. **C** You might not agree with what Douglas is saying in this passage, but he controls his tone carefully; remember, he is engaged in a debate at a time when people turned out in droves, expecting not colossal home runs, spectacular slam-dunks, hockey fights, or touchdown passes, but brilliantly conceived, expertly delivered rhetoric. If you use POE, you can narrow it down to three choices by eliminating (A) and (E). Choice (D) may be tempting, but be careful not to apply a 21st-century point of view to 19th-century reality. It may be tempting to see Douglas's defense of states' rights as a mask for his true feelings on slavery or, at least, as a poor veil for a racist bias. However, none of that is appropriate to the task at hand. The tone is best described as the tone of a debate; in other words, the speaker attempts to step back and let the force of his words (the voice of reason, if you will) carry the day. Also, remember that a polemic is a controversial argument.

3. **A** The speaker uses inductive reasoning (reasoning derived from detailed facts to form general principles) that goes something like this: you all agree that it was right for Illinois to vote as it chose and abolish slavery; thus, every state should be able to make its own choice on this issue. Moreover, every state should be able to make its own choices on just about everything.

4. **D** In this instance, the word it is referring to the choice of New York to make the distinction between *a negro who held property and one who did not* (line 33), so (D) is the best answer. Each of the other answer choices points to a different antecedent and is therefore not correct.

5. **A** The long sentence in lines 37–42 accomplishes many of Douglas's goals at once. It appeals to the principle of *popular sovereignty* (line 39), defines the term (lines 39–41), accuses Congress of *interfering* (line 41), and encourages his readers to *act conscientiously and rigidly* (line 38). Thus, (A) is the correct answer because this question highlights the word EXCEPT in capital letters. There is no evidence of a classification taking place in this sentence.

6. **C** Check lines 18–37. The author shows that Maine and New York have very different laws regarding African Americans, and that Maine and Illinois are not interfering with each other. Lines 39–42 define popular sovereignty as a guarantee *to each State and Territory the right to do as it pleases on all things, local and domestic*. This supports either (B) or (C). Choice (B) is too strong, since it uses the word prove, and the author has not necessarily shown that the laws are *successful*. Therefore, (C) is the best answer.

7. **E** The correct answer may not have been readily apparent, but using POE allows you to eliminate (A) through (D). Douglas uses no anecdotes, much less clever ones; likewise, there are no symbols, paradoxes, or metaphors. The authorities in this case are not only the other states (meaning the voters in the other states), but also the founding fathers: *Washington, Madison, or the framers of this government.*

8. **D** Douglas states his own opinion on slavery (his official opinion, at least) at the beginning of the passage (*there is no man in the State who would be more strenuous in his opposition to the introduction of slavery than I would*). Douglas also presents a clear position on voting: *I would never consent to confer the right of voting and of citizenship upon a negro.* Finally, there is a clear position on property: *I would not make any distinction whatever between a negro who held property and one who did not.* Of course, this implies that he would allow African Americans to have property, but he states that, propertied or not, they should not be able to vote. With this information, it is possible to answer the question with certainty; the correct answer is (D).

9. **E** Use POE! The last paragraph claims that Abraham Lincoln's policies will bring about the end of America's greatness and plunge the nation into Civil War. The *new doctrine* (line 70) is in opposition to *popular sovereignty* (line 54) and thus would lead to a consolidation of power, (A). Westward expansion, (B), is suggested in lines 57–59, and the author states that popular sovereignty enabled such expansion (line 65–66), so Lincoln's *new doctrine* may hinder that. Choice (C) is explicitly stated in line 71. Choice (D) is also stated directly in line 73. Population, (E), is mentioned in lines 56–57, but there is no direct link between Lincoln's policies and population growth.

10. **C** In a way, this is simply a reprise of question 7, but here Douglas pushes his scare tactic even further by saying that Lincoln and his party are deliberately infringing on states' rights to incite a civil war. Hopefully you were not fooled by (B). While it is true that Douglas is blaming the war (that hadn't yet begun) on Lincoln and his political party, he is not shifting any blame; nowhere does he imply that anyone was blaming or accusing Douglas and his party of trying to provoke a war, and to shift blame, Douglas would have to have had blame at some point.

11. **A** In this passage, Douglas is arguing for the application of the doctrine of *popular sovereignty* against the claims of Abraham Lincoln, which is why (A) is correct. He does not spend his time talking at length about Lincoln's failings, so (C) is incorrect. Douglas offers a nuanced argument, but he does not spend his time exploring *the various meanings of a universal principle*, so (D) is out as well. Because Douglas actively criticizes Congress (in lines 41–42, for example), (B) can also not be correct. Finally, (E) may be referring to the comparison of different states at the beginning of the passage, but this does not describe *the development of the passage as a whole*, so eliminate (E).

12. **D** The first paragraph lays out the definition of *convivencia* ("coexistence" among Muslims, Christians, and Jews in medieval Spain), so (D) is correct. Choices (A) and (B) are incorrect because the author does not want to say that medieval history is unimportant, just that it is portrayed incorrectly in popular histories, which he hardly wants to *reinforce.* Notice the way the test-writers used words and phrases that sounded correct *(discount the importance of and the popular perception of),* but were not part of complete, correct answer choices. Remember that if an answer is slightly wrong, it is entirely wrong on the AP English Language and Composition Exam. Choices (C) and (E) don't appear in the passage, which does not discuss historical sources or have *various historical accounts.*

13. **D** The author strings together quotes from various authors in order to retell the traditional *fairy tale* of medieval *convivencia*, which he then goes on to attack. This is why (D) is correct. While the author is frustrated with the *narrative of medieval history offered by most historians of medieval Spain*, he is not

confused by the narrative, so eliminate (A). Though the author criticizes the works of others, he does not offer his own interpretation in this excerpt, so eliminate (C). Choice (E) may be appealing in that the author does survey the story told by many scholars, but his account is hardly *comprehensive* in describing the entire *history of medieval Spain*, so (E) can be eliminated. Choice (B) is also incorrect; although the author is interested in how the *proponents of convivencia misinterpret* history, he is less concerned with their understanding of evidence. Besides, that's not the primary reason he used quotes in this paragraph.

14. **C** The primary purpose of the footnotes in the first paragraph is to document the sources for the expressions in quotes, so (C) is correct. While footnotes can *demonstrate the range of sources* in a work, this is not the case here, so (A) can be eliminated. Choice (D) is not likely to be true because that is a relatively shallow reason for including footnotes and not one that can be easily detected. In fact, most of the wrong answers are too subjective and judgmental to be correct.

15. **E** The second footnote clarifies that the expression *culture of tolerance* originates in the subtitle of Maria Rosa Menocal's book. While the author is interested in undermining the claims of Menocal, (A) is not correct. Neither are the other choices, which do not accurately portray the author's purposes for including this information here.

16. **A** *Genre* refers in this case directly to *fairy tale*, so (A) is correct. The AP Exam writers love to embed these grammatical/vocabulary questions into the multiple-choice section. Remember to take your time rereading a few lines above and a few lines below the sentence in which genre appears. Then, begin eliminating every word that you know does not relate to *genre* directly, such as *exotic journeys*, (E), and *children*, (C).

17. **E** The author does not mention documentary evidence or methodology, so eliminate (A) and (C) right away. He does claim that some scholars have distorted the relationship between Islam and Christianity during this period, but he does not do so in terms of (B) or (D), which are not precise. The author believes that *convivencia* exaggerates historical reality and distorts the history of medieval Spain into a fairy tale, so (E) is the correct answer.

18. **C** Don't forget the word EXCEPT (printed entirely in capital letters) or you will have trouble with this kind of question. Four of these answer choices will be accurate in describing the tone of the second paragraph and one will not. The author shifts his tone between sharp criticism of academic works and elaborate metaphors and humorous insults. He certainly does insist on some of his claims, so (A) is accurate and can be eliminated. *Acerbic*, (B), means sharp or bitter, and accurately describes much of this paragraph, as does *vituperative*, (E), which means harsh and abusive in its criticism. Eliminate these answer choices as well. At no point does the author express a distinct feeling of relief, so (C) must be correct.

19. **B** This question asks you to identify the author's main point in this passage, which is that the proponents of *convivencia* have encouraged people to believe a *fairy tale* about medieval Spain rather than its real history. Choice (A) is merely the author's introduction of the concept of *convivencia*, while (D) and (E) are more like asides than the main point. While (C) is appealing, it is making a specific point about *Orientalism and exoticism* that the author sustains throughout the second paragraph, not the entire passage. Choice (B) emphasizes the disconnect the author identifies between *convivencia* as a myth and the historical record, which he does not believe supports this view of *convivencia*.

20. **B** By calling *The Ornament of the World a syrupy confection* that *simmers under a thick layer of Orientalized cheese*, the author uses a metaphor built around food imagery to attack the book as unserious. Thus, (B) is correct. Remember that alliteration, (A), is the repetition of the same sound at the beginning of a word; and allegory, (C), is an extended series of symbols in a story. There is not a directly paradoxical (contradictory) claim in the sentence, so eliminate (D). Finally, the author does not ascribe human characteristics to a nonhuman subject, so eliminate (E).

21. **D** As you saw in the previous question, the author directly states that the chapter titles of the *The Ornament of the World* emphasize the extent to which the book *simmers under a thick layer of Orientalized cheese*, so (D) is correct. While the titles do refer to Islamic history, (A), and use poetic images, (B), the titles are not included to demonstrate either of these features. The author makes many accusations in this excerpt, but he does not accuse Menocal of hyperbole or failed metaphors, so eliminate (C) and (E) as well.

22. **E** This is a challenging question. The author inserts *and in the delicious irony* as an aside in the final sentence of the second paragraph. Throughout the paragraph, he alluded to sickly sweet food products in the overly dramatic characterizations of *convivencia*: he criticizes *Menocal's syrupy confection* and says that it *simmers under a thick layer of Orientalized cheese*. This metaphorical language is extended by his choice of the word delicious here, so (E) is correct. The phrase is too short and too unimportant to do any of the tasks mentioned in the other four answer choices.

23. **B** This is a critique of a particular historical perspective, but it is hardly comprehensive or complete enough to be considered a treatise, so eliminate (A). And while the author is certainly writing a *dismissal*, he is not qualifying it in the sense of limiting or restricting a critique, so eliminate (C) because it is only partially correct. (Remember that when *qualified* appears on the exam, it rarely refers to qualifications or credentials.) Because there is no *analysis* of evidence or *comparison* at work in the passage, both (D) and (E) can be eliminated as well. Choice (B) is correct because the author sustains an aggressive attack on a position while employing humor and irony throughout.

24. **D** You have two tasks on this question: ensure that the statement relates to the topic of the paragraph and make sure it is engaging (has a hook). The topic of this paragraph, much like the main idea of the entire passage, is that stadium subsidies are harmful to cities. Choices (A) and (C) can be eliminated because they do not convey the downside of building a new stadium. Choice (D) engages the audience with a real world example of a city that is experiences the consequences of stadium subsidies, while the statements in (B) and (E) are both a bit general. Eliminate (B) and (E). Choice (D) is correct.

25. **A** The main idea of the passage is that stadium subsidies have a serious downside in terms of a municipality's budget. Keep (A) because it directly references budgetary consequences. Choices (B), (D), and (E) can be eliminate because they have nothing to do with local budgets. Choice (C) may seem tempting, but it only states that stadiums cost a lot of money, not that they are paid for with tax-payer funds. Eliminate it. Choice (A) is correct.

26. **C** The author's main point is that the benefits of a new professional sports stadium do not justify using local bonds to fund them. While (A), (B), (D), and (E) are about constructing a new stadium, they do not tie in the idea of using local funds. Eliminate them. Choice (C) is correct.

27. **E** Sentence 6 shows how an oppositional perspective can be dismissed. Sentence 7 does the same thing with another possible piece of oppositional evidence. Since these sentences are doing the same thing, we need a transitional word that shows agreement. Choices (A), (B), (C), and (D) can be eliminated because they all should be used when one sentence shows a contrast to another. *Furthermore* provides the necessary agreement transition, so (E) is correct.

28. **B** For this question, you want to keep the focus on what might justify a city making a poor financial choice. Further, that decision should be due to pressure from a sports franchise. Use POE. Choice (A) is incorrect because it relates neither to making a poor financial choice nor pressure from a sports team. Eliminate it. Choice (C) references a poor financial decision, but there is no evidence that it is under the pressure from a professional sports franchise. Eliminate it. Choice (D) is about decision makers not supporting using stadium subsidies, so it can be eliminated. Choice (E) can also be eliminated because it does not have anything to do with pressure from a professional sports franchise. Choice (B) indicates that cities cave from pressure of sports teams because they do not want to lose their local team to another city. This accomplishes the goal, so the correct answer is (B).

29. **D** The proposed sentence starts with the phrase *whatever the case*, which implies that it comes after the discussion of more than one potential reason. Choices (A), (B), and (C) can all be eliminated because they occur before the discussion on potential reasons has concluded. Choice (E) can be eliminated because the proposed sentence is relevant to the discussion. The sentence should go at the end of the paragraph, which delves into the question of why cities might offer stadium subsidies. Choice (D) is correct.

30. **D** Since this is an EXCEPT question, you want to find the one answer choice that stands apart from the rest. Choices (A), (B), (C), and (E) are all supportive of the author's claim that tax-payer funded stadium subsidies are bad for cities. Choice (D), however, looks into the benefits of building a new stadium. This would contradict the author's main purpose. Choice (D) is, therefore, correct.

31. **A** For this question, you want to find evidence of a team actually leaving a city because it did not get a subsidy to build a new stadium. Choice (A) is an example that perfectly fits this scenario. Keep it. Choices (B), (C), and (D) are irrelevant to the issue at hand. Eliminate them. Choice (E) does discuss stadium subsidies, but takes a left turn by mentioning a team may leave even after getting what it wants. This is not as directly aligned with the claim as (A), so eliminate (E). Choice (A) is correct.

32. **B** Since the question mentions a *call to action*, look for an answer choice that references a remedy, or at least doing *something*, to combat the practice of offering stadium subsidies. Choice (A) does not do this, but rather states that the practice will be an inevitability for years to come. Eliminate (A). Choice (B) is at least solution-oriented (*lawmakers must find a way*), so that is worth keeping. Choice (C) is incorrect because, while it opposes stadium subsidies, it is certainly not solution-oriented. Choice (D), like (A), is more a statement of inevitability, bereft of any semblance of a solution. Eliminate (D). Finally, (E) is supportive of stadium subsidies and therefore contradicts the author. Eliminate it. The only choice remaining is (B), which is the correct answer.

33. **B** For this question, you want to find an answer choice that touches on both the patients' healthcare needs and their lack of information on the topic (and therefore the need to learn more). Choice (A) contradicts much of the passage because it suggests that a patient's convenience is more important than receiving proper medical treatment form a quality doctor. Eliminate it. Choice (B) is plausible because it focuses on the complexity of the healthcare system (*no two doctors are alike, diverse factors*), in which patients would need to be advised as to which doctor is most appropriate for their needs.

Choice (C) is extreme and contradicted by the rest of the passage, which focuses on ways patients can learn about their doctors. Eliminate it. Choice (D) is incorrect because the idea of interchangeable doctors would undermine the need to evaluate them, which contradicts the main idea of the passage. Finally, eliminate (E) since the factors in this answer choice are irrelevant to helping the patient navigating the complex world of healthcare. Choice (B) is correct.

34. **E** Sentence 2 is concerned with subjective evaluations of doctors, while sentence 3 looks at newer "*objective*" ways to measure doctor quality. Since you are looking for a contrast, find an answer choice that provides a contrast. Choice (E) is the only transition word that contrasts. Choices (A), (B), (C), and (D) are incorrect because they all transition to similar ideas rather than contrasting ones. Choice (E) is correct.

35. **C** Since this is an EXCEPT question, you want to find the one answer choice that stands out from the rest. Choices (A), (B), (D), and (E) all deal with methods of evaluating physicians. Choice (C) is the one choice that is irrelevant to the evaluation process, so it is the correct answer.

36. **B** The main idea of the paragraph is that the new trend in doctor evaluations comes from the perspective of patient satisfaction and health outcomes. Therefore, it is from the perspective of the healthcare consumer. Choice (A) is irrelevant to the rest of the paragraph. Eliminate it. Furthermore, eliminate (C) because it focuses on feedback from the medical community, rather than from patients, which is the focus of this paragraph. Choice (D) is tempting because the author goes on to explain that these are flawed approaches, but that does not occur until the fourth paragraph, and it is therefore not connected to the main idea of the third paragraph. Eliminate (D). Finally, (E), the idea that evaluations are too time-consuming, is not relevant to the main idea of the paragraph. Eliminate it. Choice (B) indicates that the assessment is from the perspective of the consumer, so (B) is correct.

37. **B** Use POE on this question. If an answer choice does not give evidence of an unfair system, eliminate it. Choice (A) suggests that what patients say in their feedback is consistent with other types of evaluations, which would indicate that patients are accurate and therefore, fair evaluators of physicians. Eliminate it. Choice (B) states that patients are not necessarily qualified to evaluate physician quality. If they are in a position to do so, then this would be evidence of an unfair system. Keep (B). Choice (C) should be eliminated because it suggests a fair system that one of the forms of evaluation currently in use (measuring long-term patient outcomes) is relatively effective (at least more so than patient surveys). Choice (D) is incorrect because a quote from a health-consumer advocate would likely argue that patients provide relevant, effective feedback and should be considered for evaluation. In other words, this type of evidence would defend the fairness of the current system. Finally, (E) can be eliminated because it is largely irrelevant to the issue of fairness. Choice (B) is correct.

38. **E** In the third paragraph, the writer claims that some patient populations could be harmed by the current system of evaluation because it would disincentivize doctors from taking on patients with conditions that are more chronic (obesity, congenital diseases) because the effects of those conditions will likely persist despite medical intervention. Therefore, some doctors may not want to take on these patients because their health circumstances would reflect poorly on their physicians. This is the opposite of (A), so eliminate it. Choice (B) is something that would make the system fairer to doctors, but it does not explain why some patients could be avoided by physicians. This answer, along with (C), is irrelevant. Eliminate both. Choice (D) is incorrect because it undermines the idea that chronic conditions are not entirely treatable by even a quality physician. Choice (E) is correct because it best describes the disincentive system that is created by tracking patient outcomes.

39. **A** The fourth paragraph describes the problems with the current system of physician evaluation. Therefore, this sentence would make a great topic sentence as it gives a general claim about the all-around flaws of doctor evaluation. Choices (B), (C), (D), and (E) are incorrect as they would awkwardly misplace a topic sentence into the middle or end of a paragraph it was intended to introduce. Choice (A) would place this as a topic sentence, and thus is correct.

40. **A** The main argument of the passage can be found in the first paragraph: patients need a fair way to know which doctors are most effective. This purpose is reflected in (A), which is the correct answer. Choice (B) is incorrect because it goes too far: patient input does not need to be completely removed from the process, but there are flaws in relying solely on patient input. Choice (C) is incorrect because it focuses on one detail from the third paragraph, rather than the passage as a whole. Eliminate (D) because the passage states that measuring the patient experience is a flawed method for evaluating physicians. Finally, eliminate (E) because the purpose of the passage is to find ways to inform health-care consumers, not to treat ailments.

41. **E** The main argument of the passage is that zoos have many benefits that outweigh the problems of keeping animals in captivity. Choice (A) is incorrect because the author does not tout the entertainment quality of zoos. Choice (B) articulates an oppositional argument. Eliminate it. Choices (C) and (D) do not relate to the benefits the author goes on to mention (research, education, conservation), so they are both incorrect. Choice (E) does the best job conveying the author's central claim and is therefore correct.

42. **B** For this question, look for an answer choice that conveys how successful zoos have been in repopulating animal species. Choices (C) and (E) can be eliminated because they each indicate failure. Eliminate both. Choice (D) is incorrect because it is irrelevant to explaining how the zoos have provided a necessary service. Although both (A) and (B), describe success, (A) is too measured, indicating only moderate outcomes. Eliminate (A). Choice (B) is correct because it notes that the programs have had dramatic effects (successes) recently.

43. **E** Since this is an EXCEPT question, use POE. The answer to this question should be an answer choice that makes zoos look bad, while the incorrect choices are all supportive of the author's defense of zoos. Choices (A), (B), (C), and (D) all support zoos and can be eliminated. Choice (E) shows a problem with zoos, and is therefore the correct answer.

44. **C** Sentence 8 builds directly from sentence 7: both sentences argue that some important research comes out of zoos. Therefore, look for a transition that shows agreement between ideas. Choices (A), (B), (D), and (E) are incorrect because they are all transitions to be used when showing contrast. Choice (C), *In fact*, shows agreement, so the answer is (C).

45. **E** For this question, locate an answer choice that sees zoos as beneficial. Choice (A) is incorrect because the current sentence does not provide closure and conveys a troubling tone if not followed up with a more solution-oriented sentence. Choice (B) is incorrect because its matter-of-fact content is not the author's central claim. Choice (C) is the opposite of the author's claim about the benefits of zoos, so it should be eliminated. Choice (D) is incorrect because, while the content is consistent with the author's perspective, its tone is not at all consistent with anything the author has presented. Choice (E) is correct as it is consistent with the central claim and the author's tone.

HOW TO SCORE PRACTICE TEST 2

Section I: Multiple-Choice

________ × 1.5000 = ________

Number of Correct (out of 45) — Weighted Section I Score (Do not round)

As of the printing of this book, there have been no official administrations of this test. Therefore, this scoring should only be used as an estimate.

Section II: Free Response

(See if you can find a teacher or classmate to score your essays using the guidelines in Chapter 4.)

Question 1 ________ × 4.5833 = ________
(out of 6) (Do not round)

Question 2 ________ × 4.5833 = ________
(out of 6) (Do not round)

Question 3 ________ × 4.5833 = ________
(out of 6) (Do not round)

AP Score Conversion Chart English Language and Composition

Composite Score Range	AP Score
112–150	5
98–111	4
80–97	3
55–79	2
0–54	1

Sum = ________
Weighted Section II Score (Do not round)

Composite Score

________ + ________ = ________

Weighted Section I Score + Weighted Section II Score = Composite Score (Round to nearest whole number)

Part VII
Practice Test 3

Practice Test 3

AP® English Language and Composition Exam

SECTION I: Multiple-Choice Questions

DO NOT OPEN THIS BOOKLET UNTIL YOU ARE TOLD TO DO SO.

At a Glance

Total Time
1 hour

Number of Questions
45

Percent of Total Grade
45%

Writing Instrument
Pencil required

Instructions

Section I of this examination contains 45 multiple-choice questions. Fill in only the ovals for numbers 1 through 45 on your answer sheet.

Indicate all of your answers to the multiple-choice questions on the answer sheet. No credit will be given for anything written in this exam booklet, but you may use the booklet for notes or scratch work. After you have decided which of the suggested answers is best, completely fill in the corresponding oval on the answer sheet. Give only one answer to each question. If you change an answer, be sure that the previous mark is erased completely. Here is a sample question and answer.

Sample Question	Sample Answer
Chicago is a (A) state (B) city (C) country (D) continent (E) village	Ⓐ ● Ⓒ Ⓓ Ⓔ

Use your time effectively, working as quickly as you can without losing accuracy. Do not spend too much time on any one question. Go on to other questions and come back to the ones you have not answered if you have time. It is not expected that everyone will know the answers to all the multiple-choice questions.

Many candidates wonder whether or not to guess the answers to questions about which they are not certain. Multiple-choice scores are based on the number of questions answered correctly. Points are not deducted for incorrect answers, and no points are awarded for unanswered questions. Because points are not deducted for incorrect answers, you are encouraged to answer all multiple-choice questions. On any questions you do not know the answer to, you should eliminate as many choices as you can, and then select the best answer among the remaining choices.

GO ON TO THE NEXT PAGE.

This page intentionally left blank.

ENGLISH LANGUAGE AND COMPOSITION
SECTION I
Time—1 hour

Directions: This part consists of selections from prose works and questions on their content, form, and style. After reading each passage, choose the best answer to each question and completely fill in the corresponding oval on the answer sheet.

Note: Pay particular attention to the requirement of questions that contain the words NOT, LEAST, or EXCEPT.

Questions 1–12. Read the following passage carefully before you choose your answers.

From the preface to *White Trash: The 400-Year Untold History of Class in America,* by Nancy Isenberg. pp. xiv-xvi. Viking.

Americans today have a narrow and skewed understanding of white trash. One of the most powerful and most familiar symbols of backwards attitudes associated with this unfavored group is that captured in newspapers and in television footage of 1957, showing the angry white faces of protest amid school integration in Little Rock, Arkansas. In 2015, tattooed KKK protestors defending the Confederate flag outside the Charleston, South Carolina, statehouse evoked similar feelings, demonstrating the persistence of an embarrassing social phenomenon. The stock of the Food Network's popular performer Paula Deen, a Georgia native known for her cholesterol-rich recipes, suddenly took a nosedive in 2013, when it was revealed that she used the "N-word"; almost overnight, her downhome reputation sank and she was rebranded as a crude, unsophisticated redneck….

These white trash snapshots offer an incomplete picture of a problem that is actually quite old and regularly goes unrecognized. In their conversations about viral events such as those noted above, Americans lack any deeper appreciation of class. Beyond white anger and ignorance is a far more complicated history of class identity that dates back to America's colonial period and British notions of poverty. In many ways, our class system has hinged on the evolving political rationales used to dismiss or demonize (or occasionally reclaim) those white rural outcasts seemingly incapable of becoming part of mainstream society….

First known as "waste people," and later "white trash," marginalized Americans were stigmatized for their inability to be productive, to own property, or to produce healthy and upwardly mobile children—the sense of uplift on which the American dream is predicated. The American solution to poverty and social backwardness was not what we might expect. Well into the twentieth century, expulsion and even sterilization sounded rational to those who wished to reduce the burden of "loser" people on the larger economy.

In Americans' evolving attitudes toward these unwanted people, perhaps the most dramatic language attached to the mid-nineteenth century, when poor rural whites were categorized as somehow less than white, their yellowish skin and diseased and decrepit children marking them as a strange breed apart. The words "waste" and "trash" are crucial to any understanding of this powerful and enduring vocabulary. Throughout its history, the United States has always had a class system. It is not only directed by the top 1 percent and supported by a contented middle class. We can no longer ignore the stagnant, expendable bottom layers of society in explaining the national identity….

Over the years, populist themes have emerged alongside more familiar derogatory images, but never with enough force to diminish the hostility projected onto impoverished rural whites. We have seen in recent decades the rise of tribal passions through the rediscovery of "redneck roots", a proud movement that coursed through the 1980s and 1990s. More than a reaction to progressive changes in race relations, this shift was spurred on by a larger fascination with identity politics. Roots implied that class took on the traits (and allure) of an ethnic heritage, which in turn reflected the modern desire to measure class as merely a cultural phenomenon. But as evidenced in the popularity of the "reality TV" shows *Duck Dynasty* and *Here Comes Honey Boo Boo* in recent years, white trash in the twenty-first century remains fraught with the older baggage of stereotypes of the hopelessly ill bred.

GO ON TO THE NEXT PAGE.

1. All of the following stylistic features are evident in the first paragraph of the essay EXCEPT
   (A) historical allusions
   (B) informal diction
   (C) metaphorical language
   (D) descriptive adjectives
   (E) vivid imagery

2. The author does NOT emphasize the negative view of white trash by using the words
   (A) "embarrassing social phenomenon" (line 10)
   (B) "outcasts" (line 25)
   (C) "marginalized Americans" (line 28)
   (D) "a strange breed apart" (line 41)
   (E) "the hopelessly ill-bred" (line 63)

3. The author develops the first two paragraphs of the essay by first providing
   (A) a comparison of two different trends, then contrasting them
   (B) a historical overview of a phenomenon, then responding with overlooked details
   (C) a common perception of a problem, then offering a more complete explanation
   (D) a detailed discussion of an event, then giving a wide-ranging investigation of its consequences
   (E) an analysis of the root causes of a conflict, then answering with an alternative explanation

4. The author primarily supports her point of view with
   (A) extended metaphors
   (B) linguistic evidence
   (C) statistical analysis
   (D) emotional appeals
   (E) appeals to authority

5. Lines 33–35 ("Well into the twentieth century … on the larger economy") indicate the author's belief that
   (A) the growth of the welfare state has reinforced the low social status of poor rural whites
   (B) most people in the twentieth century thought well of forced sterilization
   (C) poor rural white teenagers have been often expelled from school
   (D) one objection to white trash has been that class's inability to support itself without public assistance
   (E) arguments based on reason may not always appeal to all members of society

6. According to the author, the problem of white trash can best be characterized as
   (A) a question of socioeconomic status
   (B) the defining characteristic of America
   (C) one of the most vexing problems in our history
   (D) a perception that has not changed over time
   (E) a phenomenon exploited by television programs

7. The chief effect of the word "stigmatized" in line 28 is to
   (A) change the subject to something other than white trash
   (B) invoke a feeling of religiosity
   (C) comment from an objective standpoint
   (D) emphasize their outsider status
   (E) lend a tone of belittling humor to the text

8. The author's attitude toward white trash can best be described as
   (A) supportive but impatient
   (B) analytical but sympathetic
   (C) curious but judgmental
   (D) observant but hostile
   (E) probing but resigned

9. In the fourth paragraph, Isenberg notes that America's perception of white trash is
   (A) often discussed
   (B) always changing
   (C) never dismissed
   (D) usually accurate
   (E) occasionally analyzed

10. It can be inferred from this passage that
   (A) white trash people have been exploited for entertainment only very recently
   (B) uneducated people are responsible for their own fate
   (C) most members of the lower classes have been mistreated
   (D) not every American citizen has benefitted from the American dream
   (E) some members of the 1% rose out of the lower ranks of society

GO ON TO THE NEXT PAGE.

11. The fifth paragraph implies that the definition of white trash has

(A) changed from a definition based on class to a definition based on ethnicity
(B) emerged as a populist term rather than an elitist term
(C) been influenced by the growth of modern entertainment
(D) been confused with tribalism despite their vague relationship
(E) held fast despite the rise of identity politics

12. It can be inferred from the first sentence of the fifth paragraph ("Over the years…impoverished rural whites") that the author believes that

(A) the elite perspective has been derogatory toward rural whites
(B) populist themes have been dismissive of rural whites
(C) rural white members of the lowest classes are not totally responsible for their public perception
(D) many rural whites have intentionally tried to change how they're perceived
(E) socioeconomic positions are solely inherited

GO ON TO THE NEXT PAGE.

Questions 13–23. Read the following passage carefully before you choose your answers.

"The 40-Year-Old Burnout." Malesic, Jonathan. *The Chronicle of Higher Education.* October 5, 2016.

Oddly enough, my burnout began after a year away from the stresses of my job. I had just been on sabbatical in a bucolic region far from my college. When I returned to work, I was teaching, directing a teaching center, chairing a core-curriculum committee, and giving frequent conference presentations.

At first, it was exhilarating. I'm not a morning person, but on my first day back that August, I showed up early for an 8 a.m. meeting, wearing a trim-cut linen suit, eager to do what I loved.

That energy and confidence didn't last. The duties I took on to serve my colleagues and demonstrate my indispensability amounted to a heavy overload with no extra pay. I was also living apart from my wife, who was teaching in the town where I had spent my sabbatical. I felt every bit of our two-body problem. I started having recurrent and medically inexplicable sharp pains in my torso. My temper shortened. My doctor prescribed a couple of medications (neither one helped) for anxiety and acid reflux. I soon didn't fit into the linen suit, ultimately gaining 30 pounds in a year.

Without getting to see my wife regularly, I depended more on my job to affirm my worth as a person. Maslach and Leiter write that without close relationships, workers "will be far more dependent on clients and colleagues for signs of appreciation." In my case, I became more sensitive to students' base-level indifference to the required theology courses I taught. Their disinterest in the subject felt like an attack on my dignity. When I took the Maslach Burnout Inventory, I scored in the 98th percentile for emotional exhaustion.

Eventually, I came to dread every class meeting. I thought often of faking an illness and canceling class. (I never did.) My aim became simply getting to the end of class in one piece. Other teachers have described their burnout in similar terms. Maryellen Weimer, among the best scholars of college teaching, writes that she retired early after "struggl[ing] to stay alive in the classroom." In *The Truth About Burnout*, an exhausted high-school teacher reports being "just in a basic survival mode."

The language of survival is not mere hyperbole. The chronic stress associated with burnout diminishes the brain's executive function, making it harder to plan. When that happens, you rely on stress hormones to solve problems, just as you would if you encountered danger in the wild. In my final semester, I could get through class fueled by adrenaline, but after returning to my office, I crashed — hard. Then I went home and lay motionless for hours.

Planning the next day's class sessions felt like doing a crossword puzzle in cuneiform. I stared at the textbook without reading, racking my brain for ideas about how to get my students to learn. My store of teaching wisdom was inaccessible in those moments.

All semester I completely forgot about simple but effective techniques I had used for years — like requiring short weekly reading responses to spur reading compliance and foster discussion. I wrote haphazard lesson plans on index cards and scrap paper. After class, I threw them away.

Student evaluations of my teaching remained positive, but I knew I was working below my previous standards in the classroom. And my writing and college service all but stopped. As I learned, competence offers no protection against burnout. In fact, Maslach discovered that the most competent and engaged workers are often at the greatest risk for burnout. Their willingness to labor for love and not money will, over time, expose them to chronic stress. That is especially true in universities, where there are few explicit limits on working hours.

Another researcher, Janie Crosmer, has found that burnout is more acute in younger faculty members than in older ones (and in women more than men). It's easier to do too much too soon than to build barriers between your work and psyche.

But it shouldn't be entirely up to the individual to keep burnout at bay. The factors that Maslach and Leiter say cause burnout — an overloaded schedule, lack of control, insufficient reward, breakdown of community, absence of fairness, and conflicting values — are characteristics of workplaces, not individuals. Some of those factors certainly shaped my experience. Academic culture fosters burnout when it encourages overwork, promotes a model of professors as isolated entrepreneurs, and offers little recognition for good teaching or mentoring. The persistent financial stress on colleges and universities only exacerbates the problem, because, as Maslach and Leiter put it, "individual employees become the 'shock absorbers' for organizational strains," including financial ones.

The response to faculty burnout should, therefore, not be to shrug and say that academic work is a labor of love, and some people just aren't cut out for it. Instead, the response should be to find ways to give these highly skilled workers the rest, respect, and reward they need to stay healthy and effective. Institutions cause burnout, and only a whole effort of an institution can deal with it. A good start would be for colleges and universities to support and reward the things they say they value — like, for example, teaching. That would be more useful than drafting another strategic plan that will be ignored a year later.

13. The word "bucolic" in line 3 was most likely chosen because of its
    (A) ambiguous double meaning
    (B) tonal contrast with the author's pain in the following paragraphs
    (C) harsh sentiment that reflects the equally harsh truths of the passage
    (D) obviously superior status to other similar words
    (E) sense of objectivity

GO ON TO THE NEXT PAGE.

14. The primary purpose of quoting Maslach and Leiter in the fourth paragraph is to
    (A) suggest an alternate academic explanation for the author's emotional collapse
    (B) demonstrate how the loss of vocation can cause loss of confidence in one's writing skills
    (C) provide academic evidence for the author's personal experience
    (D) build the author's ethical character in the eyes of the reader
    (E) introduce a point-of-view that becomes essential to understanding the essay later

15. According to the author, his attempt to "demonstrate my indispensability" most directly resulted in
    (A) extra work without compensation
    (B) separation from his wife
    (C) health problems
    (D) thoughts of cancelling class
    (E) extended periods of sleep

16. In describing faculty burnout in the final two paragraphs, the author emphasizes
    (A) its inevitability
    (B) the role of organizations
    (C) the financial cost to individuals
    (D) the need for individual responsibility
    (E) the byproduct of entrepreneurship

17. The word "that" in the last sentence of the ninth paragraph ("That is especially true in universities…") refers to
    (A) the sense of chronic stress felt by young professors
    (B) the need for limits on hours worked at universities
    (C) the confusion of love with money
    (D) the habit of overwork that leads to chronic stress
    (E) the desire for a successful academic career

18. The sentence "The chronic stress associated with burnout diminishes the brain's executive function" (lines 40–42) is best supported by which of the following statements?
    (A) "you rely...to solve problems" (line 43)
    (B) "All semester…I had used for years" (lines 53–54)
    (C) "Their willingness…to chronic stress" (lines 64–65)
    (D) "Academic culture…teaching or mentoring" (lines 78–81)
    (E) "The response…is a labor of love" (lines 86–87)

19. This essay alternates between
    (A) conciliatory agreement and point-by-point refutation
    (B) general principles and objective evidence
    (C) comparison and contrast
    (D) process analysis and spiritual reflection
    (E) personal confession and academic analysis

20. According to the author, Crosmer found that young female faculty members are most likely to experience burnout because of
    (A) their competence, which fails to protect them despite their belief to the contrary
    (B) their inability to affirm their spouses
    (C) their habit of building barriers between their work and psyche
    (D) their tendency to take on excessive responsibilities at work
    (E) their absence due to maternity leave

21. All of the following contribute to the approachable tone of the essay EXCEPT
    (A) the use of similes
    (B) the first-person point of view
    (C) the varied syntax
    (D) the diction emphasizing feelings and stress
    (E) the use of quoted speech from known authorities

22. The 10th, 11th, and 12th paragraphs of this essay display a turn from
    (A) literal language to metaphorical language
    (B) first-person to third-person point of view
    (C) argument to counterargument
    (D) appeal to authority to bandwagon appeal
    (E) paradox to aphorism

23. The intended audience for this essay is most likely
    (A) those who aspire to graduate from college
    (B) those who have suffered professional burnout
    (C) those who are seeking to avoid burnout
    (D) those who are doing social science research
    (E) those who work in or have benefitted from higher education

GO ON TO THE NEXT PAGE.

Questions 24–31 are based on the following passage.

This passage below is a draft.

(1) Iceland is a country that not many people used to visit, but that seems to be changing. (2) These days, almost everybody in the world knows somebody who's visited the tiny island. (3) In 2014, over 12% of the entire nation worked in the tourism industry, roughly 24,000 to 32,000 people, depending on the month. (4) Nearly a million people each year visit the Blue Lagoon, stroll the streets of Reykjavik, and enter the Mál og Menning bookshop to try to make sense of the thousands of titles published in Icelandic.

(5) The funny thing is that Iceland is so small. (6) There are only 300,000 citizens total, and many of them feel that their culture is being lost in a wave of foreign tourists, primarily from the U.S. and the U.K, even as their livelihoods increasingly depend on those visitors. (7) The practical reason for the recent boom has been the arrival of low-cost airlines that promote Iceland as a convenient stop between the U.S. and Europe. (8) *Come to Iceland—it's one of those places you'll never forget!* (9) It's a marketing gimmick, and it's amazing that no one has thought to use it until now.

(10) In the meantime, the biggest danger in the influx of tourism is the loss of Icelandic identity, but one can argue that it's been disappearing for decades. (11) Long gone are the days when the native people shivered through the winter in sod huts, reading books to one another by the fire. (12) Iceland was brought into the modern era, first by the cod fishing business many decades ago, then more recently by international banking. (13) Since the economic crash of 2008–2009, tourism has largely taken up the slack. (14) So the truth is that Icelanders were pulling away from themselves long before the arrival of the tourist hordes—and they're the first to admit it.

24. To improve coherence, the author would like to move sentence 6 (reproduced below) to a better place in the passage.

There are only 300,000 citizens total, and many of them feel that their culture is being lost in a wave of foreign tourists, primarily from the U.S. and the U.K, even as their livelihoods increasingly depend on those visitors.

Where would this sentence best be placed?

(A) Before sentence 2
(B) Before sentence 3
(C) After sentence 7
(D) Before sentence 9
(E) After sentence 10

25. In sentence 9 (reproduced below), the author would like to more precisely express the meaning of the sentence.

It's a marketing gimmick, and it's amazing that no one has thought to use it until now.

Which of the following revisions would best express the author's meaning?

(A) (as it is now)
(B) When confronted with such marketing gimmicks, remember that there is a lot of money at stake.
(C) It's a marketing gimmick, which is the one thing that nobody had thought to use until now.
(D) Such marketing slogans are gimmicks, and it's surprising that nobody had taken advantage of Iceland's geographical position between Europe and the U.S. before now.
(E) It's nearly inconceivable that such a marketing gimmick has worked on an intercontinental level.

26. In sentence 14 (reproduced below), which of the following versions of the underlined text best represents the author's opinion on the topic of the passage?

So the truth is that Icelanders were pulling away from themselves long before the arrival of the tourist <u>hordes—and they're the first to admit it.</u>

(A) (as it is now)
(B) hordes, even though they are quick to admit it.
(C) hordes, even if they themselves won't quite admit it.
(D) hordes—even though they themselves won't quite admit it.
(E) hordes.

27. Which of the following sentences, if placed after sentence 4, would provide the best amplification of the most recent idea?

(A) Other good things to do in Reykjavik include visiting the Harpa Concert Hall and the Hallgrimskirkja cathedral.
(B) The city is often cold, even in summer, so it's important to dress warmly.
(C) You will most likely hear English spoken more than Icelandic, particularly in the capital.
(D) In fact, Iceland has nearly the highest literacy rate of any country on earth, and nearly ten percent of its population will publish a book during their lives.
(E) Some tourists are delighted by the colorful houses that line the narrows streets of the world's northernmost capital.

GO ON TO THE NEXT PAGE.

28. In sentence 5 (reproduced below), the author wants an effective transition from the first paragraph to the second paragraph.

<u>The funny thing is that</u> *Iceland is so small.*

Which of the following versions of the underlined text best achieves this purpose?

(A) (as it is now)
(B) Such stretches of visibility accent the worst parts of any society, especially when
(C) This newfound popularity hits especially hard given that
(D) Moreover,
(E) The reason for this swelling of tourists is the fact that

29. The writer wants to change a phrase at the beginning of sentence 10 (reproduced below) to set up the beginning of a new paragraph.

<u>In the meantime</u>*, the biggest danger in the influx of tourism is the loss of Icelandic identity, but one can argue that it's been disappearing for decades.*

Which of the following choices best accomplishes this goal?

(A) (as it is now)
(B) Nonetheless,
(C) Furthermore,
(D) Overall,
(E) However,

30. In sentence 8 (reproduced below), the author wants to write a more effective example of a marketing slogan based on the claim of the previous sentence.

Come to Iceland—it's one of those places you'll never forget!

Which of the following versions of the underlined text best achieves this purpose?

(A) (as it is now)
(B) *See the incredible history and taste the flavors of Iceland!*
(C) *Iceland—see it, feel it, love it!*
(D) *Summer or winter, Iceland is one of a kind!*
(E) *Go and book a long layover in Iceland—you may find that you'll never want to leave!*

31. In sentence 12 (reproduced below), the author would like to support the claim with more evidence.

Since the economic crash of 2008–2009, tourism has largely taken up the slack.

Which of the following sentences would best provide that support?

(A) Sentence 1
(B) Sentence 3
(C) Sentence 5
(D) Sentence 6
(E) Sentence 8

GO ON TO THE NEXT PAGE.

Questions 32–39 are based on the following passage.

This passage below is a draft.

(1) In the United States, food is increasingly being discussed in new ways. (2) For the last several years, the paleo movement has been growing in size and volume. (3) Focusing primarily on ancestral traditions, those who identify as "paleo" view the modern American industrial food system as fundamentally flawed. (4) They discuss the hundreds of thousands of years of our species spent as hunters and gatherers, evolving to eat meat whenever possible—and when it wasn't, to collect leafy greens, legumes, and berries.

(5) Indeed, there is evidence that the human gut seems to be better suited to absorb animal products than grain products. (6) As the amount of food products containing processed refined flour has increased, so too has record-setting obesity, increased levels of gluten sensitivity, skyrocketing rates of type-2 diabetes, and metabolic syndrome. (7) Certainly, eating animal fats leads to greater satiety, which prevents overeating daily caloric requirements. (8) Furthermore, some people who pursue a fully vegetarian lifestyle complain of excessive gas, bloating, fatigue, and other health problems. (9) Then again, many other vegetarians do not experience those problems, so perhaps there is individual variance at play too.

(10) Opponents of the paleo movement often stand by the low-fat gospel that dominated the public discourse in the 1980s and 1990s. (11) Others, such as vegans, take the moral stance that killing animals is bad. (12) Of course, these individuals don't express the same concern for the lives of plants, which are also killed for food. (13) Maybe because plants don't have four legs or look super cute.

(14) There is overlap between meat enthusiasts and meat opponents. (15) Both carnivores and vegans oppose the excessive use of sugars, which ultimately may affect our health more than anything else. (16) The issue of determining a proper human diet is clouded by many other factors, such as individual genetic heritage. (17) The paleo movement loves to point to the Inuits as an example of a healthy modern society that has existed, until recently, on nothing but protein and animal fat.

32. In sentence 2 (reproduced below), the writer wants to add a description of the origin of the term paleo.

    For the last several years, <u>the paleo movement has been growing in size and volume.</u>

    Which of the following versions of the underlined text best accomplishes this?

    (A) (as it is now)
    (B) it's been the paleo movement growing in size and volume: deriving from the Paleolithic Era, the name describes the ancient time when humans lived as hunter-gatherers.
    (C) the paleo movement (which took its name from the ancient Paleolithic Era; when humans lived as hunter-gatherers) has been growing in size and volume.
    (D) the paleo movement, deriving its name from the ancient Paleolithic Era, when humans lived as hunter-gatherers, growing in size and volume.
    (E) the paleo movement—the name of which derives from the ancient Paleolithic Era, when humans lived as hunter-gatherers—has been growing in size and volume.

33. The writer wants to add the following sentence to the first paragraph (sentences 1–4) to provide additional explanation.

    It relies too heavily upon refined white flour, various sugars, and processed vegetable oils.

    Where would this sentence be best placed?

    (A) Before sentence 1
    (B) After sentence 1
    (C) After sentence 2
    (D) After sentence 3
    (E) After sentence 4

GO ON TO THE NEXT PAGE.

34. In sentence 1 (reproduced below), the author wants to capture the audience's interest while also providing an effective transition to the main idea of the passage.

In the United States, food is increasingly being discussed in new ways.

Which of the following versions of the sentence best achieves this purpose?

(A) (as it is now)
(B) In the United States, with its record-setting obesity and skyrocketing rates of type-2 diabetes, food is increasingly being discussed in new ways.
(C) At the dawn of the new millennium, the United States finds itself wallowing in a massive public health crisis—and citizens are starting to discuss ways to fix this problem through diet.
(D) *Boom, boom, boom*—that's the sound of millions of overweight people hitting the floor every morning, and it should be enough to frighten anyone paying attention to the future of the United States.
(E) The United States has always been a country that alternates between self-denial and self-indulgence, a fact that is clear from our long history of Puritanism and hedonism.

35. To improve coherence, the author wants to remove a sentence from the second paragraph (sentences 5–9). Which sentence, if deleted, would contribute best to this goal?

(A) Sentence 5
(B) Sentence 6
(C) Sentence 7
(D) Sentence 8
(E) Sentence 9

36. The writer wants to adjust sentence 13 (reproduced below) so that it more closely matches the tone of the rest of the passage.

Maybe because plants don't have four legs or look super cute.

Which of the following versions of the sentence best achieves this purpose?

(A) One potential elucidation is the lack of mammalian appendages and minimized aesthetic appeal.
(B) Maybe because plants don't possess four limbs or appear attractive.
(C) One possible reason for this is the fact that mammals, which have legs, eyes, and emotional connectivity, more closely resemble humans than plants do.
(D) My best guess is that plants don't tug at the heart-strings in the same way that adorable mammals do.
(E) It's possible that mammals, with all of their adorable charms, look like humans more than plants.

37. The writer wants to add another sentence after sentence 17 to emphasize the main idea of the final paragraph (sentences 14–17). Which of the following would accomplish that?

(A) As usual, however, one needs to pay attention to the sources of information.
(B) On the other hand, the vegetarian movement cites cultures that follow mostly plant-based diets, such as India.
(C) Such indigenous cultures provide a better snapshot of human health than do just about any other groups.
(D) It stands to reason that this diet is admittedly superior to other diets.
(E) On the other hand, it's impossible to know with any certainty what constitutes a healthy diet.

38. The writer wants to add a word or phrase to the beginning of sentence 14 (reproduced below), adjusting the capitalization as needed, to emphasize the transition from the previous paragraph.

There is overlap between meat enthusiasts and meat opponents.

Which of the following best accomplishes that goal?

(A) Question of force aside,
(B) And another thing is
(C) Furthermore,
(D) Still,
(E) In effect,

39. The writer wants to add more information to the last paragraph (sentences 14–17) to support the main idea of the paragraph. All of the following pieces of evidence help achieve this purpose EXCEPT which one?

(A) The rate of cardiac disease among the Inuit is close to zero.
(B) Both carnivores and vegans oppose the use of chemicals in the processing of food.
(C) The impact of the food industry upon the environment is something that people on both sides of the debate care deeply about.
(D) Elements of paleo beliefs and vegetarian beliefs can be found in cultures around the world.
(E) Many people alternate between the two diets to find out what works for them.

GO ON TO THE NEXT PAGE.

Questions 40–45 are based on the following passage.

This passage below is a draft.

(1) In the twenty-first century, somebody once said, we are losing World War III—and most of us didn't even know we were fighting in it. (2) That's because this war is being fought on digital, not physical, turf. (3) While much of it is invisible, some of its most visible moments occur when personal data gets stolen in security breaches.

(4) The number and extent of such breaches has been increasing exponentially. (5) Health insurer Anthem suffered the loss of 80 million Americans' personal medical data. (6) In New York state, 885 million mortgage records were mistakenly exposed to the public for years—documents that included Social Security numbers and bank account numbers.

(7) Indeed, the word "breach" perhaps doesn't carry the significance that it should. (8) Therefore, many of these security breaches are *attacks* on our institutions, carried out by bad actors. (9) These include hostile foreign groups such as intelligence agents from Russia, about 100,000 Chinese doing the same, plus international hacker collectives that nobody knows their funding.

(10) These breaches often begin with "phishing"—a simple email sent by the hacker, but which contains a malicious link. (11) If the user clicks on it, the link downloads malware onto the user's hard drive. (12) This allows the hackers to enter whatever network the user is a part of.

40. In sentence 3, which of the following versions of the underlined portion of the sentence best clarifies the author's source?

In the twenty-first century, <u>somebody once said</u>, we are losing World War III—and most of us didn't even know we were fighting in it.

(A) (as it is now)
(B) some have told us
(C) it is said
(D) Fred Cohen once wrote
(E) it can be assumed

41. The author wants to insert additional information after sentence 6 that will support the main idea of the second paragraph. Which of the following pieces of evidence best accomplishes this task?

(A) Even Panera suffered a breach that affected 50 million customers.
(B) Perhaps the worst breach occurred in 2015, when foreign entities attempted to attack the U.S. Department of State, resulting in a two-day digital battle that has been compared to the twenty-first-century version of hand-to-hand combat.
(C) All of these are good examples of just how rampant the breaches are becoming.
(D) Others have occurred at MyHeritage, Quora, Under Armour, and many other sites, both large and small.
(E) It takes an extraordinary amount of effort to combat these attackers.

42. The writer wants to add a word or phrase to the beginning of sentence 5 (reproduced below), adjusting the capitalization as needed, to emphasize the suddenness of the breaches.

Health insurer Anthem suffered the loss of 80 million Americans' personal medical data.

Which of the following best accomplishes that goal?

(A) Acceleratedly,
(B) At full speed,
(C) To most,
(D) Quickly,
(E) With no apparent warning,

43. The writer wants to add the following sentence to the third paragraph (sentences 7–9) to provide additional explanation.

No mere accident, a breach is commonly associated with a foreign invader breaking through systems of defense.

Where would that sentence be best placed?

(A) Before sentence 7
(B) After sentence 7
(C) Before sentence 9
(D) After sentence 9
(E) The sentence should not be added.

44. In sentence 9 (reproduced below), which of the following versions of the underlined text best establishes parallelism and clarity?

These include hostile foreign groups <u>such as intelligence agents from Russia, about 100,000 Chinese doing the same, plus international hacker collectives that nobody knows about their funding.</u>

(A) (as it is now)
(B) such as Russian intelligence agents, for example, about 100,000 Chinese espionage agents, and shadowy international hacker collectives whose agendas and financial backing are unclear.
(C) such as Russian intelligence, Chinese espionage (rumored to number nearly 100,000 agents), and shadowy international hacker collectives whose agendas and financial backing are unclear.
(D) for example Russian intelligence, Chinese espionage (rumored to number nearly 100,000), and shadowy international hacker collectives whose agendas and financial backing are unclear.
(E) such as Russian intelligence, Chinese espionage (rumored to number nearly 100,000), plus shadowy international hacker collectives whose agendas and financial backing are unclear.

45. The writer wants to add more information after sentence 11 to explain additional steps in the breach process. Which of the following accomplishes this goal best?

(A) Once a network is compromised, the raiders are then free to access other files in the directory.
(B) But this happens only rarely, since most people know not to click on suspicious emails.
(C) Compared with employee negligence, however, the losses are quite small.
(D) Good phishing targets people who are naturally less suspicious of strangers than others are.
(E) It's inconceivable that this practice continues to work, but it does.

END OF SECTION I

AP® English Language and Composition Exam

SECTION II: Free-Response Questions

DO NOT OPEN THIS BOOKLET UNTIL YOU ARE TOLD TO DO SO.

At a Glance

Total Time
2 hours, plus a 15-minute reading period

Number of Questions
3

Percent of Total Grade
55%

Writing Instrument
Pen required

Instructions

Section II of this examination requires answers in essay form. To help you use your time well, the coordinator will announce the time at which each question should be completed. If you finish any question before time is announced, you may go on to the following question. If you finish the examination in less than the time allotted, you may go back and work on any essay question you want.

Each essay will be judged on its clarity and effectiveness in dealing with the requirements of the topic assigned and on the quality of the writing. After completing each question, you should check your essay for accuracy of punctuation, spelling, and diction; you are advised, however, not to attempt many longer corrections. Remember that quality is far more important than quantity.

Write your essays with a pen, preferably in black or dark blue ink. Be sure to write CLEARLY and LEGIBLY. Cross out any errors you make.

The questions for Section II are printed in the green insert. You are encouraged to use the green insert to make notes and to plan your essays, but be sure to write your answers in the pink booklet. Number each answer as the question is numbered in the examination. Do not skip lines. Begin each answer on a new page in the pink booklet.

GO ON TO THE NEXT PAGE.

ENGLISH LANGUAGE AND COMPOSITION
SECTION II
Total Time—2 hours, 15 minutes

Question 1

Suggested reading and writing time—55 minutes.
It is suggested that you spend 15 minutes reading the question, analyzing and evaluating the sources, and 40 minutes writing your response.
Note: You may begin writing your response before the reading period is over.

(This question counts for one-third of the total essay section score.)

In recent years, the American political landscape has grown more extreme. Both politicians and the public have grown more opposed to one another, with both sides exhibiting mutual distrust and an unwillingness to see from the other viewpoint. Some of the causes of this polarization can be ascribed to technological changes, while others can be seen in the actions of individuals or organizations.

Carefully read the following six sources, including the introductory information for each. Then synthesize the information from at least three of the sources and incorporate it into a coherent, well-developed essay that discusses the extent to which people's political beliefs can be influenced by external factors.

Your argument should be the focus of your essay. Use the sources to develop your argument and explain the reasoning for it. Avoid merely summarizing the sources. Indicate clearly which sources you are drawing from, whether through direct quotation, paraphrase, or summary. You may cite the sources as Source A, Source B, and so forth, or by using the descriptions in parentheses.

Source A (Barnays)
Source B (Zetlin)
Source C (Locke)
Source D (Pew Research Center)
Source E (Minnesota)
Source F (Inbar, Pizzaro, Bloom)

GO ON TO THE NEXT PAGE.

Source A

Bernays, Edward. *Propoganda*. 1928.

The following passage is excerpted from a book about how to manipulate public opinion. Bernays is regarded by historians as "the father of public relations."

To-day, however, a reaction has set in. The minority has discovered a powerful help in influencing majorities. It has been found possible so to mold the mind of the masses that they will throw their newly gained strength in the desired direction. In the present structure of society, this practice is inevitable. Whatever of social importance is done to-day, whether in politics, finance, manufacture, agriculture, charity, education, or other fields, must be done with the help of propaganda. Propaganda is the executive arm of the invisible government

Universal literacy was supposed to educate the common man to control his environment. Once he could read and write he would have a mind fit to rule. So ran the democratic doctrine. But instead of a mind, universal literacy has given him rubber stamps, rubber stamps inked with advertising slogans, with editorials, with published scientific data, with the trivialities of the tabloids and the platitudes of history, but quite innocent of original thought. Each man's rubber stamps are the duplicates of millions of others, so that when those millions are exposed to the same stimuli, all receive identical imprints. It may seem an exaggeration to say that the American public gets most of its ideas in this wholesale fashion. The mechanism by which ideas are disseminated on a large scale is propaganda, in the broad sense of an organized effort to spread a particular belief or doctrine.

GO ON TO THE NEXT PAGE.

Source B

Zetlin, Minda. "Want to raise emotionally healthy kids? Try to keep them off these two social networks." *Inc.* May 22, 2017.

The following passage is excerpted from a magazine dedicated to analyzing small businesses and startups.

Of the five most popular social platforms, only YouTube was seen as having a net positive effective on young people's lives, according to survey responses. Instagram, on the other hand, had the most negative net effect, followed by Snapchat. It's easy to see why. Negative body image is a huge risk for young people, especially girls, all of the time—but that risk is intensified on social media. It makes sense that young people faced with a stream of (often enhanced) photographs of others will likely compare their own bodies with the ones in the photos and find fault with themselves by comparison.

A second big issue for young people on social media is fear of missing out, or FOMO, something that can grip adults too, but may be especially dangerous for young people. Here, too, it's easy to see why a photo stream could be a big problem: People often post messages or links to Facebook or Twitter from the comfort of their sofas, but are more likely to post photos when they're out doing something fun.

GO ON TO THE NEXT PAGE.

Source C

John Locke, *An Essay Concerning Human Understanding*, 1690.

The following passage is excepted from a book of political philosophy by a famous British thinker.

Let us then suppose the mind to be, as we say, white paper, void of all characters, without any ideas:—How comes it to be furnished? Whence comes it by that vast store which the busy and boundless fancy of man has painted on it with an almost endless variety? Whence has it all the materials of reason and knowledge? To this I answer, in one word, from *experience*. In that all our knowledge is founded; and from that it ultimately derives itself. Our observation employed either, about external sensible objects, or about the internal operations of our minds perceived and reflected on by ourselves, is that which supplies our understandings with all the materials of thinking. These two are the fountains of knowledge, from whence all the ideas we have, or can naturally have, do spring.

GO ON TO THE NEXT PAGE.

Source D

"How political typologies shift with age." Pew Research Center.

The graph below was amassed from survey data collected in 2014 about American voters.

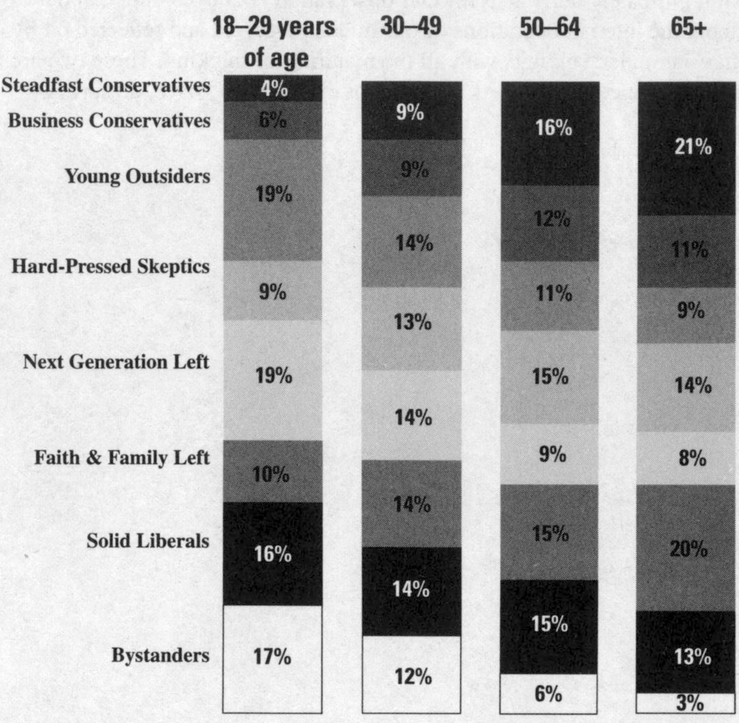

Source: 2014 Political Typology
PEW RESEARCH CENTER

GO ON TO THE NEXT PAGE.

Source E

Polling Place Rules—Office of the Minnesota Secretary of State Steve Simon.

The following rules regarding voting are found on a website operated by the state of Minnesota.

Do not enter a polling place unless you are authorized

Only authorized people are allowed inside a polling place during voting hours, such as voters and their minor children, poll workers and someone assisting a voter. People may not gather or linger in the polling place or within 100 feet of the building.

For a complete list of who's allowed inside, see Minnesota Statutes 204C.06

Do not campaign in or near the polling place

You have the right to vote without anyone in the polling place trying to influence your vote.

No one can campaign inside the polling place or within 100 feet of the building. If the polling place is on public property, no one can campaign anywhere on the property, even beyond 100 feet. However, the prohibition of signs and campaign materials within 100 feet does not apply to adjacent private property.

Do not wear campaign materials

In the polling place, you cannot display campaign T-shirts, buttons or literature which relate to specific candidates, official political parties, or ballot questions on the ballot that day. You will need to either cover up or remove these items while in the polling place.

Do not initial or sign your ballot, or mark it with a sticker

Voters may not place pre-printed stickers on their ballot in the write-in space (Minnesota Rules 83230.1450).

Taking photos is discouraged

There is no law that strictly prohibits taking photos or videos in the polling place to record your own voting experience.

GO ON TO THE NEXT PAGE.

Source F

"Conservatives are more easily disgusted than liberals." Yoel Inbar and David A. Pizarro, Cornell University. Paul Bloom, Yale University. 2008. Psychology Press.

The following passage is excerpted from an article by a group of academics who argue that innate genetic differences explain differing political opinions.

Given the important role that disgust plays in many people's moral judgments and beliefs, is it possible that individual differences in the propensity to experience disgust might be associated with systematic differences in moral ideologies? Some have argued that differing conceptions of what classes of behaviours properly belong in the moral domain are the fundamental cause of the heated and seemingly intractable disagreements between political liberals and conservatives (Haidt & Graham, 2007: Lakoff, 2002). According to Haidt and Graham (2007), for instance, political conservatives, in contrast to liberals, see the maintenance of purity as an inherent moral good and thus regard disgust, the consequence of violations of purity, as a morally relevant emotion.

Leon Kass, a noted conservative bioethicist, has argued for what he calls "the wisdom of repugnance." According to Kass, disgust at a practice such as human cloning can be "an emotional expression of deep wisdom, beyond wisdom's power completely to articulate it" (Kass, 2001). Similarly, self-described conservatives surveyed by Haidt and Graham (2007) said that whether "someone did something disgusting" was quite relevant to deciding that an action was right or wrong, a view that was not shared by self-described liberals.

These findings point to the possibility that conservatives are more likely to experience disgust in response to specific *behaviours* that violate ideals of purity.

GO ON TO THE NEXT PAGE.

Question 2

Suggested time—40 minutes.

(This question counts for one-third of the total essay section score.)

The passage that follows is an excerpt from C.S. Lewis' The Screwtape Letters, a fictional series of letters from an elderly devil to a younger devil advising him on the best way to corrupt humans. C.S. Lewis (1898–1963) was a devout Christian who was widely credited for bringing religious ideas to an audience of intellectual religious skeptics. Read the passage carefully. Then, in a well-developed essay, analyze the rhetorical strategies that Lewis uses to convey his message.

My dear Wormwood,

I am delighted to hear that your patient's age and profession make it possible, but by no means certain, that he will be called up for military service. We want him to be in the maximum uncertainty, so that his mind will be filled with contradictory pictures of the future, every one of which arouses hope or fear. There is nothing like suspense and anxiety for barricading a human's mind against the Enemy. He wants men to be concerned with what they do; our business is to keep them thinking about what will happen to them.

Your patient will, of course, have picked up the notion that he must submit with patient to the Enemy's will. What the Enemy means by this is primarily that he should accept with patience the tribulation which has actually been dealt out to him—the present anxiety and suspense. It is about *this* that he is to say "Thy will be done," and for the daily task of bearing this that the daily bread will be provided. It is your business to see that the patient never thinks of the present fear as his appointed cross, but only of the things he is afraid of. Let him regard them as his crosses: let him forget that, since they are incompatible, they cannot all happen to him, and let him try to practice fortitude and patience to them all in advance. For real resignation, at the same moment, to a dozen different and hypothetical fates, is almost impossible, and the Enemy does not greatly assist those who are trying to attain it: resignation to present and actual suffering, even where that suffering consists of fear, is far easier, and is usually helped by this direct action....

One can therefore formulate the general rule: In all activities of mind which favour our cause, encourage the patient to be un-selfconscious and to concentrate on the object, but in all activities favourable to the Enemy bend his mind back on itself. Let an insult or a woman's body so fix his attention outward that he does not reflect "I am now entering into the state called Anger—or the state called Lust." Contrariwise let the reflection "My feelings are now growing more devout, or more charitable," so fix his attention inward that he no longer looks beyond himself to see our Enemy or his own neighbours.

Do what you will, there is going to be some benevolence, as well as some malice, in your patient's soul. The great thing is to direct the malice to his immediate neighbours whom he meets every day and to thrust his benevolence out to the remote circumference, to people he does not know. The malice thus becomes wholly real and the benevolence largely imaginary. There is no good at all in inflaming his hatred of Germans if, at the same time, a pernicious habit of charity is growing up between him and his mother, his employer, and the man he meets in the train. Think of your man as a series of concentric circles, his will being the innermost, his intellect coming next and finally his fantasy. You can hardly hope, at once, to exclude from all the circles everything that smells of the Enemy; but you must keep on shoving all the virtues outward till they are finally located in the circle of fantasy, and all the desirable qualities inward into the Will....

Question 3

Suggested time—40 minutes.

(This question counts for one-third of the total essay section score.)

Anthropologist Margaret Mead (1901–1978) was known primarily for her work studying the customs of nonliterate, primitive peoples in the South Pacific and Southeast Asia. When asked her opinion of the modern American family, she stated, "Nobody has ever before asked the nuclear family to live all by itself in a box the way we do. With no relatives, no support, we've put it in an impossible situation."

Write a carefully reasoned persuasive essay that defends, challenges, or qualifies Mead's assertion. Use evidence from your observation, experience, or reading to develop your position.

STOP

END OF EXAM

Practice Test 3: Answers and Explanations

PRACTICE TEST 3 ANSWER KEY

1. C
2. C
3. C
4. B
5. D
6. A
7. D
8. B
9. B
10. D
11. A
12. C
13. B
14. C
15. A
16. B
17. D
18. B
19. E
20. D
21. E
22. B
23. E
24. B
25. D
26. E
27. D
28. C
29. D
30. E
31. B
32. E
33. D
34. C
35. C
36. C
37. B
38. D
39. A
40. D
41. B
42. E
43. B
44. C
45. A

PRACTICE TEST 3 EXPLANATIONS

Multiple-Choice Questions

1. **C** There are no examples of any other type of metaphorical language in this paragraph. However, there are definitely *historical allusions* (to the Little Rock Nine), *informal diction* (*nosedive* and *redneck*), and *vivid imagery* (*tattooed KKK protestors*). Eliminate (A), (B), and (E). An *appositive* is a noun phrase used to describe another noun in greater detail. In this paragraph, the appositive phrase is *a Georgia native known for her cholesterol-rich recipes*, which describes *Paula Deen* in more detail. Eliminate (D). Choice (C) is correct.

2. **C** This is essentially a question about tone. Hopefully you noticed right away that language such as *embarrassing, a strange breed apart*, and *hopelessly ill-bred* are all harshly judgmental. Eliminate (A), (D), and (E). The remaining two answer choices, *outcasts* and *marginalized* Americans, are quite close in meaning. However, marginalized is a bit more formal and carries with it a connotation of powerlessness. Also, (C) at least gives "white trash" the dignity of being called *Americans.* Choice (C) is correct.

3. **C** The first paragraph explores some examples of what is considered uncouth "white trash" behavior. However, pay close attention to the first sentence: *Americans today have a narrow and skewed understanding of white trash*. This implies that the author is going to correct this misperception later, which she does in the beginning of the second paragraph, stating that such *snapshots offer an incomplete picture of a problem.* That problem, she explains, is that *Americans lack any deeper appreciation of class.* Choice (C) is correct.

4. **B** Isenberg pays special attention to the words that have been used to describe white trash throughout history. She notes the use of terms such as "waste people" and "loser" people. Later, she notes that *the words "waste" and "trash" are crucial to any understanding of this powerful and enduring vocabulary.* This constitutes linguistic evidence. Choice (B) is correct.

5. **D** The quoted sentence indicates that, in the twentieth century, some people viewed white trash as a drain on the national economy. In other words, they weren't making enough money to support themselves, and so required public assistance such as Roosevelt's "alphabet soup" programs, Social Security, Medicare, food stamps, etc. Choice (A) is tempting, but it goes a step too far with the words *welfare state*, which is out of scope. Eliminate (A). Choices (B), (C), and (E) depend on a misreading of the words *well, expelled,* and *reason*. Eliminate all three. Choice (D) is correct.

6. **A** In the second paragraph, Isenberg notes that *[b]eyond white anger and ignorance is a far more complicated history of class identity that dates back to America's colonial period.* The phrase *class identity* can be reworded as *socioeconomic status.* Choices (B) and (C) are too extreme; while the history of white trash is important to U.S. history, the author never states or implies that it's more important or more vexing than any other. Eliminate (D) because it's the opposite of the author's position, particularly in the fifth paragraph, which is that the definition of white trash has changed over time. And while it's true that the white trash phenomenon has been exploited by television programs, that's not how the problem can be *best* characterized, so eliminate (E). Choice (A) is correct.

7. **D** In the medieval and Renaissance era, *stigmatized* meant "to brand or tattoo." (Also, *stigmata* are the strange Christ-like wounds that are said to magically appear on the hands of Christian saints.) In this sentence, the context of *marginalized Americans* with an *inability to be productive* should've told you that the word was doubling down on the idea of white trash people equaling social outsiders.

8. **B** The author spends a lot of time providing supporting evidence for her topic sentences—you know, the same type of essay writing 101 that you've practiced *ad nauseum* in your English classes. At the same time, you should've gotten the sense that she's trying to draw a fuller, more comprehensive picture of who these poor people really are, and how they've been treated throughout history—and that requires some sympathy. Choice (B) is correct.

9. **B** At the beginning of the fourth paragraph, Isenberg notes *Americans' evolving attitudes toward these unwanted people.* This indicates that our view of white trash has not remained static—it has changed over the years. The answer can't be *often discussed*, because the author notes at the end of the paragraph that *we can no longer ignore* white trash, so eliminate (A). It can't be *never dismissed* for the same reason, so eliminate (C). Choices (D) and (E) are vague and/or out of scope; eliminate both. Choice (B) is correct.

10. **D** For *infer, imply,* or *suggest* questions, be sure to choose the safest possible answer. In other words, the choice that makes the smallest possible conclusion. Near the beginning of the third paragraph, Isenberg discusses this group's *inability to be productive, to own property, or to produce healthy and upwardly mobile children—the sense of uplift on which the American dream is predicated.* From this, the reader can infer that *not every American citizen has benefitted from the American dream.* Choice (A) assumes that white trash had never been exploited for entertainment until recently. Choice (B) is out of scope, since responsibility for one's life is never discussed. Also out of scope is (C), because other types of lower-class people aren't mentioned. And (E) is also out of scope; the origins of the elite classes are never discussed. Choice (D) is correct.

11. **A** The author spends the second and the third paragraphs describing her belief that "white trash" was above a term derived from class structure, though many Americans want to deny the existence of that hierarchy. In the fifth paragraph, discussing more recent changes, Isenberg states that *[tribal r] oots implied that class took on the traits (and allure) of an ethnic heritage.* In other words, the definition of the word was originally from a certain class status, but now the word reflects white rural Christian ethnicity more than anything else. If you selected (B), remember that *this shift was spurred on by a larger fascination with identity politics*, which is not necessarily the same as populism. If you selected (E), consider the same sentence. This change in the definition of white trash didn't *hold fast despite the rise of identity politics*—it transformed itself *because* of the rise of identity politics. Choice (A) is correct.

12. **C** The *hostility* projected onto impoverished rural whites is the key phrase here. This indicates, very subtly, that Isenberg views that some of the responsibility for the plight of lower-class rural whites can be placed on other people or organizations. This does not mean that she views white trash as totally unresponsible for their own condition. It does mean that rural poor whites have also been fighting an uphill battle with regard to a society that wants to either ignore them or condemn them. Choice (A) comes from the previous paragraph rather than the first sentence of the fifth paragraph. Choice (B) is a misinterpretation of the sentence, since rural whites are still dismissed despite populist themes, not because of them. Choice (D) is a trap, because you don't know that the change in image was brought about intentionally by rural whites. And (E) uses the word *solely*, which is extreme—and wrong. Choice (C) is correct.

13. **B** *Bucolic* means *arcadian* or *relating to the country*, and it carries a strong connotation of rural tranquility. Picture a shepherd on a rock, peacefully watching over his flock. This mention of a break from his normal life serves as a preface to the breakdown that Malesic experiences at his university. It carries no *double meaning, harsh sentiments*, or *objectivity*, so eliminate (A), (C), and (E). Choice (D), *obviously superior*, is an extremely judgmental answer that can be eliminated. Choice (B) is correct.

14. **C** In the prior sentence, the author states that *Without getting to see my wife regularly, I depended more on my job to affirm my worth as a person.* Then he cites two experts, Maslach and Leister, to restate this same point—that we turn to colleagues more often for approval if we aren't getting it at home—but now from an academic standpoint, not a personal one. Choice (C) is correct.

15. **A** Note the words *most directly* in the question. The author states that *The duties I took on to serve my colleagues and demonstrate my indispensability amounted to a heavy overload with no extra pay.* Choice (A) most accurately describes what this amounted to. While the other answer choices all describe terrible consequences of the author's burnout as described in the passage, none of them are stated as having been directly related to accepting more work without extra pay. Choice (A) is correct.

16. **B** The final two paragraphs address the role of institutions in causing faculty burnout. Malesic states that *The factors that Maslach and Leiter say cause burnout…are characteristics of workplaces, not individuals.* Later, he explicitly states that *Institutions cause burnout, and only a whole effort of an institution can deal with it.* The other answer choices are either out of scope, misinterpreted, or the opposite of the intended meaning. Choice (B) is correct.

17. **D** Remember that if the exam asks for what a pronoun such as *that* refers to, look in prior sentences to the antecedent. In this case, the antecedent is found directly before: *Their willingness to labor for love and not money will, over time, expose them to chronic stress.* A trap answer here is (A), but just remember that it's not the chronic stress that's especially true in universities—according to the author, it's the *willingness to labor for love and not money* that is so unusually prevalent there. Choice (B) is also a trap. While the author does seem to imply that the lack of limits is problematic, this is not to what *that* refers. Choice (D) is correct.

18. **B** Keep the task in mind: you're looking for evidence that *chronic stress associated with burnout diminishes the brain's executive function.* There are many forms of evidence, and personal experience is one of them, despite being anecdotal. Choice (B) describes one specific teaching technique that the author had forgotten about, even though he'd used it for years. This is evidence of his diminished ability to think and plan during his burnout. Choice (B) is correct.

19. **E** The author spends much of the essay supporting his personal experience with evidence from research in the social sciences. Descriptions of the events that led to his own crackup are broken up with occasional interpositions from experts such as Maslach and Leiter, as well as Jamie Crosner. Using POE, you can eliminate *point-by-point refutation*, found in (A), as well as *comparison and contrast and process analysis*, found in (C) and (D). Choice (B), *general principles and objective evidence*, may look appealing, but Malesic relates little objective evidence, preferring instead to offer his own personal experience as evidence. Choice (E) is correct.

20. **D** The author notes that *It's easier to do too much too soon than to build barriers between your work and psyche.* Choice (A), *their competence*, is mentioned elsewhere but misinterpreted here. Choice (B), the *inability to affirm their spouses*, is also mentioned elsewhere but has also been misinterpreted here. Eliminate both. Choice (C) is the opposite of the correct answer, so eliminate it. Choice (E), *absence due to maternity leave*, is not mentioned. Choice (D) is correct.

21. **E** As the question indicates, Malesic's tone is approachable. A general rule of thumb is that the use of informal diction, varied sentence structures, figurative language such as similes, and the pronoun *I* all indicate a relaxed tone. These are all stylistic choices. The only answer choice that doesn't reflect style, but instead reflects a method of persuasion, is the appeal to authority. Choice (E) is correct.

22. **B** The first nine paragraphs of this essay are marked by liberal use of *I, me,* and *my*, which are all first-person pronouns. This is fitting, since the author is relating his personal story. By the final three paragraphs, however, the author has largely ended that story, and is instead exploring general causes of and responses to professional burnout. At that point, he begins using third-person nouns and pronouns instead. Choice (B) is correct.

23. **E** Be careful on this one, and keep in mind the name of the publication. The essay was originally published in *The Chronicle of Higher Education*, whose audience is primarily *those who work in or who have benefitted from higher education.* While it's tempting to choose answers about professional burnout, (B) and (C), neither one addresses education. Choices (A) and (D) are out of scope, so eliminate them. Choice (E) is correct.

24. **B** Sentence 3 states that *In 2014, over 12% of the entire nation worked in the tourism industry, roughly 24,000 to 32,000 people, depending on the month. Meanwhile, sentence 6 states that Iceland has only 300,000 citizens total.* It's a bit odd to provide the total population in the paragraph following, since some readers, using division, can arrive at that calculation on their own. Better to put the total population before sentence 3, since readers will intuitively ask for 12% of what number. Moving sentence 6 to the places indicated by any of the other choices would break up the continuity of the surrounding sentences. The correct answer is (B).

25. **D** There is a problem with the sentence as written: *It's a marketing gimmick, and it's amazing that no one has thought to use it until now.* That problem is pronouns. The word *it* appears three times, and in two of the cases—the first and the last—the reader is not sure what *it* is referring to. Choice (D) clarifies that issue by replacing the first *it* with *Such marketing slogans,* and by replacing the last *it* with *Iceland's geographical position between Europe and the U.S.* The correct answer is (D).

26. **E** First, remember that this is the final sentence of the passage. Second, the underlined portion of the sentence (which is literally the last words of the entire passage) consists of *and they're the first to admit it.* This comment would indicate that seems to have been some conflict or controversy discussed beforehand about whether or not Icelandic people were being honest with themselves about increased tourism to their island. However, there is no such discussion in the passage. For that reason, any answer related to Icelandic people admitting something to themselves would be incorrect. Since (A), (B), (C), and (D) all use the word *admit,* the correct answer is (E).

27. **D** The question asks for the best amplification of the most recent idea, which is the fact that there are *thousands of titles published in Icelandic.* This indicates that the population is very literate, and that publishing is a healthy business. (Recall that the population of the island is quite small.) The best choice will continue this train of thought. Choice (D) notes the high rate of literacy, as well as the high rate of individual publishing, so (D) is correct.

28. **C** It should be obvious that *The funny thing is* cannot be correct because its tone doesn't match the rest of the paragraph. The best answer will feature a tone that matches the rest of the passage, which is to say formal and featuring a fairly high level of vocabulary. *This newfound popularity* is the best choice because it satisfies both of those criteria—and also establishes a solid transition from the previous

paragraph, which is about Iceland's growing popularity as a tourist destination. The correct answer is (C).

29. **D** Sentence 10 introduces *the biggest danger in the influx of tourism,* which indicates that what follows is the most important takeaway from the passage. Thus, choose a transition that indicates the greatest possible sense of importance. *In the meantime,* (A), *nonetheless,* (B), and *furthermore,* (C), do not accomplish this. However, (E) shows contrast but not importance. *Overall,* (D), is the best option.

30. **E** Read the question carefully: the author wants to write a more effective example of a marketing slogan *based on the claim of the previous sentence.* The previous sentence states that the reason for Iceland's newfound popularity has been cheap airlines *that promote Iceland as a convenient stop between the U.S. and Europe.* The only marketing slogan that mentions this concept is (E).

31. **B** Sentence 3 states that *In 2014, over 12% of the entire nation worked in the tourism industry.* This is hard evidence—data—for the rising rates of tourism to Iceland, so it supports the idea that *tourism has taken up the slack.*

32. **E** A very common way to provide more description of a noun is to place that information between a pair of dashes or commas immediately after the word that it is describing. Choice (B) uses an unnecessary *it's been,* while (C) uses a semi-colon incorrectly—it should separate two independent clauses. Lastly, (D) forms a sentence fragment and can be eliminated for that reason.

33. **D** The word *it* is the key to answering this question, since *it* must refer to the thing that depends too heavily upon flour, sugars, and vegetable oil. That thing is, of course, our *modern American industrial food system,* which is found in sentence 3. Therefore, the sentence should be added after sentence 3, so the answer is (D).

34. **C** Choice (A), as it is now, is too vague, since *new ways* doesn't provide enough description, so it won't capture the audience's interest. Eliminate (B) because that information is also given in sentence 6, creating a redundancy. Eliminate (D) because while very descriptive and interesting, it doesn't address the main idea of the passage, which is diet. Eliminate (E) because a discussion of Puritanism is off-topic and doesn't transition to paleo well. Choice (C) creates a problem and solution, which is echoed later in the paragraph about a food system that is fundamentally flawed. And the last word in (C) is *diet,* which is squarely on topic, so (C) is correct.

35. **C** Sentence 6 is a list of the poor health effects that result from a diet of refined flours. Sentence 8 is also a list of the poor health effects that result from a diet of refined flours. To improve coherence, these should be placed next to each other. Sentence 7 interrupts this chain of thought by discussing animal products and their satiety. This, of course, could be relevant, but not in this particular paragraph, and especially not in this place. The answer is (C).

36. **C** Matching tone is always tricky, but one way to do this question is to simply look at diction, or word choice. The rest of the passage features a strong formal tone as a result of very specific nouns and verbs. Choice (C) provides the same diction. *Maybe because,* in the original sentence, is changed into *One possible reason for this is the fact that. Legs* is transformed into the more descriptive l*egs, eyes, and emotional connectivity.* Choice (E) is tempting, but it features an incorrect comparison. Likewise, (A) tries for the same formality but overshoots the mark, incorrectly using elucidation when a less complex word would've been more appropriate. The correct answer is (C).

37. **B** The main idea of the final paragraph is that there exists overlap between meat-eaters and vegetarians. It's even-handed, not argumentative, so it's best to choose an answer that establishes a balance. Since sentence 17 sings the praises of the Inuits' love of protein and fat, then it should be followed by a sentence that similarly sings the praises of the vegetarian lifestyle of another specific culture. Choice (B) does all of this, specifically mentioning India as a successful mostly vegetarian culture, so (B) is the answer.

38. **D** *Still* is an example of a transition word that acknowledges a counterargument while turning the topic back to the original argument. It means the same as *nonetheless*. This is the best transition for this sentence, because the previous paragraph examines the counterargument—the opponents of the paleo movement—while the upcoming paragraph describes that the paleo movement does have merit. The answer is (D).

39. **A** This is an EXCEPT question. The final paragraph discusses the merits of both side of the argument. Because the last sentence is currently a one-sided example—the Inuit culture of meat-eaters—the next sentence should bring things back to a more balanced view of the topic. The only answer choice that continues to describe the strength of the paleo movement is (A), *the rate of cardiac disease among the Inuit is close to zero*, so select (A).

40. **D** To clarify a source could mean a number of different things, but in this question, notice that the original sentence didn't even give the name of the person speaking. Choice (D) tells you that it was Fred Cohen, so (D) is correct.

41. **B** The topic sentence notes that the breaches have been getting exponentially worse. This indicates that the evidence that follows should grow in severity—put the smallest breach first, the medium breach second, and the most horrible breach last. Choice (B) explicitly says *Perhaps the worst breach occurred in 2015*. No other example in any other answer choice grows in severity quite as obviously, so the answer is (B).

42. **E** The question notes that the word is supposed *to emphasize the suddenness of the breaches*. Choice (A), *acceleratedly*, isn't typical American English usage, so eliminate that. Choice (B), *at full speed*, isn't a phrase used to describe how things are suffered; eliminate it. Choice (C), *to most*, has nothing to do with speed. Choice (D), *quickly*, could work in this sentence, but it's not nearly as descriptive or as precise as (E), *with no apparent warning*, so (E) is the answer.

43. **B** The sentence being added, *No mere accident, a breach is commonly associated with a foreign invader breaking through systems of defense*. This is definition of a breach. Meanwhile, sentence 7 says that *Indeed, the word "breach" perhaps doesn't carry the significance that it should*—a beautiful setup for a discussion of the meaning of the word. Put the new sentence after sentence 7. Choice (B) is correct.

44. **C** Look for mistakes in parallelism. Choice (A) inserts the phrase *doing the same*, to the second of the three terms; eliminate it. Choice (B) notes *for example* between the first and second items; eliminate that one too. Choice (D) also inserts *for example* just before the first item, using incorrect punctuation; eliminate it. And (E) uses *plus* instead of *and*; eliminate that too. Choice (C) is correct.

45. **A** This question asks you to choose a sentence that continues the process analysis, a specific mode in writing. Process sentences and paragraphs typically uses transition words such as *next* or *then*. Indeed, *then* can be found in (A), as well as a description of the next step of the process—the invasion of the attackers to all the files within a system. The answer is (A).

HOW TO SCORE PRACTICE TEST 3

Section I: Multiple-Choice

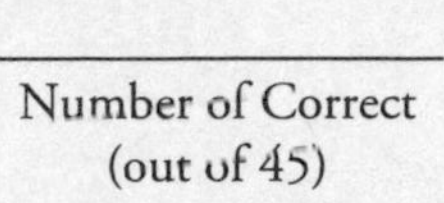

__________ × 1.5000 = __________

Number of Correct (out of 45) — Weighted Section I Score (Do not round)

As of the printing of this book, there have been no official administrations of this test. Therefore, this scoring should only be used as an estimate.

Section II: Free Response

(See if you can find a teacher or classmate to score your essays using the guidelines in Chapter 4.)

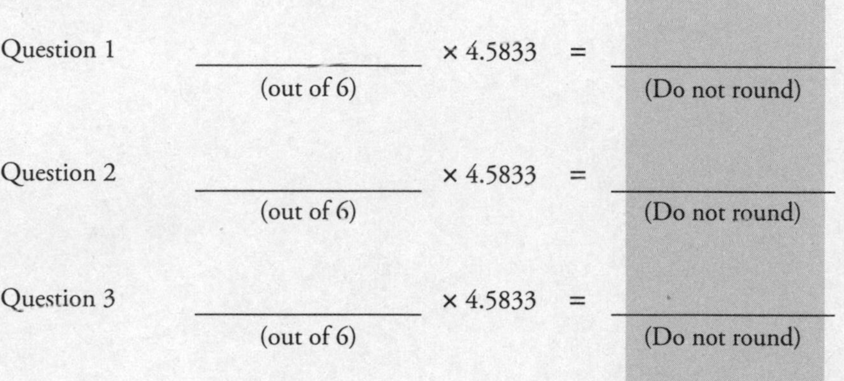

Question 1 __________ (out of 6) × 4.5833 = __________ (Do not round)

Question 2 __________ (out of 6) × 4.5833 = __________ (Do not round)

Question 3 __________ (out of 6) × 4.5833 = __________ (Do not round)

Sum = __________ Weighted Section II Score (Do not round)

AP Score Conversion Chart English Language and Composition

Composite Score Range	AP Score
112–150	5
98–111	4
80–97	3
55–79	2
0–54	1

Composite Score

__________ + __________ = __________

Weighted Section I Score + Weighted Section II Score = Composite Score (Round to nearest whole number)

Completely darken bubbles with a No. 2 pencil. If you make a mistake, be sure to erase mark completely. Erase all stray marks.

1. YOUR NAME: ______________________________
(Print) Last First M.I.

SIGNATURE: ______________________________ DATE: ___/___/___

HOME ADDRESS: ______________________________
(Print) Number and Street

____
City State Zip Code

PHONE NO. : ______________________________
(Print)

IMPORTANT: Please fill in these boxes exactly as shown on the back cover of your test book.

2. TEST FORM

3. TEST CODE

A	0	0	0

0 1 2 3 4 5 6 7 8 9 (first column)
A B C D E F G (second column)
0 1 2 3 4 5 6 7 8 9 (remaining columns)

4. REGISTRATION NUMBER

0 1 2 3 4 5 6 7 8 9 (each column)

5. YOUR NAME

First 4 letters of last name | FIRST INIT | MID INIT

A B C D E F G H I J K L M N O P Q R S T U V W X Y Z (each column)

6. DATE OF BIRTH

Month	Day		Year	
JAN				
FEB				
MAR	0	0	0	0
APR	1	1	1	1
MAY	2	2	2	2
JUN	3	3	3	3
JUL		4	4	4
AUG		5	5	5
SEP		6	6	6
OCT		7	7	7
NOV		8	8	8
DEC		9	9	9

7. SEX

MALE

FEMALE

The Princeton Review

FORM NO. 00001-PR

Section 1

Start with number 1 for each new section.
If a section has fewer questions than answer spaces, leave the extra answer spaces blank.

1. A B C D E
2. A B C D E
3. A B C D E
4. A B C D E
5. A B C D E
6. A B C D E
7. A B C D E
8. A B C D E
9. A B C D E
10. A B C D E
11. A B C D E
12. A B C D E
13. A B C D E
14. A B C D E
15. A B C D E
16. A B C D E
17. A B C D E
18. A B C D E
19. A B C D E
20. A B C D E
21. A B C D E
22. A B C D E
23. A B C D E
24. A B C D E
25. A B C D E
26. A B C D E
27. A B C D E
28. A B C D E
29. A B C D E
30. A B C D E
31. A B C D E
32. A B C D E
33. A B C D E
34. A B C D E
35. A B C D E
36. A B C D E
37. A B C D E
38. A B C D E
39. A B C D E
40. A B C D E
41. A B C D E
42. A B C D E
43. A B C D E
44. A B C D E
45. A B C D E
46. A B C D E
47. A B C D E
48. A B C D E
49. A B C D E
50. A B C D E
51. A B C D E
52. A B C D E
53. A B C D E
54. A B C D E
55. A B C D E
56. A B C D E
57. A B C D E
58. A B C D E
59. A B C D E
60. A B C D E
61. A B C D E
62. A B C D E
63. A B C D E
64. A B C D E
65. A B C D E
66. A B C D E
67. A B C D E
68. A B C D E
69. A B C D E
70. A B C D E
71. A B C D E
72. A B C D E
73. A B C D E
74. A B C D E
75. A B C D E
76. A B C D E
77. A B C D E
78. A B C D E
79. A B C D E
80. A B C D E
81. A B C D E
82. A B C D E
83. A B C D E
84. A B C D E
85. A B C D E
86. A B C D E
87. A B C D E
88. A B C D E
89. A B C D E
90. A B C D E
91. A B C D E
92. A B C D E
93. A B C D E
94. A B C D E
95. A B C D E
96. A B C D E
97. A B C D E
98. A B C D E
99. A B C D E
100. A B C D E
101. A B C D E
102. A B C D E
103. A B C D E
104. A B C D E
105. A B C D E
106. A B C D E
107. A B C D E
108. A B C D E
109. A B C D E
110. A B C D E
111. A B C D E
112. A B C D E
113. A B C D E
114. A B C D E
115. A B C D E
116. A B C D E
117. A B C D E
118. A B C D E
119. A B C D E
120. A B C D E

Completely darken bubbles with a No. 2 pencil. If you make a mistake, be sure to erase mark completely. Erase all stray marks.

1. YOUR NAME: ______________________________
(Print) Last First M.I.

SIGNATURE: ______________________________ DATE: ___/___/___

HOME ADDRESS: ______________________________
(Print) Number and Street

____
City State Zip Code

PHONE NO. : ______________________________
(Print)

IMPORTANT: Please fill in these boxes exactly as shown on the back cover of your test book.

2. TEST FORM

3. TEST CODE

0	A	0	0	0
1	B	1	1	1
2	C	2	2	2
3	D	3	3	3
4	E	4	4	4
5	F	5	5	5
6	G	6	6	6
7		7	7	7
8		8	8	8
9		9	9	9

4. REGISTRATION NUMBER

0	0	0	0	0	0
1	1	1	1	1	1
2	2	2	2	2	2
3	3	3	3	3	3
4	4	4	4	4	4
5	5	5	5	5	5
6	6	6	6	6	6
7	7	7	7	7	7
8	8	8	8	8	8
9	9	9	9	9	9

5. YOUR NAME

First 4 letters of last name					FIRST INIT	MID INIT
A	A	A	A		A	A
B	B	B	B		B	B
C	C	C	C		C	C
D	D	D	D		D	D
E	E	E	E		E	E
F	F	F	F		F	F
G	G	G	G		G	G
H	H	H	H		H	H
I	I	I	I		I	I
J	J	J	J		J	J
K	K	K	K		K	K
L	L	L	L		L	L
M	M	M	M		M	M
N	N	N	N		N	N
O	O	O	O		O	O
P	P	P	P		P	P
Q	Q	Q	Q		Q	Q
R	R	R	R		R	R
S	S	S	S		S	S
T	T	T	T		T	T
U	U	U	U		U	U
V	V	V	V		V	V
W	W	W	W		W	W
X	X	X	X		X	X
Y	Y	Y	Y		Y	Y
Z	Z	Z	Z		Z	Z

6. DATE OF BIRTH

Month	Day		Year	
JAN				
FEB				
MAR	0	0	0	0
APR	1	1	1	1
MAY	2	2	2	2
JUN	3	3	3	3
JUL		4	4	4
AUG		5	5	5
SEP		6	6	6
OCT		7	7	7
NOV		8	8	8
DEC		9	9	9

7. SEX

MALE

FEMALE

The Princeton Review®

FORM NO. 00001-PR

Section 1

Start with number 1 for each new section.
If a section has fewer questions than answer spaces, leave the extra answer spaces blank.

1. A B C D E
2. A B C D E
3. A B C D E
4. A B C D E
5. A B C D E
6. A B C D E
7. A B C D E
8. A B C D E
9. A B C D E
10. A B C D E
11. A B C D E
12. A B C D E
13. A B C D E
14. A B C D E
15. A B C D E
16. A B C D E
17. A B C D E
18. A B C D E
19. A B C D E
20. A B C D E
21. A B C D E
22. A B C D E
23. A B C D E
24. A B C D E
25. A B C D E
26. A B C D E
27. A B C D E
28. A B C D E
29. A B C D E
30. A B C D E
31. A B C D E
32. A B C D E
33. A B C D E
34. A B C D E
35. A B C D E
36. A B C D E
37. A B C D E
38. A B C D E
39. A B C D E
40. A B C D E
41. A B C D E
42. A B C D E
43. A B C D E
44. A B C D E
45. A B C D E
46. A B C D E
47. A B C D E
48. A B C D E
49. A B C D E
50. A B C D E
51. A B C D E
52. A B C D E
53. A B C D E
54. A B C D E
55. A B C D E
56. A B C D E
57. A B C D E
58. A B C D E
59. A B C D E
60. A B C D E
61. A B C D E
62. A B C D E
63. A B C D E
64. A B C D E
65. A B C D E
66. A B C D E
67. A B C D E
68. A B C D E
69. A B C D E
70. A B C D E
71. A B C D E
72. A B C D E
73. A B C D E
74. A B C D E
75. A B C D E
76. A B C D E
77. A B C D E
78. A B C D E
79. A B C D E
80. A B C D E
81. A B C D E
82. A B C D E
83. A B C D E
84. A B C D E
85. A B C D E
86. A B C D E
87. A B C D E
88. A B C D E
89. A B C D E
90. A B C D E
91. A B C D E
92. A B C D E
93. A B C D E
94. A B C D E
95. A B C D E
96. A B C D E
97. A B C D E
98. A B C D E
99. A B C D E
100. A B C D E
101. A B C D E
102. A B C D E
103. A B C D E
104. A B C D E
105. A B C D E
106. A B C D E
107. A B C D E
108. A B C D E
109. A B C D E
110. A B C D E
111. A B C D E
112. A B C D E
113. A B C D E
114. A B C D E
115. A B C D E
116. A B C D E
117. A B C D E
118. A B C D E
119. A B C D E
120. A B C D E

The Princeton Review

Completely darken bubbles with a No. 2 pencil. If you make a mistake, be sure to erase mark completely. Erase all stray marks.

1. YOUR NAME: ______________________________
(Print) Last First M.I.

SIGNATURE: ______________________ DATE: ___/___/___

HOME ADDRESS: ______________________________
(Print) Number and Street

____
City State Zip Code

PHONE NO. : ______________________________
(Print)

IMPORTANT: Please fill in these boxes exactly as shown on the back cover of your test book.

2. TEST FORM

3. TEST CODE

0	A	0	0	0
1	B	1	1	1
2	C	2	2	2
3	D	3	3	3
4	E	4	4	4
5	F	5	5	5
6	G	6	6	6
7		7	7	7
8		8	8	8
9		9	9	9

4. REGISTRATION NUMBER

0	0	0	0	0	0	0
1	1	1	1	1	1	1
2	2	2	2	2	2	2
3	3	3	3	3	3	3
4	4	4	4	4	4	4
5	5	5	5	5	5	5
6	6	6	6	6	6	6
7	7	7	7	7	7	7
8	8	8	8	8	8	8
9	9	9	9	9	9	9

5. YOUR NAME

First 4 letters of last name					FIRST INIT	MID INIT
A	A	A	A		A	A
B	B	B	B		B	B
C	C	C	C		C	C
D	D	D	D		D	D
E	E	E	E		E	E
F	F	F	F		F	F
G	G	G	G		G	G
H	H	H	H		H	H
I	I	I	I		I	I
J	J	J	J		J	J
K	K	K	K		K	K
L	L	L	L		L	L
M	M	M	M		M	M
N	N	N	N		N	N
O	O	O	O		O	O
P	P	P	P		P	P
Q	Q	Q	Q		Q	Q
R	R	R	R		R	R
S	S	S	S		S	S
T	T	T	T		T	T
U	U	U	U		U	U
V	V	V	V		V	V
W	W	W	W		W	W
X	X	X	X		X	X
Y	Y	Y	Y		Y	Y
Z	Z	Z	Z		Z	Z

6. DATE OF BIRTH

Month	Day		Year	
JAN				
FEB				
MAR	0	0	0	0
APR	1	1	1	1
MAY	2	2	2	2
JUN	3	3	3	3
JUL		4	4	4
AUG		5	5	5
SEP		6	6	6
OCT		7	7	7
NOV		8	8	8
DEC		9	9	9

7. SEX

MALE

FEMALE

The Princeton Review

FORM NO. 00001-PR

Section 1

Start with number 1 for each new section.
If a section has fewer questions than answer spaces, leave the extra answer spaces blank.

1. A B C D E
2. A B C D E
3. A B C D E
4. A B C D E
5. A B C D E
6. A B C D E
7. A B C D E
8. A B C D E
9. A B C D E
10. A B C D E
11. A B C D E
12. A B C D E
13. A B C D E
14. A B C D E
15. A B C D E
16. A B C D E
17. A B C D E
18. A B C D E
19. A B C D E
20. A B C D E
21. A B C D E
22. A B C D E
23. A B C D E
24. A B C D E
25. A B C D E
26. A B C D E
27. A B C D E
28. A B C D E
29. A B C D E
30. A B C D E
31. A B C D E
32. A B C D E
33. A B C D E
34. A B C D E
35. A B C D E
36. A B C D E
37. A B C D E
38. A B C D E
39. A B C D E
40. A B C D E
41. A B C D E
42. A B C D E
43. A B C D E
44. A B C D E
45. A B C D E
46. A B C D E
47. A B C D E
48. A B C D E
49. A B C D E
50. A B C D E
51. A B C D E
52. A B C D E
53. A B C D E
54. A B C D E
55. A B C D E
56. A B C D E
57. A B C D E
58. A B C D E
59. A B C D E
60. A B C D E
61. A B C D E
62. A B C D E
63. A B C D E
64. A B C D E
65. A B C D E
66. A B C D E
67. A B C D E
68. A B C D E
69. A B C D E
70. A B C D E
71. A B C D E
72. A B C D E
73. A B C D E
74. A B C D E
75. A B C D E
76. A B C D E
77. A B C D E
78. A B C D E
79. A B C D E
80. A B C D E
81. A B C D E
82. A B C D E
83. A B C D E
84. A B C D E
85. A B C D E
86. A B C D E
87. A B C D E
88. A B C D E
89. A B C D E
90. A B C D E
91. A B C D E
92. A B C D E
93. A B C D E
94. A B C D E
95. A B C D E
96. A B C D E
97. A B C D E
98. A B C D E
99. A B C D E
100. A B C D E
101. A B C D E
102. A B C D E
103. A B C D E
104. A B C D E
105. A B C D E
106. A B C D E
107. A B C D E
108. A B C D E
109. A B C D E
110. A B C D E
111. A B C D E
112. A B C D E
113. A B C D E
114. A B C D E
115. A B C D E
116. A B C D E
117. A B C D E
118. A B C D E
119. A B C D E
120. A B C D E

NOTES

NOTES

NOTES

NOTES

NOTES

NOTES

NOTES

NOTES